The Changing Face
of Japanese Management

For many western managers the approach taken by successful Japanese organizations and their managers has tended to inspire awe, envy and incomprehension in equal measure. But what is so special about 'Japanese' management? And how 'special' is the response of Japanese managers to global business pressures?

This text addresses these questions. It presents case examples generated from interviews with Japanese managers in Japan, Europe and the USA, contextualizing their comments by reference to recent research in the fields of international and intercultural management. The book explains how and why individual managers variously perceive threats or opportunities in the business and career environments currently evolving both inside and outside Japan. It combines vivid images of the expected with the exceptional, the traditional with the new and unfamiliar.

The Changing Face of Japanese Management offers management students with little prior knowledge of Japanese business and society critical insights into what is happening inside Japanese management today. It also offers clear and immediately transferable insights to management practitioners who are preparing to work or negotiate with Japanese business partners.

Keith Jackson is a tutor and researcher at the Centre for Financial and Management Studies (CeFiMS) at The School of Oriental and African Studies, University of London. He is currently involved in developing an online MBA community based in Konstanz (Germany).

Miyuki Tomioka is currently working for an international management and business consultancy in Japan. She specializes in strategy, e-commerce, and mergers and acquisitions in the global pharmaceuticals and biotechnology industries.

Working in Asia

General Editors:
Tim G. Andrews
Bristol Business School, University of the West of England
and **Keith Jackson**
School of Oriental and African Studies, University of London

This series focuses on contemporary management issues in the Asia-Pacific region. It draws on the latest research to highlight critical factors impacting on the conduct of business in this diverse and dynamic business environment.

Our primary intention is to provide management students and practitioners with fresh dimensions to their reading of standard texts. With each book in the *Working in Asia* series, we offer a combined insider's and outsider's perspective on how managers and their organizations in the Asia-Pacific region are adapting to contemporary currents of both macro- and micro-level change.

The core of data for the texts in this series has been generated by recent interviews and discussions with established senior executives as well as newly fledged entrepreneurs; with practising as well as aspiring middle managers; and with women as well as men. Our mission has been to give voice to how change is being perceived and experienced by a broad and relevant range of people who live and work in the region. We report on how they and their organizations are managing change as the globalization of their markets, together with their business technologies and traditions, unfolds.

Drawing together the combined insights of Asian and western scholars, and practitioners of management, we present a uniquely revealing portrait of the future of working and doing business in Asia.

Titles in the series include:

The Changing Face of Multinationals in Southeast Asia
Tim G. Andrews, Nartnalin Chompusri and Bryan J. Baldwin OBE

The Changing Face of Chinese Management
Jie Tang and Anthony Ward

The Changing Face of Japanese Management
Keith Jackson and Miyuki Tomioka

The Changing Face of Japanese Management

Keith Jackson and Miyuki Tomioka

Routledge
Taylor & Francis Group

LONDON AND NEW YORK

First published 2004 by Routledge
11 New Fetter Lane, London EC4P 4EE

Simultaneously published in the USA and Canada
by Routledge
29 West 35th Street, New York, NY 10001

Routledge is an imprint of the Taylor & Francis Group

© 2004 Keith Jackson and Miyuki Tomioka

Typeset in Times by Keystroke, Jacaranda Lodge, Wolverhampton
Printed and bound in Great Britain by The Cromwell Press, Trowbridge, Wiltshire

British Library Cataloguing in Publication Data
A catalogue record for this book is available from the British Library

Library of Congress Cataloging in Publication Data
Jackson, Keith, 1957–
    The changing face of Japanese management/ by Keith Jackson and Miyuki
Tomioka.
        p. cm. – (Working in Asia)
    Includes bibliographical references and index.
    1. Industrial management–Japan. 2. Organizational change–Japan.
    3. Corporate culture–Japan. I. Tomioka, Miyuki. II. Title. III. Series.

HD70 .J3J33 2003
658′ .00952—dc21   2003005702

ISBN 0–415–28744–8 (hbk)
ISBN 0–415–28745–6 (pbk)

To our parents, Alan, Miyu-chan, P:) & S:)

Contents

Boxes

# **Introduction**

What is this book about?

This book is about Japanese managers. It focuses on how and why they tend to make the business and career decisions they make.

Who is this book for?

The book has been written for students of management who have little practical knowledge of Japanese business and society but who have a particular interest in the complexities of managing change and diversity, specifically in Japan and Asia, but also in the general context of international human resource management.

The book is also written for management practitioners who want more insight into working with Japanese business partners so as to reduce the risk of communication breakdown or business failure.

As this is designed as an introductory textbook, we frequently refer and guide readers to other relevant and easily accessible texts in the fields of Japanese and international management and business.

What's special about Japanese management?

One answer to this question is as follows. From the 1970s until the early 1990s, many non-Japanese management experts and practitioners saw in 'Japanese-style' management some recipes for global business success, and nothing sells like success! Consider this US American view:

> A country the size of Montana, Japan has virtually no physical resources, yet it supports over 115 million people (half the population

> of the United States), exports $75 billion worth more goods than it
> imports, and has an investment rate as well as a GNP growth rate
> which is twice that of the United States. Japan has come to dominate
> in one selected industry after another – eclipsing the British in
> motorcycles, surpassing the Germans and the Americans in
> automobile production, wresting leadership from the Germans and the
> Swiss in watches, cameras, and optical instruments, and overcoming
> the United States' historical dominance in businesses as diverse as
> steel, shipbuilding, pianos, zippers, and consumer electronics.
>
> (Tanner Pascale and Athos, 1981: 20)

After making a comparative analysis of Japanese and western
organizations across a range of industries, the authors came to the
conclusion that 'a major reason for the superiority of the Japanese is their
managerial skill' (1981: 21). There appeared to be some distinctive
techniques which gave Japanese companies – and above all in
manufacturing – global competitive advantages. For example, an analysis
of the Toyota Production System (TPS) gave insights into techniques such
as for Just-In-Time (JIT) inventory control, relationship-based supply
chain and quality management, quality circles and *kanban* wastage
reduction systems, all integrated and underpinned by *kai-zen*, a
management philosophy emphasizing the value of continuous and
detailed product and process improvement and organizational learning
(cf. Bird, 2002). To many western managers in the 1970s and 1980s, the
approach taken by Japanese organizations who 'waged business' against
them provoked awe and envy in equal measure.

But 'organisations are people' (Ohmae, 1982). So, western attention also
fell on the distinctive features of Japanese-style human resource
management (HRM): for example, the 'three sacred treasures' of lifetime
employment, seniority promotion (i.e. promotion according to age and
length of service), and the stability offered by having enterprise
(i.e. in-house) trade unions (Bird, 2002; Briscoe, 1995). Enlightened
interest focused above all on how these three treasures were strategically
integrated in an approach to HRM based on cultural cohesiveness and
trust (Ouchi, 1981).

Aware of the strengths of Japanese-style management, Tanner Pascale and
Athos (1981) made a forward calculation: 'In 1980, Japan's GNP was
third highest in the world [behind the USA and the then West Germany]
and if we extrapolate current trends, it would be number one by the year
2000' (1981: 20). This has not happened. Japan is currently in economic
recession, and although it is likely to remain one of the three most

powerful economies in the world for at least another human generation (cf. Hawthorn, 1998), it is curious to observe how such burgeoning HRM strengths and sources of global competitive advantage could falter and – judging by what *The Economist* magazine and other sources of expert analysis tell us today – become perceived as such weaknesses.

Why since the mid-1990s has there been this growing sense of crisis in Japanese management? In trying to answer this question we can refer to changing circumstances: e.g. what we loosely term 'globalization' and the emergence of new (e.g. technology-based) industries and rival national economies such as China. Jack Welch, former chair and CEO of General Electric, states that: 'Organizations are changing by necessity. Globalization is simply a fact of life.' We were curious about how 'simple' it has been for Japanese managers to adapt to this 'fact of life'.

So we come back to focus on people; in this case, Japanese managers, and how and why they make the decisions they do, or don't do. How are they responding to the current 'crisis', accepting the word in its original meaning as a point in time where a 'critical' (i.e. balanced and informed) decision is required (cf. Ayto, 1990)? How similar or different is the experience of Japanese managers to their counterparts worldwide as they too negotiate the challenge of globalization and other pressures to change? Which managers see business and career opportunities? Which perceive mainly threats?

What's special about Japanese managers?

This, we believe, is the more interesting question and answering it is the focus for discussion in this book. In considering what informs the ways in which Japanese managers learn and make decisions, we work with notions of 'culture': i.e. what Geert Hofstede memorably and (for the time) topically defined as 'the collective programming of the mind which distinguishes the members of one human group from another' (1984: 21). In trying to understand better what makes Japanese managers 'tick' we also work with notions such as 'problem' – which we define as a 'gap' in our knowledge or understanding; for example, in respect of how Japanese managers think today – or 'dilemma', where individuals are faced by a limited set of choices: e.g. should I stay in this failing company/country or should I move on and look for another job?

In addressing such crises, problems and dilemmas we explore how Japanese managers tend to feel constrained in their choices: for example, in terms of choosing and negotiating a career path. In an attempt to explain these constraints we develop the notion of face: hence, the 'face of Japanese management'. We look at how this face is changing. We look at the impact of 'tradition', remembering that tradition in the context of Japanese-style management effectively means the management systems and procedures that have emerged since the national reconstruction after World War Two. And we listen to different generations of Japanese managers talk about shaping up for an increasingly 'globalized' future by giving voice to their individual perceptions, experiences and expectations. We expect that managers who read this book – and by 'managers' we mean both those who are currently practising and those who form the coming generation of international managers – may find echoes of their own concerns and experiences in what their Japanese counterparts have to say.

Our approach

The core material for this book is derived from a series of structured and semi-structured interviews and discussions held with Japanese managers in Japan and Europe since the mid-1990s. Their individual stories are central to the discussion in each chapter. To protect the identity of our respondents, several testimonies have been aggregated and all names have been changed. The voices of these managers are contextualized by reference to current management literature, drawn mainly from the field of international management and international HRM. We have not tried to draw rigid conclusions: the book is about change and tracing what is currently happening in the context of Japanese management. It is, therefore, a 'work in progress'. Overall our aim is to offer some representative and (we hope) vivid insights into how change is being managed and experienced by Japanese managers.

We have no particular axes to grind. However, we try to avoid over-generalizations: the term 'Japanese management' is itself becoming increasingly suspect in our ever more globalized business and employment environments. We also think that understanding 'management' requires some practical understanding of how and why people work, and why they have ambitions and aspire to achieve professional fulfilment. For this reason we have concentrated our research on Japanese managers of middle-ranking responsibility and/or at a mid-stage (indeed, crossroads) in their career. We assume that many people reading this book will be able to empathize with these managers.

How the book is structured

The book is designed to offer several pathways. Generally speaking, and in response to the book's title, the first four chapters describe what the face of Japanese management is changing *from*, while the last four chapters suggest what it is changing *to*.

In linear sequence, Chapters 1 to 3 present some fundamental concepts which should help to describe, explain and (in very general terms) predict some distinctive features of Japanese management behaviour. These are: *culture* (Chapter 1); *attention to face* (Chapter 2); *experience of upbringing and education* (Chapter 3).

We then focus on the notion of 'career'. From Chapter 4 onwards we progress our discussion by reference to the generic 'HRM cycle' (cf. Devanna *et al.*, 1984; Storey, 1989). Namely:

- *recruitment, selection and organizational induction* (Chapter 4);
- *training and development* (Chapter 5);
- *performance appraisal* (Chapter 6);
- *rewards and promotion* (Chapter 7);
- *organizational exit* (Chapter 8).

Pairs of chapters are linked thematically and designed to mirror each other as follows:

- Chapter 1 mirrors Chapter 5: the theme linking both is *the cultural context for management learning and communication.*
- Chapter 2 mirrors Chapter 6: the theme linking both is *balancing trust and control in Japanese-style HRM.*
- Chapter 3 mirrors Chapter 7: the theme linking both is *becoming an international manager.*
- Chapter 4 mirrors Chapter 8: the theme linking both is *managing a career.*

Each chapter has a brief Introduction (with discussion objectives) and a brief Summary, with questions or thoughts for reflection. We consider it good practice to begin by reading the Summary and then read critically through the discussion in the chapter.

Each chapter contains a number of boxes. These provide contextual information about Japanese business and society and can be read or discussed separately from the chapter text.

The bibliography lists the sources of information or quotes referred to in the text together with a selection of titles used in our teaching or in preparing our research for this book. We have tried to use only up-to-date online sources and apologize for any of these which since writing 'die out'.

Acknowledgements

In contrast, we thank wholeheartedly the following people: Catriona King and Rachel Crookes at Routledge for their patience and support; Tim Andrews as a co-editor and teaching colleague; Richard Mead as a colleague and an inspiration; Yoko Akashi as an inspiration pure and simple; and the hundreds of students and colleagues we have worked with and who have been so generous with their thoughts, their personal and professional experiences, and not least their dreams, over the past ten years.

1 First encounters

Introduction

> All people are the same. It's only their habits that are
> different.
>
> attributed to Master Kong Zhu (Confucius),
> Chinese, fifth century AD

Experience tells us that it is both efficient and respectful to approach
international management or business encounters by concentrating on the
essential similarities between people (e.g. their purpose in coming or
working together) rather than give too much attention to superficial
differences in behaviour. When we encounter, work or negotiate with
managers or customers from cultural backgrounds different to our own
we should remind ourselves that they too want to 'win'.

The influence of Confucian thought is still great in East Asia – and Japan
lies (from a western perspective) in East Asia. But the emphasis he gives
to observing different 'habits' could persuade us to focus our discussion
of Japanese management on different ways of behaving; for example,
addressing the 'kiss, bow or shake hands' type of anxieties that beset

most of us as we cross national and cultural boundaries on a mission to persuade or impress (cf. Morrison *et al.*, 1995). We know that 'getting off to a good start' helps boost confidence, and that confidence goes a long way in business. However, by crossing national or cultural boundaries we inevitably encounter behaviours and attitudes that baffle us. For Japanese in Britain it may be something as banal as people blowing their nose in public. The key is to perceive cultural differences as a source of learning and not as a personal or professional threat.

Soichiro Honda, co-founder of the global giant, the Honda Motor Corporation, suggested a more recent uptake on the Confucius message. When pushed, Honda surmised that Japanese and US American management styles were 'ninety-five percent the same' and yet 'different in all important aspects' (Tsutsui, 1998: 13). Was he talking about 5 per cent difference in technique? Or 5 per cent in attitude? In this first chapter we try to identify and explain in practical terms some of these '5 per cent' of differences. We refer (critically) to notions of national culture. However, we focus on the perceptions and experiences of individual managers, believing in this and subsequent chapters that herein lies the potential for a more effective and longer-lasting understanding of how and why Japanese managers tend to make the personal and professional decisions they do.

Our objectives for this first chapter are:

- to offer an insight into how international management researchers and other experts describe Japanese management culture;
- to equip non-Japanese managers and students of management with references and conceptual tools which should help them better recognize, explain and (where feasible) predict some of the behaviours and attitudes they are likely to encounter when working with Japanese business partners;
- to encourage us to question our own assumptions about 'culture'.

SECTION 1: CROSSING BOUNDARIES

When observing and discussing how individuals behave either collectively or individually in different situations or contexts, the question of 'culture' arises. 'Culture' is a highly complex notion; it is 'one of the two or three most complicated words in the English language' (Williams,

1985) and in international management literature 'over 450 definitions of the word culture exist' (Herbig, 1998). What international managers want to know – and particularly HR, sales and marketing managers, together with managers on international assignments – is how people's experience of culture influences their choices of behaviour in standard and non-standard situations.

Accordingly, discussions of culture become particularly significant when considering how people individually and/or collectively respond to a crisis. Japanese managers currently face a professional crisis: the established assumptions about job and career security are changing rapidly and radically; furthermore, the nature and boundaries of traditional Japanese markets are changing as globalization takes hold. How individual Japanese managers are responding to this crisis is the focus of discussion in this book. In this first section we offer an introductory discussion of Japanese management culture from a non-Japanese perspective.

Open your mind

To understand Japanese management effectively we need to open our mind to other perspectives and norms of behaviour. Indeed, this is a pre-requisite for trying to understand any national culture effectively, including our own. For example, if this book were written using Japanese script it would be possible to read each page from left to right and top to

Figure 1.1 *NI-HON*

bottom one line at a time (as we assume you are doing now). However, it would also be possible for the same text to be arranged such that it could be read from right to left, top to bottom, and not one line at a time but one idea or written character (*kanji* and other symbols of Japanese writing) at a time. So, for example, the two *kanji* (Figure 1.1) could be written one above the other and still give the meaning: *ni-hon* or 'Japan'. Attention to the form or the process, as much as to the message or the content, is one key to understanding Japanese-style business and management communication.

Time

Time shapes our experience of culture. In time, we talk about culture-specific traditions. The temptation for westerners to *exoticize* Japan and Japanese management culture comes partly from history and cultural tradition. When, during the last quarter of the previous millennium, news and artefacts started coming back to Europe and then North America from Japan and other Asian cultures, a notion of *orientalism* – as something mysterious 'from the East' – arose. But as with all such relative points of reference, 'from the East' means 'east' of where we personally stand. Where we stand determines our perspective and where we draw boundaries on the cultures of others.

Space

Space is another key factor in shaping cultural experience. Geographically, the islands of Japan lie in East Asia. The Chinese, also East Asians, have for the last few thousand years been confident that they stand in the middle and everybody else to the east or west, north or south of them: hence the idea of China as 'the middle kingdom'. It was the Chinese who first named today's Japan the islands of *Nihon* (*Nippon*) as the islands where (from a Chinese perspective) the sun rises. Correspondingly, the two *kanji* illustrated above signify (from left to right) 'sun' and 'origin'. This information reached Europe via Marco Polo.

Language

Our experiences of time and space are understood and communicated through language. Accordingly, language is a powerful expression of individual and collective cultural identity. Most of what we know of our native or 'mother' tongue we learn during our most formative years: probably until the age of twelve or fourteen. This explains why many adults find it difficult to learn a foreign language with fluency and confidence. Language takes the form of both verbal symbols (e.g. speech and writing) and non-verbal symbols (e.g. gestures and eye-contact). After crossing geographical and political boundaries, and perhaps time zones, it is our encounter with a different language that usually reinforces our sense of having crossed a cultural boundary.

Cultural boundaries

We should recognize that cultural boundaries need not coincide with national boundaries, though in the case of Japan, nation and culture are (as we shall see) easily confused. In fact, we can encounter a different 'language' by crossing organizational boundaries (e.g. in the jargon of lawyers or doctors). Even within organizations each department or section may have its own jargon or 'in-jokes', its myths and traditions, fluency in which distinguishes 'insiders' from 'outsiders'. The notion of culture-specific 'insiders' who share context-specific information is a key element in understanding Japanese management culture and the behaviour of Japanese managers, as we discuss in detail in Chapter 2.

Defining cultural boundaries

According to Giddens (1989: 31) a culture can be defined by reference to the *values* that members of a given group hold (e.g. how they claim to think the world ought to be) and the *norms* they follow (e.g. what members of the group currently choose to be appropriate and/or inappropriate behaviour in a given situation). These norms of behaviour are often determined by a 'significant minority' of members whose views carry more weight on account of their relative status (e.g. age, experience) or of their perceived or ascribed authority: e.g. parents, teachers, religious leaders, the 'boss'; and also people we individually choose as role models such as sports heroes or charismatic business leaders. Among many Japanese managers, Soichiro Honda (mentioned in our introduction) has such status. Among Americans it might be Jack Welch, former chief of GE. With the growing internationalization in management studies, aspiring managers will take their inspiration from a range of sources.

We should note that behavioural norms tend to be more superficially held than values, and so are more adaptable to immediate circumstances. For example, many cultures share the value that killing people is 'wrong'. However, in circumstances of extreme crisis (e.g. war), individuals who share this value may suddenly adopt contradictory norms (e.g. go out and kill people). In short, values and norms are subject to change according to time, place or circumstances and, not least, each individual's experience and perception of what is or might be allowed by the 'significant minority' of the culture-specific reference group: i.e. those who might call the individual to account for errant behaviour. The influence of reference groups in Japanese management behaviour is a focus for our discussion in Chapter 2.

Giddens (1989) also explains how a culture can be distinguished by reference to the *material goods* that the members of the group create or use. These material goods (or *artefacts*) can be recognized in personal choices of food, dress, and other commodities such as cars, mobile phones, and so on. Material goods can also be recognized in the form of architecture, road design, signposting and other social facilities. Language is also a collective and culture-specific creation or artefact.

Approaching cultures

As suggested above, when we travel around on business – or even when we turn on a television set – we encounter different cultures. In describing encounters with culture, Trompenaars and Hampden-Turner (1998) identify three layers of intercultural contact. First in line comes the encounter with *explicit products*; then at a deeper level the encounter with sets of *norms and values*; and then, at a deeper level again, with *core assumptions*. One difference between these three layers and those outlined by Giddens is the significance given to 'core assumptions'.

Core assumptions

We each acquire a set of culture-specific core assumptions in much the same way as we learn our 'native' or so-called 'mother' tongue. Accordingly, these core assumptions are transmitted from generation to generation (often in the form of stories or myths) and serve to explain and actualize the efforts made by individuals – singly and above all collectively – to survive against natural elements – 'the Dutch with rising water, the Swiss with mountains' (Trompenaars and Hampden-Turner, 1998: 23). To these we can add the US Americans with their wide plains and the Japanese with their mountains and the ocean on all sides. This notion of 'survival' against hostile elements (e.g. 'competitors') can be readily translated to the field of corporate strategy (cf. Henderson, 1989).

Encountering cultures

Trompenaars and Hampden-Turner's view of culture can be applied to predict how non-Japanese managers are likely to experience their encounter with Japanese culture or indeed any other business culture. The learning value of engaging in this process is enhanced by asking ourselves critical questions such as 'why this?' and 'why not that?' at each stage in the encounter. To make the experience memorable, we could also ask ourselves 'and why do I react as I do?'

Our own tentative definition of Japanese culture will take its initial shape in response to first impressions. These will include *explicit products*, such as language, architecture, dress, food, and so on. Our ability to recognize these will be influenced by the broader environmental context given by our perception of the climate and of time differences, and so on.

After a period of familiarization – more or less long, depending on our prior experience of international travel, of Asia, and our individual sense of flexibility, adaptability and confidence – we then begin to discern a second layer of culture where *norms* and *values* become evident. According to Trompenaars and Hampden-Turner, norms are 'the mutual sense a group has of what is *right* and *wrong*' [emphasis as in original] (1998: 21–22). They go on to state that 'norms can develop on a formal level as written laws, and on an informal level as social control' (1998: 22). For example, at the airport we will notice signs and instructions directing us in what we should do, and what not. From these encounters we will begin to extrapolate and form a generalized idea of 'Japan', 'Japanese people' and 'Japanese culture'.

Norms are commonly assumed to dictate individual behaviour: the feeling of how one should or should not 'normally' behave in culture-specific situations. Further into our encounter with Japanese culture we will observe examples of *normal* Japanese behaviour: greetings, bowing, use of eye contact, and so on. From the outsider's perspective these can be 'learnt' (as in imitated) but perhaps not fully assimilated or understood. We will also begin to recognize culture-specific *values*: for example, in respect of a person's age or perceived social status. Such values can be learnt (as in recognized and respected) without requiring full commitment. For example, we can see both Japanese and western tourists wearing headscarves while visiting the Blue Mosque in Istanbul, but this does not make them committed Muslims. We can adapt to norms without changing our fundamental values; and culture-specific norms can be adapted, though to change values generally takes considerably longer. In

Japan, our experience of learning norms and values will converge as we begin to pick up some Japanese phrases such as 'thank you' (*arigato*) and 'excuse me' (*sumimasen*) and learn how and when to use them; for example according to who we are speaking to and in what context.

The fluency of our understanding of culture-specific norms and values will be determined by our experience of *time* and *space*: for example, how long we get to stay in Japan and in what situations and contexts we are able to make our experiences. Given sufficient time and space, we may even begin to tune into some of the core assumptions that, according to Trompenaars and Hampden-Turner's model, decisively distinguish cultures from each other: for example, distinctive attitudes among Japanese people towards the natural environment. Crucially, our individual understanding of culture-specific norms, values and core assumptions will be determined by our own motivation, confidence and ability to achieve a given level of fluency in identifying, tolerating and interpreting or managing them: in other words, the type of skills and attitudes useful for managing so-called 'culture shock' (cf. Mead, 1998: 412–417).

SECTION 2: CRITICAL INCIDENTS

> Traveling abroad . . . helps us to understand from where we come.
>
> (Tanner Pascale and Athos, 1981)

Two managers told us about their first encounters with Japanese management and business culture.

A Swedish manager explained her first view of Japanese office life. It was from a 'limousine bus' bringing her group from Tokyo's Narita airport to the city centre.

> As we got closer to the city centre we got caught up in a traffic jam. It was getting dusk and so we had plenty of time to look out and into the office blocks near the raised section of the highway. I could see floor upon floor of offices, very brightly lit, open-plan and laid out in large blocks of desks. The staff seemed to sit and work very close to each other; in some offices there was a PC or a laptop on every desk so everything appeared rather cramped. There were piles of paper and ring- and box files stacked along the windows. I thought: is this what Japanese efficiency looks like? Higher up in the building were what appeared to be the larger, perhaps single-person offices and meeting

rooms – all plainly visible, it was like an open picture book! On each floor there was what looked like a small room for coffee – I saw a vending machine – and people standing around, smoking and chatting. As we were hardly moving in the traffic I had plenty of time to take all this in. It was seven-thirty in the evening and I was thinking to myself: why are they hanging around? Why don't they go home or somewhere more pleasant?

The first direct person-to-person business contact in a foreign culture is often one of the most fraught. Many books offer step-by-step remedies towards negotiating the difficult first meeting (cf. Morrison *et al.*, 1995; Rice, 1991). Sometimes a little knowledge causes a large anxiety.

One British manager told us ruefully:

> I remember that at my first meeting with Fujimori-san (his Japanese negotiating partner) he gave me his business card and I gave him mine. During our discussion he gave me a date, time, and number for me to call him to arrange another appointment. I wrote this down on his business card. Looking back, I still don't know whether I offended him by doing so because I later got a call from his secretary to say he was unexpectedly busy and would have to get back to me to arrange a new appointment. He never did.

This manager had read about the importance given to the exchange of business cards in Japan (Box 1.1). Was Fujimori-san offended that his business card (and, by implication, his company and his hard-earned status within this company) had been 'besmirched'? Or was he indifferent to the treatment of his business card but decided, after conferring with his superiors, that the UK manager's offer or product was not good enough? Both answers are possible. But which, for future reference, is more likely?

When we recognize a 'problem' (i.e. a gap in our knowledge and understanding) during our encounters with other cultures we may choose to perceive it as a threat (i.e. towards our ability to achieve our chosen business objectives) and/or as an opportunity to learn more, both about the 'target' culture and about ourselves. Problematic encounters like this can be called 'critical incidents' or 'case studies': i.e. encounters that allow us 'to empathize with people who are having difficulties in various intercultural settings' (Brislin and Yoshida, 1994: 10). Intercultural management training focuses on preparing managers for dealing with critical incidents with confidence and with a minimum of distraction from their business objectives. We hope this book is a contribution in this direction.

Box 1.1 *O-meishi*

The exchange of business cards (in Japanese, *o-meishi*) is an integral part of the first intercultural business encounter. It is customary to read the business card you have received carefully and demonstrably and, if sitting down to a table, to lay it face up in front of you throughout your business discussion. As one business language book explains: 'Business cards are very important in Japan, where one of their most important functions is to immediately identify a person in terms of both the company worked for and the person's relative status within that organisation' (Young, 1998: 17).

The relationship between a Japanese manager's *meishi* and his or her social status is closely related to the notion of 'face', discussed in Chapter 2. We asked a Japanese colleague about what a non-Japanese manager should do to get over the problems of the first meeting: 'If you are in doubt about what is or is not appropriate behaviour, we suggest you do what is natural for you, and then ask what's expected, and then decide to what extent it's in your and your business partner's interests for you to adapt your behaviour. In short, be consistent and show respect. Any "mistakes" you make will be understood as honest mistakes.'

SECTION 3: EXPLAINING JAPANESE MANAGEMENT BEHAVIOUR – A CASE STUDY

It's often happened that when we're negotiating with a group of Japanese, the whole group appears non-committal. It's difficult to know where the questions are coming from and why. In fact, we [the American delegates] often spend hours afterwards in the hotel bar trying to figure out who the main man is, who the decision makers are in the Japanese group, and who we have to impress or persuade when we meet up again next day.

(US American manager, negotiating a product distribution contract in Tokyo, 2001)

How can expert analyses of Japanese management culture, as compared (for example) to US or Anglo-American management culture, help explain the tensions in this common situation?

Applying theories about Japanese management culture

In studies of international management, there is no getting round the problem of balancing theory and practice. The scene above is an extract from practice or individual experience: a slice of reality told to us in a hotel lobby one afternoon in Tokyo (April 2000). A theory should help generalize from individual experience or observation – the process of generalization allows us to compare one experience with our own previous experiences, or our own experiences with those of other people. A theory is a generalization that, to be practically useful, should help us describe and explain our and other people's experiences. Ideally, a theory (or model, also a generalization) should help us to predict the outcome of similar future experiences.

Schneider and Barsoux (1997) present a comprehensive overview of models and theories that should help managers better describe, explain and (ideally) predict the behaviour and attitudes of their international counterparts. For example, they outline models of international management cultures that describe how people from different cultural backgrounds differ in their perception and expectation of their individual and collective relationship to time, space, nature and the environment. They also outline how experience of different cultures tends to shape each individual's approach towards the management of risk or uncertainty and, correspondingly, towards negotiating or solving business problems.

Hofstede and Hall

According to Dahl (2002), two models remain prominent as implements in the intercultural and comparative international management toolbox. The first is Hofstede's '5 Dimensions' model (Hofstede, 1980; 1984; 1991/94; 2001): the five dimensions for comparative analysis being *power distance*; *uncertainty avoidance*; *individualism* versus *collectivism*; *masculinity* versus *femininity*; and *long-term orientation* versus *short-term orientation*. Hall's analysis highlights distinctive features in culture-specific perceptions of *space*, *time* and *language* or *communication* (Hall, 1976; 1983; Hall and Hall, 1987/90). We apply these criteria in more detail below and refer back to them at various stages in this book.

It is important to note that Hofstede's analysis is comparative: which is to say, in order to state anything practically meaningful about 'Japanese' management culture we need to compare it with another national culture we are familiar with – usually our own, though the extent to which each of us reliably 'knows' our 'own' culture is open to debate (cf. Trompenaars and Hampden-Turner, 1998). Hall's analysis tends to treat specific national cultures in isolation (a so-called emic approach). There are intercultural experts (in Europe) who suggest that Hall's analyses tend to be 'Americo-centric'. In a sense, this quality offers a useful balance in our discussion of contemporary Japanese management cultures, given that (among prominent Japanese experts) many discussions of Japanese culture have tended to be 'Japan-centric' (cf. Box 3.1). Furthermore, American models and values have had a formative influence on Japanese management thinking and behaviour since the end of World War Two, a theme we develop in Chapters 3 and 7.

For a concise summary of the methodology and results of Hofstede's analysis see Mead (2000) and Lane, DiStefano and Maznewiski (2000). For an update on Hall's thinking – and not least his views on selecting and preparing managers for expatriate assignments to cope with 'culture shock' – see Sorrells (1998).

Being critical with theories

One danger inherent in applying models and theories is that of over-generalization. As stated already, there is a temptation for us to apply general conclusions to individual cases, coming to conclusions about other people's individual behaviour such as 'typical' (British, Japanese, etc.). As managers we need to ask ourselves critically how practically useful such generalizations are: for example, do they help us communicate more effectively with our counterpart from another culture? Do they help both of us achieve a specific 'win-win' outcome to intercultural business negotiations?

Applying business models

It is natural to generalize; this is how we as human beings make sense of our complex lives. Generalization is usual procedure in creating models for effective management. For example, the well-known '4Ps' or '7Ps' marketing mix models have been created and developed on the basis of the collective and cumulative experience of many individual managers over many years. Management models and theories are generalizations. Why do we need them? First, because they help us translate the complex everyday processes of management into a concise form with a terminology that together offer a clear and shared point of reference for discussion among managers of diverse backgrounds and experience. By extension, models facilitate communication between ourselves and others: for example, the 'marketing mix' models can be projected to a room of five or fifty managers, or to infinite numbers via the internet, for focusing a discussion or for group training purposes. For future reference the marketing mix model offers a starting point for individual managers of diverse experiences to generate their own marketing analysis according to their own or their organization's needs and circumstances. Similarly, managers can relate their experiences of encounters with Japanese management culture by referring to models such as those generated by Hofstede and Hall; without, however, claiming that all Japanese managers behave in this way. In our experience, it is the 'exceptions to the rule' which provide most learning value.

Avoiding stereotypes

We should be critically aware of the gap between our own experiences and what we know of others' experiences. Furthermore, we should be wary of creating or relying on 'stereotypes' – as we shall see, the notion or image of the Japanese *salaryman* is one such stereotype (cf. Box 8.1). Mead (1998) warns us that relying on stereotypical images to inform our attitudes towards the behaviour of people with cultural backgrounds different from our own is 'lazy' thinking and puts at risk the efficiency and effectiveness of outcomes of our future encounters with individuals from these cultures. As stated previously, we recommend focusing on:

- the individuals we are trying to work with;
- the context for our encounter;
- our common objectives or desired outcome from this encounter.

Focusing on the problem

Against this background, let's return to the case of the US American manager and his negotiation team. As a reminder, this is a summary of what he told us; this is the 'problem' or (as defined in our introduction) the 'gap' in understanding between the US American group manager and their Japanese counterparts:

- the Japanese negotiation team appears non-committal;
- it's difficult to know where the questions are coming from and why;

- we [the American group] have to spend hours trying to identify who the real decision-makers [in the Japanese group] are;
- we're not sure who [in the Japanese group] we have to impress or how.

Here is how we can apply some of the models of comparative cultural analysis to describe and explain key aspects of this problem.

Collectivism

A fundamental aspect of the problem appears to be the apparent mismatch in dynamics between the two negotiation groups. This can be explained in part with reference to Hofstede's *collectivism/individualism* dichotomy. According to Hofstede's analysis, US American managers are twice as likely to express individualist values than their Japanese counterparts. According to Dahl (2002): 'Individualist cultures typically emphasise the goals of the individual, individual initiative and achievement, more dominantly than collectivist societies, which are more concerned with collective goals and the group as a whole . . . collectivist societies put a greater emphasis on personal relationships and group harmony.' According to Mead (2000: 149): 'Individualism and collectivism are better distinguished in terms of the social priorities that influence decision-making. [In individualist cultures] . . . the manager aims for variety rather than conformity in work and does not have strong emotional connections with the company. He/she is loyal for as long as it suits his/her interests; that is, loyalty is calculative.'

Using this analysis we could suggest that, whereas members of the US American team are willing to speak out individually – for example, each speaking out or answering questions according to his or her own curiosity or field of expertise, and perhaps even qualifying what one of his colleagues may have just said – members of the Japanese group are more likely to be committed to maintaining the appearance of a harmonious or cohesive unit: a 'solid front' which resists pressure to move the negotiation along in a direction or at a pace they feel uncomfortable with. Furthermore, and rather than speaking out openly and spontaneously, the group perhaps saves its critical questions for private discussion or for follow-up negotiation sessions where these questions can be put forward in a carefully phrased written form. As we discuss in Chapter 2, the priority for many Japanese managers is first and foremost to avoid losing – or causing – loss of face: speaking out and 'making a mistake' or committing the group to a course of action it has not (collectively) sanctioned would amount to losing and causing loss of face, a process we discuss in more detail in Chapter 2.

Aversion to risk or uncertainty

In the context of international management, we should distinguish between notions of 'risk' and 'uncertainty'. Nobody can predict the future with certainty: uncertainty is therefore a natural condition. Hofstede (2001; 1991) explains how 'Uncertainty is to risk as anxiety is to fear. Fear and risk are both focused on something specific: an object in the case of fear, an event in the case of risk. Risk is often expressed as a percentage of probability that a particular event may happen' (2001: 116). This definition thus suggests that 'risk' can be calculated. It could further be argued that a core strategic responsibility of managers is to identify and calculate risk: in other words, and on behalf of the organization, managers are expected to take 'calculated' risks. A common wisdom states that 'good' managers are those who can predict and respond to future uncertainties effectively and confidently.

Risk is where progress or profits are generated. Correspondingly, risk can be distinguished from uncertainty by reference to two main criteria: (1) the degree of focus on specific outcomes (e.g. profit); and (2) the amount of available information relevant to achieving these outcomes (i.e. context). And in addition to quantitative calculations of risk comes the more qualitative 'people risk': i.e. the extent to which managers can rely on other people involved in or influenced by their decisions to behave as they had calculated or expected (Jackson, 2003).

Based on Hofstede's analysis, Japanese managers are likely to be twice as averse to uncertainty as their US American counterparts. According to Dahl (2002), 'Countries that score low in uncertainty avoidance typically favour taking risks, trying new ways and using novel approaches. Societies that score high however tend to put greater emphasis on the "tried and tested" methods, are unlikely to take on high risks and are generally considered to be averse to ambiguity.' This conclusion would explain (again in part) why members of the Japanese team appear unwilling to speak out emphatically or critically – spontaneous utterances are more prone to ambiguity than written or prepared ones: speaking out may also commit the Japanese side to something they might later regret – or be unable to get approved if they have to refer any decisions to superior decision-makers.

Power distance

This dimension is concerned with deference, respect for authority, hierarchy, status and the tolerance of inequalities between members of a social or culture-specific group. Hofstede's analysis reveals that Japanese managers are slightly more likely to be concerned with (automatic) respect for authority and hierarchy than US American managers. The key difference between the two in practical terms is likely to be how noticeably 'the boss' chooses to behave among his/her subordinates.

Despite an explicit tradition of social and political values which emphasize equality, in an American context the boss or leading decision-maker in a group can be expected to announce him/herself and act according to the expectations of being noticed and taking a lead. This may be explained by reference to Hofstede's 'individualist' dimension. The expectation of senior figures in Japanese cultures is different. Confucian tradition emphasizes un-equality in society: for example, attributing automatic authority to older and male members of society. However, with this seniority comes an obligation modestly but firmly to concern oneself with the welfare of junior members, for example, in terms of teaching and guiding them in appropriate behaviours. In Hofstede's words: 'a key part of the initiation process for junior members to a given group is to learn obediently from the prior experience of their superiors' (Hofstede 1991: 37). Accordingly, it is likely that younger members of the Japanese negotiation team will be regarded as 'learners' and so perhaps have more licence to 'make mistakes' than their seniors.

Adler, Campbell and Laurent (1989) confirm that younger and less experienced managers in Asian cultures often perceive seniority (in terms of management position and age) as synonymous with expert knowledge – hence the significance of power (ascribed decision-making authority) and distance (e.g. age) in Confucian and in traditional Japanese management culture. This view is a core element in understanding the systems of education in core values and training in work-related values in Japan, described in Chapter 3. However, experience tells us that referring to Japan as a 'Confucian society' is about as practically useful in business contexts as referring to Brazil, France and the USA in one breath as 'Christian' societies (cf. Oh, 1991; but see also Dore, 1987).

So, how does this generalized analysis help explain the US team's frustration at identifying the 'real decision-makers'? Given the traditional promotion structures in Japanese organizations, it is possible that the oldest member of the Japanese group held the highest rank. However, given the cumulative 'inflation' of middle-ranking manager positions since the 1980s in Japan (cf. Chapter 6), the oldest member of the group might not be the major decision-maker. In fact, the key decision-maker might not be present at all. However, his (and it probably is 'his') influence will be felt by the Japanese members present and inform their choices of behaviour, a phenomenon we describe in Chapter 2. Once this absent decision-maker has conferred and agreed a course of action with his proxies, the group and their organization are able – collectively – to switch very swiftly into the implementation process.

Time orientation

This dimension is typically concerned with the time frame in which the individual operates. We have seen that major business decisions take time in Japanese organizations: Japanese managers take a long-term time orientation. The US negotiators should probably not expect to get a 'signed and delivered' deal in the space of one visit. In Hall's terms, short-term orientation is primarily concerned with the present and immediate future, such as favouring immediate benefits (e.g. year-end profits or return on investment) over long-term gain (e.g. business relations that will last and sustain both sides over the long term). Management actions for controlling the short-term future tend to be planned sequentially and causally – or *monochronically*, using Hall's terminology. There is a preference for specific objectives or goals and an explicit measurement of progress. In the US negotiating team, 'best practice' may be seen as setting firm markers of progress with interim phrases such as 'now let me just summarize what we have achieved so far' as both sides work towards 'getting to yes' (cf. Fisher and Ury, 1997).

Japanese managers and their organizations traditionally take a long-term strategic view (cf. Kono, 1990). From a western perspective, this tradition may seem to contradict the heightened aversion to uncertainty, as outlined above. However, this long-term orientation can also be interpreted as being based on confidence in the resources one has to hand to negotiate whatever the future might bring. In a Japanese context the nearest factor at hand to control and therefore prepare for what the future brings is human capital: people. Accordingly, there is a tradition in Japanese management culture to trust in the commitment and flexibility of their people to respond effectively to future business conditions. In contrast, some Japanese managers suggest that the 'western' (i.e. Anglo-American) short-term orientation displays a lack of confidence or trust in one's employees (cf. Ouchi, 1981). The question as to whether this degree of trust is still viable in Japanese management contexts is controversial and forms the focus for discussion in Chapter 6.

In terms of intercultural business negotiations the Japanese preference for long-term orientation may generate a severe (and frustrating) mismatch of agendas: the US negotiators want to 'get to yes' quickly, and not only because they have limited time in Tokyo. In contrast, their Japanese counterparts want – or are perhaps required – to take their time. Some western managers complain that Japanese companies sometimes use negotiation procedures 'to get information from us: with their incessant and detailed questions, they just try to find out how far we are in developing our products, but without actually agreeing to close any deals with us', as one member of the US American group complained. This perception might be tuning in to a distinctive Japanese approach to taking time to learn from contact with culture-specific outsiders or unfamiliar (when unthreatening) situations (cf. Chapter 5). Accordingly, Japanese managers may interpret the same scene very differently: 'We tried patience as we wanted to get to know them and so get to trust them. But they just wanted to sell and then move on to the next deal.'

High-context communication

The impression that the US negotiators get of their Japanese counterparts has to be interpreted in some form. For this to happen, this impression has to be communicated by the Japanese team. One of the key concerns for participants in intercultural communication is the ease with which what one side communicates might not be understood or (more significant and risky) be misunderstood by the other side.

In the context of patterns of culture-specific communication, Hall distinguishes between *low-context* and *high-context* cultures. High-context cultures are those where members generally do not expect a significant amount of information to be made explicit (e.g. through speech, gesture, or spoken or written instructions): 'A high context communication or message is one in which most of the information is already in the person' (Hall, 1976). Japan is profiled as a high-context culture. Specifically: 'The Japanese talk around the point', explaining that this is because they expect their interlocutors or communication partners 'to discover the point of the discourse from the context' (Hall, 1983: 63). Dahl (2002) sees direct parallels between Hall's high-context/low-context distinction and Hofstede's collectivist/individualist dimension.

The importance of context

There is little practical use in 'blaming' some generalized notion of 'culture' for communication breakdown or negotiation failure. There is likely to be more value in focusing on specific 'contexts'. According to Avruch (2002), 'culture is context, not cause'. This view supports recommendations on 'smart' ways to work with Japanese business partners in particular (cf. Yoshimura and Anderson, 1997).

What do we mean by context? According to Herbig (1998: 58), 'context' is 'the amount of information in a given communication'. Differences in culture thus become evident in the ways that people (individually or collectively) select and process information and thereby identify and interpret contexts. Working to understanding how each side interprets their shared context is, we believe, important in working to avoid intercultural communication breakdown.

The US American negotiators appeared frustrated by the lack of clear information that the context for negotiation was giving them. Part of the context is given by the location in Tokyo (i.e. as opposed to in the USA). But ultimately decisions are made in rooms or offices that are likely to be neutral in terms of reaching major decisions. This may contrast with, for example, the Chinese way of negotiation, which often involves a meal where decisions effectively are made in flow with the mood of the occasion, and for as long as this mood coheres with prior expectations (cf. Blackman, 1997).

Given the traditionally high-context nature of much Japanese business communication, face-to-face interaction is a key factor in ascertaining how closely each side's interpretations of context conform. According to Matsumoto (2002), US Americans are distinctive by their ability to achieve 'cross-context consistency' (cf. Box 1.2). In other words, US American managers might tend to 'import' prior norms and values into diverse and (most significantly) previously unfamiliar contexts rather than adapt to them. Applying Matsumoto's logic, they might not even fully perceive the degree of contextual differences. In our experience, Japanese managers probably do something similar; the significant difference being that these will pause and try to work out the (unfamiliar) context (perhaps choosing to be silent or non-committal while they do this) before proceeding with action or decision. Returning to our negotiation case study, it might be the US team's unwillingness or failure to adapt to local context that makes the negotiation process appear so difficult. As the US manager himself said (almost resignedly): 'Well, if they really want to do business with us, we'll find a way somehow.'

Box 1.2 Critical voices

Ambler and Witzel (2000) do not accept Hofstede's methodology or conclusions, stating that the dualism of the dimensional axes (e.g., collectivist *or* individualist) does not match with their and other management practitioners' experience. With regard to the dualism element they suggest that Hofstede is 'a prisoner of his own (Dutch) culture' and then pronounce that 'quite frankly, this type of research is hocus-pocus' (2000: 71).

Matsumoto (2002) takes issue with many of the established conclusions about Japanese culture. He sees it as his purpose to 'debunk' a series of cultural stereotypes that westerners commonly hold about Japanese people and their norms of behaviour. Based on his own research he concludes among other things that:

- Japanese people are as individualistic as US Americans: indeed, that in certain contexts Americans adhere more to 'collectivist values' than do Japanese;
- Japanese people are as independently-minded in their decision-making as US Americans or Australians: i.e., they do not rely on advice or collective guidance before making a personal decision;
- Japanese people are as 'emotional' as Americans: i.e., contrary to the stereotypical view that Japanese in the company of strangers tend to hide their true negative emotions behind a fixed smile.

In terms of comparing the behaviour of Americans and Japanese Matsumoto does concede that individual Japanese tend to regulate their behaviour according to context. For example, Japanese are more likely to express negative emotions with [group] 'outsiders' and positive emotions with [group] 'insiders' than their American counterparts. In contrast, 'Americans believe in cross-context consistency, they generalize this tendency to *all* contexts [and therefore infer] that Japanese people hide their emotions – or have no emotions – in general' (2002: 63). This view gives further basis to the belief that, in order to understand or criticize other cultures, one needs to be aware of one's own culture first. Also, that one should be wary of other people's over-generalizations about one's own or other cultures.

We contrasted this view with that of a Russian manager (a distributor for Japanese automobiles) who told us: 'I enjoy doing business with Japanese. I think we know how to get on. What I respect above all is that, when they give their word to a deal – a delivery date or a price – then they stick to it. Even if it means they end up losing out because of the exchange rate or something like that.' Different context, different culture, with different collective and individual expectations: this manager had learned his trade during the turbulent Gorbachev years at the end of the Soviet Union.

Distinctive features of Japanese-style management communication

Focusing on context and interpreting what is considered appropriate or inappropriate behaviour in a range of (ideally, predictable) contexts is a skill that Japanese managers learn from their earliest exposure to language learning in the family, in school, and later in the world of work (cf. Chapter 3).

For example, Yoshimura and Anderson (1997) describe the process of 'hearing one and understanding ten'. This describes the situation whereby a senior manager 'suggests' an instruction to a junior who is then expected to rack his or her brains and confer with colleagues until eventually s/he finds out and delivers what the senior wanted. This in part explains the traditionally high level of presenteeism in Japan or what Kossek and Lobel (1996) term 'face time' at work: not daring to leave before the boss; hanging around the office coffee machine (as observed by one of the non-Japanese managers cited in Section 2); or trying to glean from more experienced colleagues later in the bar exactly what the boss is asking for – a process half-jokingly called 'nomination', a term combining the English 'communication' with Japanese 'nomu' [to drink] (cf. Melville, 1999: xviii).

Tanner Pascale and Athos were among the first western observers to recognize the strategic HRM potential of these forms of learning and management communication in Japanese organizations, seeing it as '[a] development of language and forms of discourse, especially in their indirection, [which] permit high development of skills we [westerners] seldom achieve or honor' (1981: 204). In short, high-context communication is very effective in developing individual skills of interpretation and, from the HRM perspective, generates cultural cohesion while simultaneously offering a subtle instrument of control. We discuss in detail issues in balancing trust and control in Japanese management culture in Chapters 2 and 6.

Silence

Distinctive for high-context cultures such as Japan is the communicative potential of *silence*. By this we mean the period of non-verbal communication tolerated between verbal utterances. The period of silence allowed in Japanese speech tends to go far beyond the few seconds that is the normal tolerance limit in western languages. Anybody who has tried to conduct business or personal telephone conversations with Japanese people will understand this phenomenon. This, the US American manager told us, was a particularly 'irritating' aspect of the negotiation case we have been discussing. Quite simply, Japanese negotiators can usually tolerate silence longer than their Anglo-American or European counterparts.

Some Japanese and non-Japanese international management experts emphasize the 'uniqueness' of *haragei* or 'belly language' in Japanese business and management communications. This appears to have the nature of a combination of shared intuition and telepathy and has been suggested as one way in which Japanese negotiators are able to 'outfox' 'low-context people' such as 'Americans, Germans, Swiss, Scandinavians and other northern Europeans' (Hickson, 1997: 14). It is our view that this power of *haragei* has to do with cultural cohesion and collective (i.e. group) confidence rather than being a medium of communication 'unique' to Japanese (cf. Box 3.1). One interesting question is how far proponents of *haragei* have a future when more and more business communication happens via electronic means.

Practical recommendations

Based on the discussion so far, our advice to the US American negotiator and his colleagues was as follows:

- focus on the individuals in front of you: avoid working to stereotypes;
- stay positive: work towards establishing trust;
- be flexible: try to elicit and understand your partner's interpretation of the context;
- make your own purpose clear and transparent;
- be patient.

SECTION 4: CHANGES IN JAPANESE MANAGEMENT CULTURE

> It is our belief that you can never understand other cultures.
> (Trompenaars and Hampden-Turner 1998)

Problems and generalizations

In the introduction to this book we defined a 'problem' as a 'gap in knowledge or understanding'. Trompenaars and Hampden-Turner (1998), following from Hofstede (1991) and Kluckhohn and Strodtbeck (1961), have developed a model whereby a culture can be defined according to how members of that culture-specific group singly and collectively tend to identify and respond to problems or what we have previously referred to as 'critical incidents'.

The essential 'problem' for a non-Japanese business visitor to Japan is how to negotiate the different levels of encounters with Japanese culture in order to achieve his or her business objectives. We have looked at the experiences of some non-Japanese business visitors to Japan. We saw how these cultural 'outsiders' expressed a need to refer to their own culture-specific values: as rational human beings we naturally make comparative generalizations. We do this not only in order to rationalize immediately observable norms of behaviour, but also in order to predict with any accuracy how the individuals we are dealing with are likely to behave in future contexts and encounters. This is, fundamentally, a form of self-protection: a survival technique. In Japanese contexts, attention to 'face' has a similar value, as we discuss in Chapter 2.

In order to predict how we expect ourselves and other people to respond when faced by a problem or dilemma, we reflect on or own acquired sets of values and assumptions: our own culture-specific experience. The US American and Japanese negotiators we discussed in the previous section appeared to be facing (individually and collectively) the 'problem' of insufficient knowledge or understanding of each other's cultural backgrounds and (in this context) of each other's business objectives. The extent to which this situation represented a 'crisis' would be determined by how important they perceived the success of the current negotiation to be. How the individual members of each group managed the dilemmas they encountered would be determined by their experience and expectations of culture and of their individual motivation and ability.

What is 'typical' Japanese business behaviour?

What is currently happening in Japanese management culture which could make the tensions and frustrations they experienced more or less likely should this particular US American manager and his team return to negotiate with their Japanese business partners?

On his own account he might (after reflection on recent experience) have gained a clearer view of the complexities of Japanese business culture. Perhaps he will have had a similar conversation to one we had when asking a Japanese manager what he understood by 'typical Japanese' business culture. He thought for a moment and then gave us some examples, contrasting Japanese behaviour with that of managers from North America and Europe he had previously worked or negotiated with. 'So, would you say your behaviour in those situations was "typical" for Japanese managers?' 'Well, no. You see, I originally come from Osaka and there people do business differently.'

He gave us some practical examples: Osaka business people are more likely to negotiate over meals ('similar to Chinese') and are 'less formal' [than people in Tokyo] in developing business relationships, 'particularly with foreigners (*gaijin*)'. Why? He suggested it was because of Osaka's 'more cosmopolitan past'. What did this mean? Osaka used to be the main access port for imports from China and Korea and the city still has a sizeable ethnic Korean community. Also, and given its current ranking as ('only') the third-largest city in Japan – Tokyo and its neighbour Yokohama are one and two respectively – 'being number three means you can take everything in a more relaxed way' (cf. Box 3.2). Of significance to him in comparing social behaviour in Tokyo and Osaka was that 'people on escalators in Tokyo stand on the left-hand side while in Osaka we normally stand on the right. This is the one of the first things I remember when I get off the *shinkansen* in Osaka'. We concluded from this and similar conversations that there is little practical value in referring too strictly to notions of a monolithic 'Japanese' management culture.

Masculinity/femininity

But generalizations about features of so-called 'national' cultures are useful: they give us a conceptual framework and common point of reference for analysing and discussing change. However, relying on generalizations may also restrict our understanding of how we perceive and interpret events. Take, for example, Hofstede's masculinity versus femininity dimension. Our experiences in applying and teaching this concept are fraught with complication, not least because of the tendency to confuse gender relations (i.e. male/female) with culture-specific values (i.e. masculine/feminine): women managers can be analysed as expressing a mix of masculine and feminine values, as can male managers. The frequent confusion is indicative of the value- and assumption-laden complexity of using and interpreting language: the 'management of meaning' as current HRM texts have it.

Based on Hofstede's analysis, Japanese culture comes way out top in terms of adherence to 'masculine' values. In contrast, Sweden is ranked as the most femininity-oriented of cultures with a score one-nineteenth that of Japan. According to Dahl (2002): 'masculine cultures typically favour assertive, competitive and tough attitudes'. And Mead (2000: 151): 'In the more masculine cultures, the social ideal is performance, and the maintenance of economic growth has top priority. Employees may give the company higher priority than the home.' Other 'masculine' characteristics include a preference for 'strong' or 'corrective' behaviour (Hofstede 1991: 103); and furthermore in high uncertainty avoidance cultures 'managers will invest great amounts of energy into avoiding what is unfamiliar or suggests unpredictable outcomes; this includes discouraging individual behaviour which might upset the accepted behavioural norms of the social group' (Hofstede 1991: 125). This might explain some of the US American negotiator's frustration. And yes: the entire Japanese negotiating team was male.

What does this profile suggest in practical terms? The expected dominance of masculine values in Japanese management culture might in part explain the experience of one UK manager who told us: 'We find our Japanese business partners are hesitant to speak out openly in formal meetings, even though we've done business with each other many times before. They fear making mistakes in their English: to them, being misunderstood means appearing weak or incompetent. They open up much more in more informal situations, for example during a round of golf or after a few drinks.'

Masculine/feminine values

In developing his generic analysis of the masculinity/femininity dimensions of societal cultures, Hofstede lists the features of 'twin-pole parameters'. Societal cultures that tend towards the 'masculine' pole (i.e. ostensibly Japan) give priority to:

- *earnings* (e.g. monetary rewards);
- *recognition* (e.g. for a job well done);
- *advancement* (e.g. promotion);
- *challenge* (e.g. work which is difficult but gives a 'personal sense of achievement').

In contrast, societal cultures that tend towards the 'feminine' pole (such as Sweden) give priority to:

- having good relations with immediate superiors;
- co-operation within groups;
- 'living in a desirable area' (e.g. family life and quality of life outside work);
- employment security.

(adapted from Hofstede 1991/94: 81–82)

Despite Japan's clear ranking (in Hofstede's analysis) as a 'masculinity-oriented' societal culture, we believe that the individual case studies we present and discuss in the following chapters suggest the following more complex picture of (1) traditional Japanese management culture and (2) emerging Japanese management culture – or, in our terms, the emerging face of Japanese management.

1 Traditional values in Japanese management culture

- *individual recognition* for *effort* and *collective recognition* for a job well done;
- *advancement* (i.e. mainly for male managers as automatic seniority promotion);
- *having good relations* with line-managers and immediate superiors;
- *co-operation* within *groups*;
- *employment* security.

2 Emerging features of Japanese management culture (based on our research and case studies presented in this book)

- *earnings* (i.e. for those who have become disenchanted with traditional reward and promotion structures) or who wish to finance more time and energy for;

- *quality of life* (i.e. family and individual lifestyle choices, including Hofstede's 'living area' notion) together with a willingness to forgo;
- *employment security* if the alternative is to experience personal and professional;
- *challenges* and achieve;
- *individual recognition* and satisfaction for a job well done.

We accept that a conscious decision to present a balanced (i.e. approximately 50–50 male/female) ratio has had an impact on our conclusions in terms of the growing overlap between men's and women's roles in Japanese management. Also, we should remember that around the time Hofstede first published his results the common western view was that in Japan 'female managers [were] virtually non-existent' (Hofstede, 1991: 81). Until recently, this perception was mirrored in Japan itself (cf. Renshaw, 1999). Indeed, Hofstede's assertion that 'Femininity stands for a society in which social gender roles overlap: both men and women are supposed to be modest, tender, and concerned with the quality of life' (1991: 261) encourages us to suggest that Japanese management culture is becoming more femininity-oriented.

Shifts in Japanese management culture

A trend common to both men and women managers in our sample suggests that increasingly individual managers are seeking out challenges in order to experience a sense of what we term 'self-esteem' or what Trompenaars and Hampden-Turner (1998) emphasize as *achievement*. This observation encourages us to suggest that Japanese managers are becoming both less risk or uncertainty averse – perhaps necessarily as job security and automatic promotion prospects diminish – and thereby more individualized and internationalized. These are themes we develop in Chapters 5 to 8.

The development of these trends is constrained by features of uncertainty avoidance, exemplified by the traditional and residual expectation of 'lifetime employment' (Box. 5.1). Women managers appear to be leading the way in this respect. As one female respondent explained to us: 'Because of the way most career paths have been structured in Japan, Japanese women have tended to be less loyal to companies and more flexible in response to adverse conditions. And we are certainly experiencing adverse conditions at the moment!'

SECTION 5: OUR OWN APPROACH

> We all have our Biases. Our experiences dictate our
> behavior and our perceptions of the behavior of others.
> (Ptak, Cooper and Brislin, 1995)

In this chapter we have paid particular attention to a model of and definition of culture developed by Trompenaars and Hampden Turner (1998). Essentially, this model is generated by taking a 'problem focussed approach'. One advantage of the problem-focused approach to defining culture is that the more we suspend judgement (i.e. 'open our minds') and reflect on the evidence of our encounters with other cultures the more we learn about 'culture' and the nature of intercultural business and management encounters generally.

We have taken a problem-focused approach in researching and writing this book. We negotiated our interviews and conversations with Japanese managers in order to get answers to questions; but also to find out which questions we should be asking. We explained the premise for our research. We compared the answers given to us by Japanese managers to those given by non-Japanese managers and experts. We posed our questions in different *contexts*. For example, at times the interviews and discussion were set up formally, at others times more informally. We interviewed in groups of two, sometimes more. Mindful of the unevenness in gender relations in Japanese society we arranged interviews between only women, or between only men, or in mixed groups or dyads. Mindful of the centrality of language in identifying Japanese society we interviewed sometimes in English and sometimes in Japanese, and sometimes in both.

Rather than start from generalizations we chose to focus on the experiences, expectations and perceptions of individuals, and ask how these are changing. How are individual managers responding to crisis? Are they aware of it? What professional or personal opportunities and threats do they perceive in the current and emerging circumstances? What constraints do they perceive and experience in trying to make and follow through on their own career and business decisions? How do those who are considering quitting their current 'secure' job respond to the appeal from family and friends to 'common sense' as they struggle to 'do the right thing'?

To echo Trompenaars and Hampden-Turner (1998), can we ever 'know' other cultures? Almost certainly not. But we can certainly respect them and on this basis try to understand them, and in doing so learn more about how individual managers of different cultural backgrounds negotiate the problems and dilemmas that the challenges of international business and a professional career generate. This is the theme of the following chapter.

Summary

> We are what we repeatedly do . . . our habits.
> (attributed to Aristotle, Greek, fourth century BC)

In this chapter we have worked towards a definition of Japanese management culture. This process should be of practical use in helping us understand, explain and (ideally) predict some of the distinctive features of Japanese management behaviour and how non-Japanese managers might respond to these. This chapter provides a conceptual framework for interpreting and understanding the experiences of individual Japanese managers that form the core of this book.

We began this chapter by quoting from Confucius, whose philosophical and moral teaching has an enduring influence in East Asia. We ended the chapter with a quote from Aristotle, whose teaching has encouraged people in western cultures to do the best they can in the 'here and now'. In between we have begun to look at how western management experts and practitioners have tried to understand Japanese management cultures and work with Japanese managers and business partners. We have worked towards what we hope is a practical definition of culture, applying it to a case study of negotiations between Japanese and US American managers.

Consider these questions – they tune into our core values and assumptions:

- How do you feel when a foreign manager or visitor says to you 'Oh, you're so typically "X"!' ('X' being your nationality)?
- What is 'a fact'?
- What is 'common sense'?

2 The face of Japanese management

Introduction

> Avoid breaking the rules.
>
> Master Kong Zhu (Confucius)

In Chapter 1 we worked towards a definition of Japanese management culture by combining the research of management experts with the experiences of practising managers. We traced a picture of Japanese management culture which emphasizes cohesion and long-term oriented continuity, as evidenced in the traditional expectation of lifetime employment.

In this chapter we take a closer look at some of the distinctive features of Japanese management culture, taking the perspective of individual managers and employees. In particular we focus on the notion of 'face', defined by Hofstede (1994: 261) as 'a quality attributed to someone who meets the essential requirements related to his or her social position'. Hofstede suggests that face (as in 'losing face') is particularly significant in so-called 'collectivist' societies such as China, from where (he explains) the notion first entered the English language (Hofstede, 1991: 61). In this chapter we discuss 'face' in the context of the 'reference group', defined as 'a closed circle whose members mutually define themselves as insiders' (Yoshimura and Anderson, 1997: 57–58).

After illustrating what essentially the 'face' of Japanese management is, we begin to trace how this face is changing. Specifically, we suggest how interpretations of face in Japanese management and employment cultures are shifting away from an emphasis on 'collectivist' requirements and towards increased attention to 'individualist' requirements such as 'self-respect' (Hofstede, 1991: 61) or 'self-esteem' (Mead, 1998: 136). We conclude with two individual manager case studies.

Our objectives for this chapter are:

- to develop a definition of 'face' in the context of Japanese management;

- to indicate ways in which the face of Japanese management is changing.

SECTION 1: FACE AND REFERENCE GROUPS IN JAPANESE MANAGEMENT

> At first glance a manager's role is to organise, supervise
> and control people so that there is a productive outcome to
> work.
>
> (Hannagan, 1998: 4)

In order to understand why Japanese managers and employees tend to behave and make decisions as they do, singly and in groups, we need to understand something about the notion of 'reference groups' and, in the context of these groups, how individuals pay attention to 'face'. It is by reference to these social and culture-specific constructs that Japanese managers typically 'manage' (cf. as defined above) and Japanese employees typically work. As an illustration, the Japanese negotiating team discussed in Chapter 1 formed a context-specific 'reference group': how members of the group chose to behave and respond – and *not* behave and respond – was shaped by their perceptions of the context of their individual and collective attention to face.

The 'bawling out' scene

Yoshimura and Anderson (1997) describe a scene whereby a group of Japanese managers each evening line up their sales staff ('associates') 'from most junior to most senior' and ask them to give a report on what they had achieved that day. According to Yoshimura and Anderson (1997): 'Usually there wasn't much to report, because a sales associate could do only a limited amount of work in a day, but the purpose of the meeting really wasn't to convey information. The managers focused on what each associate had *not* accomplished during the day; the associates spent most of the meeting listening to their managers yell at them' (1997: 28 – emphasis as in original).

When we refer to this scene and similarly vivid scenes in our work with students and seminar participants, we ask them: 'If you were a witness to this scene, would you feel embarrassed? If you were one of the sales associates, would you feel ashamed, or angry perhaps? What kind of "management" is this? If you were one of the managers, what would you be hoping to achieve with this display of ritualistic behaviour? If you were a witness and all the participants were wearing military uniforms, would this change your interpretation of the scene?' We usually conclude that whether such scenes appear more or less strange or familiar depends on our individual experience of culture and on our expectations of how people (managers/subordinates) should or should not behave in what we can understand of this particular context or situation.

Reference groups

In the context of Japanese management culture, attention to face can be superficially regarded as each individual's endeavour to 'do the right thing'. Doing the 'right' thing is dependent on a person's interpretation of context. By understanding the context, each person should know what behaviour is appropriate. What is 'appropriate' is determined by the expectations of the dominant 'reference group' – the 'closed circle' whose members define themselves by sharing important information. Following on from our discussion of culture in Chapter 1, this information determines the context. Those who are 'insiders' have a better chance of behaving 'according to the rules' – and so avoid loss of face – than group 'outsiders'. Alternatively, those with the status of 'insiders' may have more face to lose.

How individuals perceive and respond to contexts is shaped by their experience of culture: a normal response to context in one culture is not necessarily normal in another. For example, would you tolerate being bawled out each day in the same way as those sales associates in the scene described above? Maybe yes, maybe no: it depends on the context and what is regarded as a normal response in that particular context.

The structure of reference groups

Often, senior or more experienced members of the reference group will give explicit instructions about what type of response is expected: they will make or influence individual members' decisions; they will set the 'rules'. If an individual breaks the rules, he or she risks embarrassment, or even loss of face – we explain the essential difference between these two responses below.

In this sense the reference group is, as Hofstede suggests in his definition of face, a social construct with a hierarchy of authority: think of officers commanding soldiers in battle. In saying this we are not suggesting that Japanese management culture is militaristic, although military metaphors are common enough in the 'culture' of management studies (cf. Drucker, 1999). With or without uniforms, the scene described above does recall military norms and values. In a Japanese context these could be traced back to *samurai* tradition and aspects of the *bushido* code of honourable behaviour: namely, 'courage, benevolence, politeness, veracity, sincerity, honor, loyalty and self-control' (Matsumoto, 2002: 6; Nitobe, 1969). We are not discussing warriors. Though, under crisis, something of a 'warrior' or 'fighting spirit' may be invoked – not least in strategy, marketing and/or the management of sales, as in the scene described above.

The function of reference groups

Reference groups by definition are not limited to Japanese management culture or society. What appears to be distinctive is (and as we discuss in Chapter 3) the systematic way in which Japanese children learn what it takes to work and begin a successful career in the context of families and schools as specific yet overlapping forms of reference groups. The reference group is boundaried, but the boundaries shift in response to context and to individual perception. The children observe how adults form reference groups among themselves. The reference group has a purpose and is thus a social as well as a culture-specific construct. For example, both parents and teachers form a reference group when the focus of concern is on little Hiroaki or little Keiko and how well he or she is doing at school.

Overall, the reference group in a Japanese context exists to guide and to teach individuals by sharing information and experience, transmitting values and norms. It functions as a boundaried 'learning environment', thus pre-empting the Japanese company or *kaisha* as a 'learning organisation' (cf. Nonaka and Takeuchi, 1995; 1998; cf. Chapter 5). The emphasis given to information sharing in the context of Japanese reference groups appears to confound the classic 'prisoner's dilemma'. However, and as we shall see in discussion of 'lifetime employment' and other culture-specific features of Japanese-style HRM, information sharing is the smart choice when the reward is long term (e.g. protection and prosperity) and the relationship between reference group members is based on trust (cf. Chapter 6).

Self-regulation

Accordingly, the stage at which 'little' Hiroaki and Keiko themselves become 'adult' is determined in large part by how soon they become fluent and confident in interpreting the rules and expectations of a wide range of culture-specific contexts and of culture-specific reference groups within Japanese society: in other words, when they can be relied on to regulate their behaviour according to reference group expectations and context. Japanese society is remarkably self-regulating; indeed, Japan's cities are among the safest in the world. This is true and should be kept in mind when making superficial international comparisons between Japanese employment culture and generalized (western) notions of 'quality of life' (cf. Chapter 7).

Time

The reference group sets boundaries to each individual's perception of location (or space) and time. For example, my own interest in the purpose of the reference group may be short term or long term. I may know that my current colleagues will be 'my team' for the next few years and so I will try hard to 'get on' with them. In Japan, where individual managers traditionally expect to trust their career to one company for a lifetime, 'getting on' with colleagues – or the company as a super-ordinate reference group – takes on a particular emphasis, as we illustrate in Chapter 6.

Alternatively, my team and I may be together for only a weekend project and so our focus is likely to be more on 'getting the job done'. This shorter-term orientation is probably a more common perception among managers in western organizations. In comparison to their Japanese counterparts, western managers may feel more encouraged to perceive their current company/reference group as a temporary context before 'moving on', and so their adherence to 'the rules' will probably be less vital. Furthermore, senior members of the company/reference group will expect this and so the rules will be different anyway. On this basis, the generic rules (norms and values) of Japanese-style HRM will tend to differ from western-style HRM. How this traditional expectation is faring in comparison with international trends in employment is a theme we develop in the second half of this book.

Space

In terms of space, the reference group may be perceived as being immediate or distant. For example, I may be managing a project overseas but feel I 'know' what type of professional behaviour my colleagues and superiors back at base expect of me. I should also know what my clients or local colleagues expect of me: as an 'expatriate' manager I need to negotiate my responses in tune with the expectations of a complex array of reference groups whose interests and expectations will overlap – all being focused on the project – but crucially, and almost certainly, will not coincide. In the context of Japanese organizations/reference groups, it is assumed that these diverse interests and expectations tend to coincide to a marked degree, giving rise to the 'collectivist' label all too easily attached to Japanese management culture. The argument is that Japanese managers tend to subsume their individual interests to the collective expectations of the reference group to such a degree that an appearance of extreme cultural cohesion is generated: to outsiders, 'harmony' (*wa*) appears to prevail. We discuss the extent to which this assumption still is – or ever was – valid in Chapter 6.

Mixed-ability groups

Despite the assumption or even expectation of harmony, any reference group will consist of individuals with diverse abilities and attributes (cf. Matsumoto, 2002). Inevitably, tensions will arise, and particularly in times of crisis. Tensions beg to be 'managed'. Picking up on the military metaphor again, this is where past training and current cohesion of thought and action come into play. This is also where social hierarchies (e.g. seniority based on age, length of service, qualifications, and even gender) become apparent. However, the reality is that in the face of crisis a 'junior' group member may have a 'better' idea for an effective response than a 'senior' member. The extent to which this junior member will be encouraged or even allowed to present this idea to the group will be determined by the context and the experience and expectations of the other members of the reference group.

The case study of the US American managers and their Japanese negotiation partners (Chapter 1) illustrates this (apparent) contradiction in tension. During a break in negotiation one of the junior members of the Japanese group appeared to open up and show a lively understanding of the American position. According to the American who told us this, this insight was not translated – and indeed not even mentioned – in subsequent open group discussions. To understand how the junior member of a Japanese reference group might choose to act in this context, and how and why his or her seniors might choose to respond as they did in the broader context, we need to consider again some distinctive features of Japanese-style communication.

Understanding the context

Looking again at the bawling out scene, we have concluded that these people form a 'reference group', despite the fact that, as the authors point out, 'the purpose of the meeting really wasn't to convey information'. So what was being conveyed?

Put the participants in this scene in military-style uniforms, and we (as outsiders) may believe we begin to understand. The context begins to make more sense, because uniforms are a powerful non-verbal symbol of authority and rank. From our own personal or vicarious (i.e. borrowed) experience, we know that people in uniform of a higher rank or status tend to have licence to bawl out people in uniform of a lower rank: we begin to perceive the behaviour in this scene as more 'normal'. But the question remains: what information is being conveyed? To answer this question, we need to engage in some 'cultural decoding'.

Sharing insider information

In Chapter 1 we saw how Hall and others describe Japanese management culture as being particularly 'high context' in terms of preferred communication styles. One expression of this type of culture is that meanings are assumed to be 'in the person': many core meanings are learned and expressed tacitly or without words. A uniform sends a powerful non-verbal message, but by this definition it is not particularly 'high context'.

To understand this particular bawling out scene, we as outsiders need more culture-specific or 'insider' information. Greater insight into the cultural context tells us that sales and marketing people (going back to feudal days of itinerant merchants) have low status in Japanese business life: they are regarded as staff members who, by dint of their function (e.g. person-to-person sales), may well be organized collectively around sales targets but in their behaviour might tend to be individualistic. As such, they threaten the carefully crafted cohesion of the organization as a reference group, the 'crafting' being formalized by HRM policies and practices.

In specific reference to 'sellers', Usunier (1996: 469) states that: 'In a masculine society, the absence of results will be emphasized in a fairly crude manner': ritualistic shouting at people is crude enough! However, and despite the clear results of Hofstede's research, it is unhelpful to describe Japan sweepingly as a 'masculine' society. These sales associates are not being threatened with dismissal: in fact, it is likely that their managers are keen to support them (albeit paternalistically) if they genuinely make an effort to improve their performance. In other words, the managers are willing to express what Usunier calls more 'femininity-oriented' values. We return to this complex theme in subsequent chapters.

Meanwhile, and against this culture-specific backdrop, the ritual bawling out (which the managers themselves have probably learnt from their own time – or initiation – as sales associates) may therefore be interpreted as a means of 'bestowing group identity' (Herbig, 1998: 168). 'You belong to us' is the information being conveyed. Among these particular insiders, such behaviour is normal. To outsiders, it may appear strange and opaque. We should also note that the ritual bawling out takes place *within* the same specific group within the company and not within ear- and eye-shot of members of other groups or sections within the company: the social or reference group is closed. To open it up without a specific purpose is likely to cause loss of face.

Opaque flexibility

The boundaries of reference groups are flexible, defined by common purpose and interest in sharing information. This can baffle non-Japanese outsiders. For example, rival Japanese companies are commonly believed to 'collude' and share information when operating in foreign markets. They may be fierce rivals in domestic markets, but when operating in overseas markets (i.e. in new or unfamiliar contexts) they may regard themselves as members of nation- and industry-wide reference groups and so be willing to share information and other resources. Also, Japanese companies are not averse to sharing strategic information (e.g. sales targets) to industry insiders, the purpose being to maintain some form of equilibrium, even temporarily. Again, this seems implausible to western ears unless one recognizes that the reference group is there to serve the long-term interests of individual members. In strategic terms, competitors can be regarded as useful partners in business or 'stakeholders' – western management theories have caught on to this idea. In culture-specific terms, forcing a near competitor into ruin in Japan is considered undignified and causes loss of face. Traditional Japanese companies affirm themselves by the *existence* of rivals, not by their destruction.

But this insight cannot explain all Japanese management behaviour; many aspects of behaviour remain opaque to outsiders. Consider the following scene, told to us by a non-Japanese business visitor in Tokyo in spring 2002: 'It was early morning and a row of uniformed sales staff were lined up outside the retail outlet I guess they all worked for. In unison they were shouting out to no one in particular details of their recent "failures" to offer customers as high quality service as could be expected and promising to improve their performance from that day forth.'

Again the purpose of this behaviour only makes sense if, as a reference group outsider, we understand the context. The insiders are expected to know what it means. If they don't, they are either not true insiders or they are in the wrong group. For a more detailed insight into the changing life and times of retail staff in Japan, see Matsunaga (2000). We make a case study of management in the Japanese retail industry in Chapter 8.

SECTION 2: FACE AND CONTROL IN JAPANESE MANAGEMENT

Attention to face is universal. In its original meaning 'face' referred to how we appear individually to those around us, or how we appear (individually and as a group) to the rest of society or the world. We can talk of 'national face'. This original meaning gives us the term 'façade', as in the façade of a building (Ayto, 1990). In dealing with Japanese managers, it is important not to confuse 'face' (an emotion) with 'façade' (an appearance). To do so is to fall into the ultimately fruitless trap of accepting without criticism the over-generalized label of 'inscrutable Japanese' (cf. Kodansha, 1997).

Losing face

Imagine you walk into your office to find the 'big boss' shouting at one of your line-managers in eye- and ear-shot of everyone around. Unless you are unfortunate enough to work in an office where this kind of behaviour is normal, you may feel embarrassed for the line-manager, imagining yourself in the same situation. You might also feel amusement, if you dislike this particular manager. Taking a professional stance, however, you imagine that your line-manager must be suffering more than embarrassment; he or she must be experiencing loss of face.

Embarrassment, amusement – these are emotional responses to a crisis situation. Loss of face is more significant in the context of crisis management. It is difficult to be precise. However, embarrassment may be regarded as a fleeting emotion, while loss of face is something that we feel/believe will have longer-term consequences. We don't really 'get over' the embarrassment and we can assume that some time sooner rather than later this loss of face will have consequences for our motivation and our career. In the short scene we depicted we can imagine that sooner rather than later this line-manager will quit this job or the company.

Returning to the all-important consideration of context, we can get over loss of face more easily if we know that this type of behaviour by the boss goes against the rules of the dominant reference group and that we can rely on the group's members to support and protect us over the necessary term to invalidate the original transgression. Accordingly, the notion of face loss is associated with culture-specific assumptions about time, space and (not least) trust in the judgement of fellow group members, a topic we return to in the context of staff performance management in Chapter 6.

Avoiding loss of face

In our experience, the pressure on Japanese managers to avoid doing the 'wrong thing' appears often to cloud their perceptions of what is the 'right thing' or even a 'good thing'; at least, in terms of a spontaneous judgement or response. This is because attention to face has a distinctive and central role to play in explaining Japanese management behaviour. It is essentially negative: the primary motivation is probably to *avoid* loss of face. Notice in the bawling out scene with the sales staff 'the managers focused on what each associate had *not* accomplished during the day'.

This attitude echoes Confucius: *avoid breaking the rules*. Which rules? Whose rules? The answers to these questions should be given by the context and the expectations of the reference group. Accordingly, the most effective way of avoiding loss of face is to understand the context or

Box 2.1 Yes, no, maybe

In practical terms, the emphasis given to avoiding loss of face explains the common frustration felt by non-Japanese business people as they struggle to interpret their Japanese counterparts' responses to direct or pressing questions. The Japanese word *hai* can be translated into English 'yes'. But, from a Japanese perspective it often means (as an English equivalent) 'yes, I have understood' rather than 'yes, I agree'. So, when a western manager is pushing his Japanese counterpart with a statement such as 'We need to have your agreement on this matter today', the Japanese manager's response of 'yes' should be interpreted as meaning either 'Yes, I agree, we need to work further towards an agreement' or even 'Yes, I understand why you are asking me this question.' It almost certainly does *not* mean 'We will confirm our agreement today.' Other likely non-committal responses include: 'It will be difficult' or 'I'll see what I can do' (cf. Imai, 1975).

The answer 'maybe' is likely to mean 'no'; but to say 'no' outright would cause loss of face to the questioner. If the 'maybe' does signify a 'no', as in 'No, I'm afraid your offer/product is not good enough', the sequel is likely to be silence. Silence offers further opportunity for avoiding loss of face.

associated expectations of the relevant reference group. If these are not clear, then it is probably safer to do nothing; hence the generalized image of Japanese managers and students as 'passive' or 'uncritical' by many non-Japanese colleagues and the conclusion by other experts about the Japanese 'frail sense of self' (Trompenaars and Hampden-Turner, 1998: 203).

Giving face

Ambler and Witzel (2000), Yoshimura and Anderson (1997), Rice (1991) and other experts agree: 'giving face' is something that western managers either find difficult or more often neglect when working and negotiating with their Asian counterparts. They thereby run the risk of losing out on the many advantages that good and enduring intercultural or inter-company business relationships can bring.

The following list of techniques for 'giving face' has been summarized and adapted from Rice (1991: 139), Trompenaars and Hampden-Turner (1998: 103), and Mizuno and Shiom (2002):

- Study the history, background and stated future vision of the Japanese organization you hope to do business with. Make explicit note of any significant achievements.
- Prepare yourself: try to learn your Japanese partners' names and company status in advance and refer to their names and titles after you've met them. Remember to use the 'honorific' '-san' suffix after family names (it means 'Mr', 'Mrs' or 'Ms') unless your Japanese partners say it's not required.
- Show explicit interest in the *meishi* you are given: respect them (cf. Box 1.1).
- Talk calmly – not slowly – and avoid using too much slang.
- Avoid making absolute references such as 'of course' or 'obviously': what is obvious to you may not be obvious to your negotiation partner. And you may be mistaken.
- Have an answer for every question asked, in document form, if possible. If you have no answer, apologize and give a reliable promise of an answer later.
- Don't rush to evaluative judgements about your counterparts' apparent behaviour: remain focused on the purpose of the meeting or encounter.
- Show an engaging interest in Japan, your partner's company and (in informal situations) your partner's family and hobbies.

- Don't go into discussion believing that Japanese management or negotiation cultures are 'unique': it distracts from managing the complexities necessary for establishing long-term business relationships.

Remarkable about this list of 'do's and don'ts' for dealing or negotiating with Japanese business partners is, we believe, how unremarkable the items in such lists appear. Are these suggestions not applicable to visitors or negotiation partners from any nationality or culture, including your own? Wouldn't you want to do the same for just about any nationality of business partner you were dealing with? Wouldn't you like to be treated in a similarly sensitive way? Do these suggestions for 'giving face' not resemble some of the subtle techniques used in applying HRM paradigms of employee 'empowerment'? As Rice (1991: 141) concludes: 'There's no secret about Japanese management practices. It's all common sense . . . It's all a matter of developing respect.'

Face and control

From an enlightened western perspective, a fundamental requirement of managers is that they should 'control, co-ordinate and direct' human and other organizational resources, including information. Their purpose in doing this is 'to create the conditions under which people are motivated to perform' (Goffee and Hunt, in Pitman/FT, 1997: 631–633). In the context of Japanese management culture, these management functions in effect overlap with those ascribed to senior members of the reference group.

Despite fashionable reference to HRM paradigms such as MBWA ('management by walking about'), direct and continuous control of employee behaviour and performance is not practical: control needs to be balanced with some degree of trust. Attention to face in Japanese management contexts allows trust to be emphasized over control. This – in the long term – can be considered more effective in generating 'productive outcomes to work' (cf. Hannagan, 1998: 4) and, according to Ouchi (1981), also describes one of the factors that distinguish Japanese-style HRM most clearly from western (i.e. Anglo-American) models.

A definition of trust

In the context of Japanese HRM, trust can be defined as 'something built up over time and [meaning] that one can predict others' behaviour and expect that others will treat one well in difficult situations' (Kono and Clegg, 2001: 280). By this definition we can see how trust relates to notions of face and the reference group, and through these to the question of management control. As we detail in Chapter 6, a relationship of trust arises for as long as individual behaviour (self-regulation) predictably conforms to reference group expectations. Time – as in length of reliable service – is another key factor. In return, the reference group will help the individual in times of difficulty or of professional and even personal crisis. We elaborate upon this definition of trust in Chapter 6.

The 'train girl' story

An American manager was travelling by bullet train or *shinkansen* between Osaka and Tokyo. Apart from the speed and efficiency of the service, what impressed him was the on-board catering. This is provided by staff who wheel trolleys of snacks (e.g. drinks and ready-packed meals called *bento*) through the carriages. Having completed one of several trips through one carriage, the sales assistant will each time turn and, from behind the now closed windowed door, bow to the passengers of the carriage that she (and it is probably a she) has just left. 'Why does she do this? Who's watching? As far as I could see, none of the other passengers in my carriage was watching. I was fascinated by this performance for the length of my journey!'

By taking different perspectives on the 'train girl's' behaviour, we can generate an analysis of the relationship between face, control and trust.

Perspective 1

The train girl's line-manager and colleagues (let's call them reference group 1) can predict her behaviour without having to observe or control it directly: as an employee and reference group insider, she can be trusted.

Perspective 2

The train girl's HR manager and other representatives of the transport catering company (let's call them reference group 2, noting that their interests and purpose overlap with reference group 1) can be assured that the girl is performing to required standards and indeed could act as a positive model to new recruits in the job. Members of reference group 2 are distant from actual observation and control of the girl's behaviour and so will need to rely on reports by her line-manager – another trusted group 2 member – for an assessment of her performance, a process we discuss in more detail in Chapter 6.

Perspective 3

Alternatively, company managers could rely on reports from train company staff and customers (reference group 3). We should note that only a minority of these people buy anything from her, preferring to bring with them *bento* and drinks from home or bought more cheaply at one of the multitude of station buffets and kiosks. The important thing to recognize is that, although few of these group members actually appear to observe or call the girl's behaviour to account, she is aware of their expectations and so continues to bow each time she leaves a carriage, simultaneously saying a phrase in Japanese equivalent to 'Excuse my disturbing you', before moving on to repeat the ritual in the next carriage. In repeatedly performing this ritual she is *giving* face to her company's customers, a vital element of Japanese-style business practice.

Perspective 4

The American manager as a cultural 'outsider'. He is in fact, from the girl's perspective, a member of reference group 3, even though (unknown to her) he lacks much of the culture-specific information that the other group 3 members tacitly share. The company may also send in some 'mystery shopper'-style monitors of the girl's performance. These could be also be classed as 'outsiders' to reference group 3, but on the strength of their access to insider information, members of reference groups 1 and 2. For the girl these monitors would probably belong to group 3.

Perspective 5

The girl's family and friends (several of whom may be members of reference group 1). In doing her job according to expectations, the girl avoids causing them loss of face. Of course, these people may be indifferent. If she's from a traditional family, they are likely to be satisfied that at least she has a job until she gets married and starts a family, a perspective we explore in more detail in Chapters 3 and 4.

Perspective 6

The girl herself. Her view may coincide with those of all the above-mentioned reference groups. She probably prefers to feel trusted and so will behave as expected in order to avoid losing or causing loss of face.

Perspective 7

The assessments of external experts, whose views may or may not infiltrate to any of the above. These insights are taken from Rice (1991: 110–111): 'The Japanese understand the difference between giving service and being servile . . . In the West, we tend to think of servants as doing a menial and unworthy job, but in Japan providing good service is a mark of pride in one's work and a source of respect from others.' And further: 'The philosophy of customer service is an all-consuming fixation. The customer is king [*kyakusama wa osama*] and there is fantastic loyalty to him [*sic*]. [Japanese] people see themselves as there to serve the customer' (1995: 111). This insight conforms to what Japanese managers told us when we asked them to explain the 'train girl's' behaviour. However, and with Richard Donkin in *The Financial Times* (7 February 2003, European edition), we believe we should not underestimate the 'F-word': i.e. fear – fear of losing face.

CCTV eyes

By conducting this type of comparative expectation analysis we can better understand how Japanese people work and are managed with particular reference to face. We told the train girl story to a senior German manager. His response was this:

It doesn't surprise me. In Japan, as in Germany or in Switzerland (where we also run a production plant), we need people who turn up at 7am each morning and just get on with work, reliably and conscientiously, without thinking too much about it. You know the German word *arbeiten* [to work]. Well there's another word – *Maloche* which means just getting down to it. In this part of the world we talk about *schaffige* people: *go schaffe* in Swiss German dialect means to work in the sense of turning up, being reliable and precise in your work. In my experience you need a critical mass of people with this kind of attitude – from shop floor to middle-management – in order to build up and sustain the kind of strong economy that Switzerland, Germany and Japan have. If you have this, senior management is easy – perhaps too easy sometimes.

Diffuseness

According to this respondent, the management of staff became 'easier' where it was common for employees to 'take their work personally': i.e. where the values and norms that shape their social life overlap markedly with those of their working life, what we identified in Chapter 1 as 'diffuse' work cultures or cultures where 'everything is connected to everything' (Trompenaars and Hampden-Turner, 1998: 89).

Japan is not unique in this respect. Trompenaars and Hampden-Turner equate the diffuseness of Japanese management culture with what they call the 'Latin cultures' of Southern Europe and South America. This is confirmed by one of our Turkish colleagues who, when we explained our interpretation of face in Japanese society and culture immediately recognized parallels in her own Turkish culture and society (Bayyurt, 1996). Meanwhile, Hofstede recognizes parallels between East Asian interpretations of 'face' and Greek *philotimos* or (citing Triandis, 1972: 38) 'the extent to which [a person] conforms to the norms and values of his [*sic*] ingroup' (Hofstede, 1991: 61).

The diffuse nature of Japanese management and employment culture can be compared to the experience of one of this book's authors who used to work for a mammoth wholesale/retail conglomerate in Switzerland. As employees of this company we could shop for a full range of food and non-food goods, bank our money, buy petrol, attend evening classes, join sports and other clubs, book our holidays, and even arrange funerals, all through outlets carrying our company logo. Thus, those of us who were particularly loyal to the company brand could make our personal and professional lives into a markedly diffuse experience. This corresponds to the 'company as family' perception commonly ascribed to 'masculine' employment cultures generally (Mead, 2000: 151) and to Japanese employment culture in particular (cf. Chapter 3).

What motivates the train girl?

Assuming she knows that nobody is watching to check whether she bows and apologizes each time, we need to ask: what pressure of expectation does this employee feel on her? What motivates her to interpret and conform to the expectations of the same set of anonymous customers, repeatedly, during the course of one train journey? How does she experience management control? What does this tell us about Japanese management culture?

Questions about 'motivation' are highly complex (cf. Box 6.2). However, in considering these questions in the context of Japanese employment cultures we developed the notion of 'CCTV eyes'. This concept arose out of a discussion with a colleague who had made a study of how Turkish people tend to behave in front of television cameras (Bayyurt, 1996). In her view there are parallels between Turkish and Japanese people in this situation, meaning in respect of how they predictably choose to behave in response to the expectations of a physically removed and invisible/imagined audience. In our train girl story, there are no cameras, but she still probably perceives herself as connected in a type of 'virtual control loop' where management and reference group expectations are transmitted or sensed as if through a 'closed circuit television' (CCTV) network.

The 'CCTV eyes' notion suggests that an individual's choice of behaviour is being continuously watched and evaluated: or, at least, the individual senses this is so. It represents an expression of self-regulation as an outcome of culture-specific *socialization* (as discussed in Chapter 3). The 'CCTV' notion helps explain how, in our experience, Japanese managers and colleagues appear so often guarded and sensitive to pitfalls that *might* cause loss of face.

Japan as a 'shame' culture?

It would be possible to expand this idea in terms of 'morality' or even more specifically in terms of business or management ethics. Indeed,

Benedict (1946) developed a pervasive theory of Japan as a 'shame' culture, to be contrasted with western/Anglo-American 'guilt' cultures. Trying to make sense of Japanese wartime behaviour, the suggestion was that Japanese people tend to behave in ways they felt they could 'get away with' (i.e. specific to time and immediate context or opportunity). The primary motivation was *not* to be found out (i.e. lose face). In contrast, members of 'guilt' cultures carry their sense of what is 'right' and 'wrong' through time and across contexts.

Benedict's theory is plausible, and one which is well known among Japanese people we spoke to – Japanese people tend to be extremely curious about what westerners think of them (cf. Box 3.1). However, it hardly explains the behaviour of the 'train girl' in our example: i.e. it doesn't help explain how and why Japanese people work. It furthermore suffers from the type of dualism (based on Judaeo-Christian values) that undermines, for example, the practical applicability of Hofstede's 'individualism/collectivism' dimension (cf. Box 1.2).

Box 2.2 *Tatemae* and *honne*

We can relate our discussion of face in this chapter to two distinctively Japanese concepts: *tatemae* and *honne*. According to Smith and Misumi (1994; in Hickson, 1997) *tatemae* 'refers to what might be considered ideal or correct concerning relations between two persons or groups. *Tatemae* will frequently derive from long-past events which have defined the state of relationships between the two groups in question; *honne* is what happens in practice' (1997: 365). In these terms *tatemae* may appear closer to informing perceptions of 'tradition' and of what is 'normal' or routinely expected. In contrast, *honne* will refer more closely to present context of time, space and perceived requirements.

Smith and Misumi give a practical example of how attention to *tatemae* and *honne* can impact on the management of reward systems in Japanese organizations. In accordance with tradition (*tatemae*), a manager will be promoted along a salary scale according to his (seldom her) age and experience, thereby avoiding loss of face. Simultaneously, the more flexible and less transparent bonus payment system will be used to reward (possibly younger) staff members whose performance in reality (*honne*) adds more value to the company's strategic performance.

Is this a charade? Consider this view (from Yoshimura and Anderson, 1997: 1): 'What is unique about Japan is the overwhelming sense of *contradiction* that non-Japanese come to feel. The Japanese seem capable of reacting in completely different ways on different occasions when faced with similar situations' (emphasis as in the original). Also: 'Because it is vital to do what others expect in a given context, situations arise that often strike Westerners as charades. It is very important in Japan to play them out according to what each person believes others expect to happen' (1997: 44). Unsurprisingly, 'outsiders' struggle to fathom *tatemae*, and so tend to misunderstand its complex interaction with *honne*. In Box 2.5 we see how Japanese routinely manage *tatemae* and *honne* in relation to face. In Box 6.4 we illustrate a situation where the management of face breaks down.

SECTION 3: RE-DEFINING FACE – CASE STUDIES

In the context of international management, Mead (1998: 136) defines face as: 'the positive social value a person claims by his/her conduct in social relationships. Face denotes a perception that others within your social group have of you (compared to self-esteem which refers to your assessment of yourself).'

In contrast to Hofstede's definition (cited in the introduction to this chapter) where 'face' is 'a quality' which is 'attributed' to an individual, Mead's definition emphasizes what the individual has to do – and, by implication, *not* do – to *claim* face. The individual thus makes and enacts a critical choice. For this reason we believe that Mead's definition is more appropriate in the context of our current study.

Within this definition we should first recognize that 'face denotes a perception'. Perceptions (i.e., the combination of seeing and interpreting) are highly culture-specific. For example, the colour white in Christian tradition and ritual tends to symbolize purity or virginity while in Japanese (Buddhist) tradition and ritual it can also be associated with death. So, perceptions of face in Japanese society will not always coincide with perceptions of face in non-Japanese societies.

Mead's definition covers other complexities. For example, what do we mean by 'positive value', and 'positive' in relation to which or to whose criteria? What type of 'social relationships', and in which contexts? When an individual claims face, they are likely to do so *despite* their sense or experience of prevailing social expectations.

We can apply Mead's distinction between 'face' and 'self-esteem' to the train girl example discussed above. She may in fact hate her job, but be determined to make her 'claim' to face. So, she chooses to work according to reference group expectations. Her sense of 'esteem' may be claimed and granted (by the reference group). But is this the same as claiming 'self-esteem'?

Face and esteem

Japan ranks as a culture where *esteem* has a high and socially transferable currency value (Trompenaars and Hampden-Turner, 1998: 98, citing Talcott Parsons, 1951). This explains why managers who have spent years building up a 'reserve' (one respondent's word for this) of esteem (or 'good reputation' to quote him further) in one company are very reluctant to move to what is imagined to be the closed reference culture of another Japanese company where these new arrivals have to start again effectively at zero in terms of esteem or reputation.

Kawaguchi-san

Take, for example, the case of *Kawaguchi-san* (the name has been changed). He had the following dilemma. For ten years he had been seconded by his company to a high-profile post as an economic analyst in an international non-governmental agency headquarters in Europe. This, he believed, was 'a major achievement' given that he had graduated from 'only a middle-ranking university' in Japan. Now he and his wife wished to return to Japan, partly because his current assignment was winding down and partly because they wanted to re-integrate their children into the Japanese school system. He was pessimistic, almost despondent. 'I know that with my university background, my age [forty-five], and the fact that I have been outside the company system for so many years means that I have probably missed my chance to get a good promotion. Other managers of my age won't accept me and will treat me as an outsider. The longer you spend outside a company [culture], the more difficult it is to get back in.'

Kawaguchi-san was aware that it would be difficult for any traditional Japanese company to recruit and position him at a level commensurate with his age and recent experience. To do so would probably cause loss of face to managers who had dedicated their career hitherto to working their way slowly through the ranks. With loss of face would arise a potential loss of motivation and loyalty among the 'insider' cohort.

One discussion we had with another Japanese manager became a form of counselling session. This manager was responsible for part of a large-scale CRM project that he felt was going in the wrong direction: despite demanding long hours of data research and analysis over several weeks from his team, the task leaders appeared (in our manager's view) to have made up their mind from the beginning about what the final report to the client company should contain. These task leaders (Japanese) had been drafted in from the US American office of this particular manager's company: 'they are confident and, in my view, dismissive of our [i.e. their Japanese colleagues'] more cautious client-focused [in his view] approach'. At the time this manager was so stressed out by the situation that he was (unknown to others on the project) working under medication. 'Can't you speak to the task leaders about your concerns?' 'No, I think they have the support of senior management.' 'Is there anybody in HR you can talk to about maybe getting a transfer from the project?' 'If I do that they'll think I'm weak and I'll jeopardize my future career chances.'

In these two examples we believe we can address the question about the distinction between 'esteem' and 'self-esteem'. Esteem is claimed and granted (i.e. by the reference group); self-esteem is claimed regardless of whether the reference group grants esteem or not.

Breaking the rules

In the context of our discussion so far it would appear that Japanese managers who decide to claim an enhanced sense of individual self-esteem, are likely to be commonly perceived as 'rule breakers' and thereby (perhaps) as hardly to be trusted. Consider the following two cases of managers who decided to quit the security of their Japanese companies and take more independent control over the course of their careers.

Kimura-san

Kimura-san is male, married, and at the time of the first interview his wife was pregnant with their first child. The interview and follow-up discussion was held in Japan, in both English and in Japanese and, on separate occasions, with male and with female interviewers.

Kimura-san is in his late thirties. He graduated in civil engineering from a top-ranking Japanese university. He had been working for fifteen years at a government ministry in Tokyo, a post he had gained initially (he believed) on the personal recommendation of his former university professor. When we first interviewed him he still held a middle-ranking management position in client relations and project supervision. See Box 2.3 for some background information about the role of government ministries in Japanese business.

Box 2.3 The role of government ministries in Japanese business

There are twelve ministries in Japan's central government structure. They emerged in their current roles and structures during the national reconstruction after World War Two. Some of these wield enormous power. For example, the Ministry of Construction controls a budget for public works expenditure that 'tends to be two to four times greater than that of other advanced industrial countries such as France, the United States, Germany and the United Kingdom' (Bird, 2002: 303). Large works of construction – such as high-speed (*shinkansen*) rail links, airports (e.g. Osaka's Kansai International Airport), motorways, tunnels, bridges, and the extensive (and controversial) coastline defence systems have been used by successive central governments to boost national and regional economic activity and by local politicians to sustain business relations with their most powerful constituents, notably those representing the notoriously over-manned construction industry (cf. Box 2.5). This industry still employs around 10 per cent of the national workforce and contributes around 15 per cent of GDP, a figure 'equivalent in absolute size to the US and Western European construction industries together' (Bird, 2002: 80) The Kansai airport project became the focus of tension between US American companies and their Japanese competitors – the so-called 'construction friction' of the late 1980s – when it was alleged that Japanese construction companies together with ministry officials were conspiring to keep out non-Japanese bids (Bird, 2002: 304). The perception was therefore reinforced that Japanese business and government ministries form a type of reference group whose purpose is to protect 'insider' interests and so, by extension, preserve national face.

Kimura-san's dilemma was essentially twofold. First, he regretted being involved in what he saw as the increasing number of missed opportunities – 'inefficiency' was his term – in his part of the ministry. Opportunities for greater quality and value for money were being missed.

Second, he had recently been approached by a headhunting agency and offered a job with an international (Japanese-speaking) business consultancy firm. The consultancy had been subject to a recent management buyout – the new Japanese partners had kept the name and the client portfolio of the previous company. They wanted Kimura-san for his inside knowledge about how private companies tendered for government projects. His starting salary would be less than he earned at the ministry, 'and certainly there would be less job security', but there was the prospect of earning more money 'based on performance'.

Why change jobs? 'I felt a move would help me learn more, and I would be able to offer a better service to some of the customers I already know. Also, I think I can help "modernize" the [Japanese] way of doing business.'

Why now? Kimura-san told us about the recent cost-cutting drive in his ministry. In his view service quality was suffering. Furthermore, (we inferred) promotion prospects for individual managers were diminishing. Kimura-san told us about a competition he had recently missed out on. The ministry usually sent 'the top 10 per cent' of each year's intake group [called *doki*] on MBA programmes in the USA. It wasn't clear to him exactly how this top 10 per cent were chosen. However, he vividly remembers one female colleague – 'the brightest of our year' – who had been selected and completed her MBA at an Ivy League business school. Memorable was the way that, soon after her return, she quit the ministry and took a job with a higher salary at an international investment bank in Tokyo.

'It was around this time I started thinking seriously about looking for another job. I spoke to [trusted] colleagues in the office, I spoke to people I had studied with.' Kimura-san was given the contact details of a headhunter bureau. He arranged a brief lunchtime meeting in a coffee shop at some distance from his office. They assessed his 'market value'. Encouraged by this experience, he approached a couple of other agencies. Within 'three or four weeks' the offer of the new job came. After much deliberation, and consultation with his family and close colleagues, he decided to accept.

Takeda-san

Takeda-san had just turned thirty when we first interviewed her. She is unmarried and works as client services manager (China) at one of Japan's largest and longest established trading companies (Box 2.4). The next follow-up interview was held in English in the UK. The final interview was held in Japan, also in English.

Takeda-san graduated with a degree in foreign languages from 'a middle-ranking women-only university'. Her dilemma was whether to quit her job in the trading company and take up the offer of a MBA place at a business school in the UK. She said she would like to switch to working in retailing as '[this] is an area where Japanese women have a better

Box 2.4 The role of trading companies in Japanese business

Many traditional Japanese corporations are networked around one or more central banks and trading companies: a network known as *keiretsu*, explained in Chapter 7. The role of trading companies or (*sogo*) *shosha* is to facilitate supply and distribution between various companies within the *keiretsu*. Because of this networking influence it has been traditionally difficult for group 'outsiders' – and above all foreign outsiders – to gain access to domestic Japanese distribution and other channels of influence (cf. Drucker, 1999). The *shosha* might offer financial services and training services within the *keiretsu* group and might co-ordinate the sale and marketing of the group's products in international markets. Because of this experience they can be used to facilitate joint ventures between Japanese and non-Japanese corporations. They also advise Japanese government staff about international business trends (cf. Yonekawa, 1990; Yoshihara, 1982).

Managers at *sogo shosha* need to be flexible and responsive to developments, not only within a diverse range of industrial and strategic environments in Japan, but also in international markets and trading environments. They act as a cultural interface between Japanese companies and the global business environment. According to Rudlin (in Bird, 2002: 166), 'Due to their pivotal role in the Japanese economy, the variety of work and possibility of international postings that *sogo shosha* offer, they are a highly popular employment choice for Japanese university graduates.' During the years of rapid economic growth, the benefits offered to staff of *sogo shosha* were perceived to outstrip Japanese norms: 'As well as the usual fringe benefits of dormitories, subsidized accommodation and lifetime employment, many *sogo shosha* offer employee marriage bureaux, higher than average salaries and retirement packages and very generous expatriation benefits' (Rudlin, in Bird, 2002: 166). During the current economic downturn, these benefits are among the first to be cut. Accordingly, the status of *sogo shosha* as a magnet for aspiring Japanese managers began to decrease. However, recent restructuring at traditional *shosha* such as Mitsubishi Corporation has begun to attract a new generation of graduates seeking international experience or career prospects (cf. Chapter 7).

chance of succeeding as managers'. She mentioned new companies on the retail scene such as Uniqlo (discussed as a case study in Chapter 8) as well as the more traditional department stores such as Mitsukoshi. When we asked her about any famous women she knew in Japanese management, she thought for a while and could only mention one: 'Matsunaga-san [of the mobile phone giant NTT DoCoMo.com]'.

Her then salary was 'low, for the work I'm expected to do' but the twice-annual bonuses were 'good, especially for a woman'. This is because the section she worked in had a consistent record of success. 'The hours are long. I live at home, and so I don't have much social life outside work.' She enjoyed her work, but she didn't like her line-manager at the time. In her eyes 'he's happy to take most of the credit for the success [of the section]' but it was she and a few others who did 'the real work'. She believed her boss 'spends too much time networking and making a career for himself in the company'. And furthermore: 'Most women I joined [the trading company] with have left to get married or gone to other jobs. I don't get offered other jobs or promoted, except when my boss gets promoted. He says that we are a "good team". He says I'm an expert in what I do. He tells me that I have a great future in the company if I stay with him because he expects to become one of the senior partners one day and he sees me as his "number one". He tells me I can share his success.'

Takeda-san was often asked to train new staff. Often these were male staff members being rotated between departments as part of their progress to higher-level jobs within the company. In her view this was not part of her job and she suspected she was being exploited by her boss, believing he got the recognition for her work in training up budding (all male) managers and so 'saving the company money'. She went on: 'I tried to ask the people in HR about this extra [staff training] work I did. They told me how much they appreciated what I was doing, but they never told me directly why or who decided that I had to do this extra work.' Why didn't she refuse to do the work? 'Impossible' she says, with a quiet laugh.

Leaving the company, leaving her boss, and on top of this leaving Japan (if only for one two years) is a prospect which 'frightened' Takeda-san. Was there any pressure from her family to get married or settle down in Japan? 'No, but I'm an only child and my grandmother [who lives with the family] is now very old and quite ill.' There was also the challenge of doing an MBA: 'I'd never studied business before but the [UK] university seemed keen to have me.' She doubted she'd be able to cope.

When we later spoke to her the dilemma had become both personal and professional. One of her closing comments was: 'If I don't decide and do something for me right now, it will never happen.' Takeda-san appeared to lack confidence throughout the two years we kept in touch with her. We infer this was because of her perceptions of her gender, her age, her educational background, and the years of gradual de-motivation she'd experienced in the trading company.

Nevertheless, she did quit the trading company and she did get an MBA. Last time we met she was back in Japan, still looking for the career breakthrough, but much more aware now of what she didn't want and what she wouldn't tolerate in a future job.

Case studies: first conclusions

Kimura-san and Takeda-san sought to resolve personal and professional dilemmas: what do their examples tell us about the face of Japanese management and ways in which it might be changing?

First of all we should recognize that we are not talking about rebels: as our research sample shows, their dilemmas are becoming ever more common and publicly discussed in Japanese management culture. They are both individuals who have decided that the route to career fulfilment may not lie along the established pathways of social behaviour (see Box 2.5). We are talking about women professionals who are waiting until their mid to late thirties to have children or who may choose not to marry at all. We are talking about men who are willing to quit a secure job in a 'high-ranking' organization and set up or off on their own career path: to study abroad, or join non-Japanese companies in the expectation of more challenge, more risk, more immediate financial reward, but above all more opportunity to succeed or fail by their own terms of reference.

Box 2.5 How Japanese insiders talk about 'face'

Japanese insiders are critically aware of how attention to 'face' confuses non-Japanese outsiders. In a recent article entitled 'Politicians blur facts to save face during internal disputes', Itaro Oishi explains some of the political manoeuvring behind Prime Minster Koizumi's stop-start political and economic 'reform' programmes (Oishi, 2002). The article focuses on the machinations of politicians close to the 'road construction lobby' (cf. Box 2.3) and who are resisting proposed government reforms to this sector. Senior party members are trying to 'avoid settling the matter through majority rule' and instead 'preserve the appearance of unanimity by pressuring the minority that opposes the party line [i.e. those believed to be close to the road construction lobby] to refrain from voting. The result is that the minority fails to get its way, but party members are able [publicly] to save face.'

For the further information of cultural outsiders to this process, Oishi explains that 'this tradition is only natural in a land where people set great store by harmony' and continues: 'People outside of Japan, in particular, must find it hard to understand the Japanese way of doing things, because politicians deliberately blur the facts about who has supported or opposed a certain course of action as well as the outcome.'

These practising and aspiring managers are re-assessing their own professional worth and comparing the results of this experience to what their current employers can offer. They are pursuing their own sense of self-esteem. This is, in essence, the changing face of Japanese management and the theme for discussion and analysis throughout this book.

Summary

In this chapter we have developed a praxis-oriented definition of the 'face' of Japanese management. We have discussed face in the context of 'reference groups', management control, and of some distinctive patterns of management and employee behaviour in Japan. We have suggested ways in which the face of Japanese management is changing, making a study of two individual cases of managers (Kimura-san and Takeda-san) who decided to take more control over the course of their professional careers. We will refer to these and other individual cases throughout the discussion in this book.

Consider the following questions:

1 Referring to Mead's (1998) definition of face (given in this chapter), can you recall situations at work and in your personal life where you have experienced

- loss of face?
- gaining face?
- giving face?

2 To what extent did these personal and professional experiences of face overlap?

3 Learning how to work

Introduction

> In Japan one is born twice – once to one's natural parents,
> once to an educational system.
>
> (Goodman, 1990)

In this and the following chapter we look at how Japanese managers such as Kimura-san and Takeda-san have been brought up, educated and inducted into the structures and cultures of Japanese society and business organizations. Our purpose is to understand better how their experiences of these processes impact on their ability to identify and reconcile the type of professional dilemmas discussed in Chapters 1 and 2.

The formative processes of upbringing and early-years education can be defined universally as *socialization* or 'the process whereby the helpless infant becomes a self-aware knowledgeable person, skilled in the ways of the culture into which she or he is born' (Giddens, 1989: 60). The experience of socialization underpins how we as adults later respond to personal and professional problems, dilemmas and crises.

The main agents of socialization are the family, peer relationships, schools and other education institutions, and, of course, work. As discussed in Chapter 2, the boundaries of these agencies overlap in terms of 'reference groups'. Towards the end of the formative socialization experience, say around the age of fifteen, individuals tend to become aware of what it means to 'be' Japanese, German, and so on. In a Japanese context, the ways in which individuals have learnt to self-regulate their behaviour suggests also how effectively they have 'learnt how to work' (Dore and Sako, 1998).

Our objectives for this chapter are:

- to apply a model for analysing culture-specific approaches to problem-solving in order to generate a clearer understanding of Japanese management culture;

- to illustrate how the experience of socialization commonly impacts upon the way Japanese managers tend to perceive and approach business problems and professional dilemmas.

SECTION 1: CULTURE AND PROBLEM SOLVING

At the end of Chapter 2 we presented and made an initial analysis of two individual manager case studies: Kimura-san and Takeda-san. Both managers faced a professional dilemma: whether to quit or stay on their then career path. In line with our discussion in Chapter 1, we recognize how we can identify the boundaries of cultures, and specific features that distinguish these cultures, when we observe how individuals (collectively and singly) identify and respond to problems or dilemmas.

The 'TH-T model'

Trompenaars and Hampden-Turner (1998: 8–9) offer a framework for analysing cultures taking this approach. Within this analytical framework (henceforth referred to as the 'TH-T model') there are seven dimensions:

- *universalism versus particularism*: (i.e. 'universalism' suggests that 'what is right is always right');
- *individualism versus communitarianism*: (i.e. 'Do people regard themselves primarily as individuals or primarily as part of the group?'). Note that the TH-T model avoids reference to 'collectivism' as in Hofstede's model (cf. Box 1.2);
- *neutral versus emotional*: (e.g. to what extent is it acceptable to express or show emotion in pursuing management or business objectives?);
- *specific versus diffuse*: (i.e. 'specific' cultures encourage people routinely to separate work from social or personal concerns and priorities);
- *achievement versus ascription*: 'achievement means that you are judged on what you have recently accomplished and on your record. Ascription means that status is accorded to you by birth, kinship, gender or age, but also by your connections (who you know) and your educational record (e.g. as a graduate of Tokyo University [in Japan] or an Haute Ecole Polytechnique [in France])'.

Based on our discussion so far, a superficial application of this model would suggest that Japanese culture is: *particularist* (i.e. behave according to context); *communitarian* (i.e. reference group-oriented); and *diffuse* (i.e. work and social life overlap). We illustrate the fundamentally *emotional* nature of Japanese management culture in Chapter 4. In this chapter we begin to develop our impression of emerging tensions in Japanese management culture between adherence to values of 'achievement' and to values of 'ascription'.

Time and space/environment

The sixth and seventh dimensions in the 'TH-T' model relate dilemmas to perceptions of time and of the individual's place (or sense of space) in relation to the natural environment, both notions we discussed and exemplified in Chapters 1 and 2.

Specifically, the TH-T model identifies:

- *attitudes to time*: in western cultures the passage of time is seen as linear and progressive, whereas in East Asian cultures time is perceived to progress cyclically: 'what goes around, comes around';
- *attitudes to the environment*: e.g. whether nature is something to be conquered and systematically exploited or something to be (collectively) respected or even feared.

In respect of 'attitudes to the environment' Trompenaars and Hampden-Turner give the example of how Japanese people who have a cold wear face masks in public and at work: 'they wear them so that they will not "pollute" [the environment] or infect other people by breathing on them.' They compare this context for individual behaviour with London where masks 'are worn by bikers and other athletes who do not want to be "polluted" by the environment' (1998: 11).

SECTION 2: BEING JAPANESE

Being 'a Japanese manager' assumes first of all the manager is 'Japanese'. Obvious enough, but what does this mean? Based on the conclusions from our previous discussion of culture-specific 'core' or basic assumptions, it has much to do with growing up with certain perceptions and expectations of space and time; or, employing the overlapping terminology of the TH-T model, 'attitudes to the environment' and 'attitudes to time'.

Attitudes to the environment

Over generations, each culture organizes itself 'to find the ways to deal most effectively with their environments, given their available resources' (Trompenaars and Hampden-Turner, 1998: 23). The core of a culture is generated by assumptions about human existence and how the first individual and then collective human dilemma is survival in the face of natural elements: mountains, oceans, availability of shelter and food. Effective ways of surviving and prospering become the subject of stories and traditions which are transmitted to succeeding generations during the process of each individual's upbringing and early education: in short, of each individual's experience of the socialization process.

Japanese people tend to regard nature as more powerful than individuals: nature can act as a source of fear or emulation that helps people to understand themselves and develop values and norms. The rituals of Shinto (a native Japanese system of belief) seek to appease the destructive and benevolent forces of nature, while traditional Japanese garden architecture encourages a modest and reflective view of the individual's place in the universe (cf. Hori, 1989).

Geography

The background to this attitude can be found in part in the geography of Japan. Japan as a land mass consists of four main islands and many smaller ones. The topography is Swiss-like, but continually shaped and re-shaped by volcanic and tectonic action. The national climate runs from Nordic (e.g. on the northern island of Hokkaido) to subtropical on the southernmost islands of Okinawa. In terms of human geography, most of the 125 million population live along the (south-)eastern coastal strip of the main island – Honshu – between the cities of Kobe, Kyoto and Osaka and then up the 550 or so kilometres north east through conurbations around Nagoya and on to Tokyo, Yokohama and Chiba. To travel by *shinkansen* from Osaka to Tokyo takes less than three hours.

Cities

All Japan's major cities lie on a geothermic fault line: the threat of devastation is constant. The most recent large-scale earthquake happened in 1995, killing over five thousand people in and around the city of Kobe. The 1923 Tokyo quake killed one hundred and forty thousand people. Current urban architecture is designed to minimize damage. According to seismological research – a major industry in Japan – the next big Tokyo earthquake is either ten years late or one hundred years distant.

Japan is self-sufficient only in rice and some vegetables and so most food is imported. The capital city Tokyo, with a population of between twelve and over twenty million, is the centre of political and economic power. Most internationally known Japanese corporations have their headquarters in or around Tokyo, while Osaka has a greater concentration of small and medium-sized enterprizes (SMEs) that still make up the majority of employment in Japan (cf. Box 4.2).

The sea

No one in Japan lives more than 90 kilometres from the sea. The sea sets the historical and cultural boundary for the reference group called 'the Japanese'. Japan is an Asian country but for most of its national history it has been culturally isolated and feudal in its social structures. There are countless clearwater mountain streams (Japan is a mountainous country) but there are few navigable rivers or canals. The Japanese frequently compare Britain and Japan as 'island nations' (cf. Noh and Kimura, 1989), but these are people who probably know more about the beaches of Haiwaii than of Japan or Britain. Britain was instrumental in developing the modern Japanese navy (around the beginning of the twentieth century): the basis for Japan's sudden emergence as a modern military power. Scotland is revered for golf and whisky. From their early teens, many Japanese schoolchildren wear navy-like or tartan-like uniforms. As in Britain, people in Japan drive on the left-hand side of the road.

Attitudes to time

In the mists of myth and legend, 'western culture' for Japanese originally meant 'European'. The Portuguese in the sixteenth century brought trade and some expressions such as 'obrigado' (now *arigato* – 'thank you') and *tempura* (deep-fried fish and vegetables). The Portuguese also tried to mass export Christianity to Japan, but failed.

The Dutch visitors of the seventeenth century stuck to trade. The Americans arrived (uninvited) in 1853 in the guise of Commodore Perry's infamous (in Japan, at least) 'Black Ships' that, by mooring in Yokohama Bay off the new imperial capital of Tokyo, effectively forced Japan to 'open up to the west' (cf. Tames, 1993). Most Japanese today are conscious of the achievements of the Meiji emperor whose government (from around 1870) initiated the process of learning from western industrialization and applying it to Japanese conditions. This was Japan's 'enlightenment'. The rallying cry was *fukoku kyohei* – 'enrich the country, strengthen the military' (cf. Barnard, 2003)

Germany

Appropriately for the time, Germany was Japan's chosen model for social, political and industrial development. Kudo (1998) describes their relationship until the 1940s as one between teacher and student. Between the two world wars Germany was the most reliable source of high-quality heavy and precision engineering goods and technologies, whether in the form of imports or of licensing agreements. For Germany, Japan was a new and open market controlled by a central government that appeared willing to import German goods to the exclusion of other nationalities. During the 1920s and 1930s, German steel, machine and electrical engineering, chemicals, pharmaceutical and other basic industries were restricted in what they could produce for the domestic German market but could be exported with little risk to the emerging Japanese market.

There appears to be an enduring affinity between the two work cultures: the value ascribed to hard work; the experience of recovery from economic and political disaster; the focus on quality in terms of precision, accuracy and reliability, particularly in export-oriented industries such as manufacturing and engineering. German brand names continue to have a high status in Japan (Box 3.3).

US America

Modernized and militarized Japan announced itself to western powers with a surprise victory over a Russian fleet in 1904, and again much later with the surprise attack on the US Pacific navy base at Pearl Harbor in 1941. The war in the Pacific ended with an unconditional Japanese surrender in 1945, shortly after two types of nuclear bombs had been dropped over the southwestern cities of Hiroshima and Nagasaki. Other cities had already been devastated by fire bombing.

The US occupation effectively lasted from 1945 until the end of the Korean War (1952). From that time most foreigners (*gai-jin*) seen in Japan were assumed to be US American. Since 1945 the dominant Japanese vision of 'the west' effectively passes through an American prism, a topic we return to in Chapter 7.

Box 3.1 *Nihonjinron*

The study of the 'distinctiveness' of Japanese people and culture (*nihonjinron*) arose in Japan in the aftermath of World War Two. Japan, it was claimed, had a 'uniquely' homogeneous culture and historical traditions that emerged around the co-operative effort needed to tend rice fields. Thus Japanese culture emphasized group orientation (for survival) and mutual consideration and sympathy (for social cohesion). In contrast, western cultures were 'hunter-gatherer' cultures, homogeneous mainly in their lack of understanding of things Japanese, their lack of social and ethnic cohesion, and (in some extreme views) in terms of the threat they posed to Japanese uniqueness. The popularity of this initially academic notion of Japanese 'uniqueness' took hold and, in a process of apparent self-fulfilment, its popularity grew in tandem with the growth of the Japanese economic miracle; i.e. well into the 1980s.

Nihonjinron ideas have entered studies of international management. For example, out of the Japanese traditions that emphasize collective (and emotional) sensitivity and stable and cohesive teamwork grew the style of HRM and marketing (cf. Tanouchi, 1983). In contrast, western rivals' 'hunter/gatherer' traditions came to emphasize aggressive independence and restless mobility in business and management: as Tanouchi (1983) points out, these more 'masculine' values appear emphasized more in western cultures than in Japanese, casting further doubt on some of Hofstede's conclusions (cf. Box 1.2). More recent academic research has begun to cast severe doubt over the assumed unique and homogeneous origins of 'the Japanese people' (cf. Yoshino, 2002). The picture – or facade – was seldom as clear-cut as it may have seemed, a theme we return to in Chapter 7.

Sony

The 'history of Japan' that shapes and informs the traditions of national and industrial recovery and achievement – at least in the perceptions of most mid-career managers in our sample of respondents (i.e. those born in the late 1950s) – can be illustrated by tracing the development of the Sony Corporation. Consider the follow sequence of events:

1946   On a 'shoe-string' of resources, Akio Morita co-founds the company (then known as Totsuka) together with Masaru Ibuka and twenty other employees (cf. Morita, 1986).
1949   Totsuka develops the first magnetic sound recorder and player in Japan.
1953   Morita signs a licensing agreement (with US firm Western Electric) to make transistors in Japan.
1958   Totsuka becomes the 'Sony Corporation': the name being derived from Latin 'sonus' (sound) and English 'sonny' (little boy or son).
1968   Sony develops the trinitron television tube: still a hit product.
1960   Sony Corporation America established.
1971   The strong yen shock (also known in Japan as the 'Nixon dollar' shock): the sudden re-evaluation of currencies makes Japan's exports much more expensive.
1971   Sony opens colour tv production in the USA (San Diego).
1973   The first (of several) global oil price shocks: price for crude oil jumps 400 per cent.
1974   Sony opens colour tv production in the UK (Bridgend, in South Wales).

1975   Sony develops the Betamax video cassette system, finally losing out in a ferocious format war to Japanese rival Matsushita and the VHS format (cf. Chapter 5).

1979   Sony introduces the Walkman® and establishes a reputation for invention and global marketing prowess which subsequently brought music CDs, Playstation® and Discman®.

1988   Sony acquires US media firm CBS Records Inc. to be followed one year later by Columbia Pictures Entertainment, bringing non-Japanese onto its board of directors.

(adapted from Kenney, in Bird, 2002)

Time and tradition

In western cultures the passage of time is seen as linear and progressive, whereas in East Asian cultures time is perceived to progress cyclically. With a cyclical view, the past, present and future can appear closely interrelated. When the Japanese managers in our survey look back on the recent past they see natural disasters (such as the Kobe earthquake) combined with great modernizing technological and economic leaps forward, usually in the wake of cyclical and humiliating encounters with US American forces (Perry's Black Ships and the 1945 US Occupation). They do not appear to dwell on the (distant) past, because there is the past in terms of the present to deal with.

It is for this reason that, in the context of our discussion of Japanese-style HRM, we refer to 'tradition' as meaning 'since the post-World War Two reconstruction'. Two of the aforementioned 'three sacred treasures' emerge from this period, namely: 'lifetime employment' and 'enterprise unions' (cf. Box 5.1). In general perception, they appear to have been around much longer – rather like the very recent 'traditions' of Christmas celebrations in both Japan and in western societies. We discuss in subsequent chapters how post-war generations of Japanese managers respond differently to the expectation of 'lifetime employment'. In Chapter 6 we relate some reactions of union officials to current employment trends. The third 'treasure' ('seniority promotion') has a longer social and culture-specific history, as we explain in Section 3 below.

Sony's achievement

Totsuka/Sony's achievement was to draw quickly on what resources they could from their then circumstances (i.e. the US Occupation) to launch a future-oriented enterprise which ultimately surpassed many US rivals and became 'the first Japanese electronics firm to globalize [gaining] a reputation for being more Westernized than its Japanese competitors' (Kenney, in Bird, 2002: 416).

Time and information (i.e. context) shape perceptions of reputation. Akio Morita's reputation as a master of innovation and global marketing is established: he and his company quickly learned from the Betamax disaster: we discuss the VHS champion (Matsushita) in Chapter 5. Reputation is a key resource in Japanese business and society and is commonly made visible in terms of 'rankings' (Box 3.2). Kimura-san was well aware of his status as a graduate from a 'high-ranking' university. His employer's present focus on an established (past) reputation informed the decision to invest (i.e. recruit and train for a lifetime of employment) in this particular human resource. In this context, Trompenaars and Hampden-Turner (1998) draw parallels with French management cultures where decision-makers act with a strong (present) sense of the past – call it perhaps 'tradition'. Such cultures are 'ascriptive', meaning 'that status is accorded to you by birth, kinship, gender or age, but also by your connections (who you know) and your educational record (e.g. as a graduate of Tokyo University or Haute Ecole Polytechnique)' (1998: 9; cf. Box 3.2).

Box 3.2 Rankings

Japanese society is obsessed by rankings: i.e. knowing who is top of the pile of relative equals. Ask a Japanese manager to name the 'top five' companies in his/her own company's industry, you should get a clear answer. Aspiring managers know from early childhood which 'high-ranking' high school or university they need to study at in order subsequently to work at which 'high-ranking' (or 'famous') company.

The rankings for Japanese companies have traditionally been based on domestic market share. Often the rankings show one clear leader (e.g. *Toyota* in automobile manufacture) and so the real fight takes place for market share percentages between rankings two and three (e.g. between *Honda* and *Nissan*) and so on down the rankings. Companies benchmark fiercely against each other, making them similarly successful in good times, and similarly lethargic in bad (cf. Porter *et al.*, 2000).

continued

Rankings are generated by a conscious choice and implementation of comparative measurement criteria. Therefore it is essentially a political process: Whose criteria are being applied? How are they being applied and to what purpose? How people accept and interpret rankings relies essentially on trust (cf. Chapter 6).

In Japan hitherto the political forum for generating rankings has been effectively a process 'internal' to the relevant and overlapping national and industrial reference groups. The incursion of more externally generated measures such as ROI and EVA™, criteria for determining the relative performance and so ranking of Japanese companies – and by extension of their managers – has served to undermine the credibility of established reference group criteria, a theme we develop in Chapter 7.

As an indicator of how the culture for employment is changing in Japan, Kenney (in Bird, 2002: 416) states that: 'In a break with tradition, Sony announced in 1997 that it would no longer consider a graduate's university as a major factor in the hiring process in its subsidiaries in Japan.'

Our main resource is our people

In our experience, being 'Japanese' means feeling affiliated to people in one's immediate social and national reference groups defined by standardized education and largely standardized lifestyle expectations. When pushed, Japanese people may begin to distinguish among themselves on a regional basis: e.g. between 'Kansai' Japanese from the Osaka and Kyoto area or from the southern islands of Okinawa. However, the term 'Japanese' is likely to address the sensibilities of most Japanese any non-Japanese is likely to meet.

Even more formulaic than self-reference to the Japanese as an 'island race' is mention of Japan's 'lack of natural resources' (oil, gas and so on). Crude oil is by far the largest volume import; hence Japan's extreme vulnerability to price fluctuations. It is therefore ironic and remarkable that automobiles became by far Japan's largest volume export. 'Our main resource is our people and their ideas' we were repeatedly told: people as 'human capital' (cf. Dore and Sako, 1998).

In terms of ethnicity, Japanese society appears remarkably homogeneous. Other original ethnic groups of the islands – such as Ainu in the north (Hokkaido) and Okinawans in the far south have in social and cultural terms been almost totally assimilated: another view is they have been systematically eliminated. Non-ethnic Japanese have (to date) usually been refused naturalization. Japan's total population is approximately 127 million forming around 47 million households. Nearly a quarter of these comprise the 'Tokyo Metropolitan Area'. The practical sense of 'communitarianism' – i.e. the extent to which 'people regard themselves primarily as a part of a group' (Trompenaars and Hampden-Turner, 1998: 9) – is, given the compression of living space, overwhelming.

Approximately 640,000 ethnic Koreans and 260,000 ethnic Chinese live and work in Japan, many over several generations. Many have adopted a Japanese name, often (they say) to avoid bullying at school or social discrimination. The first 'Japanese' Olympic champion (the marathon in Berlin in 1936) was in fact a Korean: Kitei Son (real name Sohn Kee-chung) who died in November 2002. Korea was a Japanese colony between 1910 and 1946.

Today, the common assumption among Japanese people appears to be that Japanese race *equals* Japanese nationality *equals* Japanese cultural identity *equals* membership of the reference or insider group that identifies itself as 'the Japanese'. Unlike its Asian neighbours, Japan assumes the status of 'an honorary western power', the only Asian member of the 'G8' economic club. It is perhaps only a matter of time before China also joins this club.

Box 3.3 Brand marketing in Japan

Non-Japanese managers and marketers still ask: How can we crack the Japanese market? De Mooij (1994) gives the following advice: recognize local cultural differences as being among the most important variables and then get yourself a reliable reputation and a brand name. She concluded even then (mid-1990s) that 'Japanese society in particular is changing fast' (1994: 96). Citing Hiromura (1990) she lists the brand names that Japanese consumers most readily recognized: ranked from 1 to 10 they were Sony, Chanel, Toyota, IBM, Luis Vuitton, Coca-Cola, Mercedes Benz, Honda, General Motors and McDonalds. Japanese brands most readily recognized by US Americans were (in descending order): Sony, Toyota, Honda, Mitsubishi, Panasonic, Toshiba, Nissan and Nikon. Herbig (1998) describes which 'faces' (e.g. radiator grilles) of cars attract Japanese customers most.

Remarkable is how little these positions change, even (or especially?) in times of economic crisis (cf. Box 8.3). According to Drucker 'Brand loyalty is probably no more common in Japan than anyplace else. But brand recognition is of far greater importance.

continued

When you ask why supermarkets in Tokyo carry Swiss chocolates, the answer is always "But everybody knows they are the best"' (1999: 87–88). 'Everybody' in this response probably means 'the people I know': i.e. 'my immediate reference groups'.

Finally, De Mooij (1994) offers advice to western advertisers trying to attract a new generation of Japanese consumers: 'stress the emerging individuality of the Eastern consumer [rather than] uphold the slowly declining traditional group orientation . . . Hard-sell themes are a rarity in Japan and there is little comparative advertising because of the Japanese reluctance to cause a competitor to lose face' (1994: 237).

Communitarian achievement

One manager (now in his late fifties) spoke to us about the revival of his career. In what he told us we recognized the power of core and culture-specific assumptions: for him, the significance of 'being Japanese'.

Takeguchi-san

Takeguchi-san spoke about his experience of 'lifetime employment' with a major Japanese shipping company. The company 'suddenly collapsed' towards the end of the 1990s. This particular manager spent some time at a loss about what to do next: he had been with the company for over thirty years and he was on a high-level overseas assignment in Southeast Asia at the time of the company's collapse and so had missed out on the internal wheeling-and-dealing by which his erstwhile senior management colleagues sought to salvage their careers, their accustomed income, and their social status. In his own words he drifted 'like a character from a Joseph Conrad novel' for a few months.

On arriving back in Japan Takeguchi-san met similar-aged former executives who had suddenly and unexpectedly found themselves in a similar vacuous position. From a 'self-help group' he developed the idea for a headhunting bureau for mature and multi-skilled executives. A key selection criterion he uses is that the candidate should 'be flexible' and 'have an international perspective'. He emphasizes 'being fluent' as a core skill. This means more than having developed foreign language skills in English or Chinese. It means: 'being culturally adaptable, being confident, not only in [respect of] foreign cultures, but also in the management [culture] which is emerging in Japan now'. According to

Takeguchi-san, the solution to Japan's current problems '[lies] within Japanese people themselves'.

Takeguchi-san took inspiration from a story his father (a railway manager) used to tell him. Two weeks after the end of World War Two, the first timetabled passenger train left Osaka station for Tokyo. Because of the devastation that had been visited on many Japanese cities along the route, the journey had been scheduled to take two days. The train arrived in Tokyo 'only forty-five minutes late'. 'Room for improvement, of course' he said, expressing a *kai-zen* attitude, 'but an example of what Japanese people can achieve even in the most difficult circumstances.'

The communitarian achievement here is not the precision of the outcome; it is the effort expended towards achieving this outcome; the notion of effort, commitment and 'doing one's best' (*ganbaru*) is central to establishing an individual's acceptance by the reference group.

Furthermore, it is not so important whether Takeguchi-san's memory is accurate. More significant is the importance he attaches to this story. Through him it becomes an aspect of Japanese management 'culture' interpreted as 'the ensemble of stories we tell ourselves about ourselves' (Geertz, 1973). Transmitted from generation to generation, such stories shape each individual's formative experiences of culture and of national cultural identity. Universally, such stories are told about heroes and heroines who overcome obstacles (dilemmas) on the path to self-fulfilment; or, in the context of our current discussion, to enhanced self-esteem.

SECTION 3: FAMILY AS ORGANIZATION – ORGANIZATION AS FAMILY

Figure 3.1 *I-E*

The Chinese character or *kanji* (Figure 3.1) [*ie* – pronounced *ee-yeh*] signifies one of the most powerful concepts in the socialization of Japanese people. It defies precise translation. It encompasses ideas in English such as 'family', 'household' and 'home'. These are core assumptions with deep historical and cultural roots, and are similar to those informing our understanding – or more precisely our *difficulty* in understanding – culture-specific concepts such as the German 'Heimat'.

Among Japanese people *ie* evokes a sense of belonging, and of obligation and loyalty within the boundaries of reference groups. Attention to *ie*, as with attention to face, prescribes the values and norms for interaction between individuals perceived to have unequal rank and status, such as superiors (managers) and subordinates (staff), but also between members of a family (distinguished by age and gender) and between participants in institutionalized situations such as teachers and students, and trainers and their trainees (distinguished by assumed expertise and knowledge). In addressing dilemmas, individuals are expected to refer to the example of their 'elders and betters'.

The origins of *ie* can be found in the 'traditional obligations of [feudal] Japanese village life' (Smith and Misumi, 1994, in Hickson, 1997). The basic social and economic unit for human survival was the household. The *kanji* itself consists of two elements: a roof of a dwelling over a domesticated animal (a pig). This arrangement 'symbolises the importance placed upon the household's economic role *over* the human aspects of a conjugal nuclear family' (Scher in Bird, 2002: 183 – our emphasis). Renshaw (1999) relates *ie* to the household organized as a patriarchal unit around small-scale rice production and in doing so implies support for *nihonjinron* assumptions about Japanese organizational structures and cultures (Box 3.1).

Ie tradition and Japanese business organizations

Taking a slightly different tack, Scher (in Bird, 2002: 183) describes how the traditional function of *ie* evolved into a prototype for Japanese business organizations. Three aspects of this prototype are worth emphasizing:

- *ie* as a multi-generational socio-economic unit where the older generations would train up the younger generations to succeed them;
- *ie* as an organization which relies on the commitment and loyalty of all members, regardless of each individual's perceived or ascribed status, in order to survive and (hopefully) prosper;
- *ie* as a unit whose material assets are indivisible (most people in feudal Japan were too poor feasibly to distribute wealth between siblings) and so needed to be handed down intact from generation to generation: *our most valuable resource is our people.*

Two further points are worth mentioning in this context. First, we need to remember that in feudal Japan (as earlier in feudal Europe) the vast majority of the population did not travel, having neither the resources, nor the occasion, nor the legal permission. Also, each individual was usually addressed according to their function or status within the *ie* unit. Even today, members of Japanese families may refer to each other only as 'mother', 'father', 'younger brother' or 'elder sister', and so on. This tradition persists in aforementioned individual forms of address such as Yamada-*kacho* ('section manager Yamada') or Sato-*sensei* ('teacher Sato'). Many surnames reflect aspects of the natural environment: the *kanji* for the surname *Ota* describes 'a large rice field', for *Kawaguchi* 'the mouth of a river'.

Comparing Japanese with Asian tradition

The Japanese version of the economic family unit (*ie*) differs from the traditional Chinese and Korean versions. Significantly, non-blood relations would be routinely included into the 'family' in order to ensure the unit's continued survival. From this basic culture-specific assumption it is easy to extrapolate to 'typical' HRM practices of Japanese organizations: namely, external recruitment, lifetime employment, in-house training, seniority promotion, and the expected commitment and loyalty of staff at all levels towards the survival of the company (*kaisha*) as 'family' (*ie*), once they had been granted the privilege of entry. Privilege because, as in times of feudal strife, having a home meant satisfying basic human needs such as physiological needs; safety and security needs; belonging and acceptance (cf. Maslow, 1970; Box 6.2).

In common with Asian tradition, one HRM principle remains hard to break: seniority according to age – 'the son should not defy the father'. Accordingly, the senior managers in a Japanese company will tend be older than junior and (possibly) more talented or expert younger managers. To avoid loss of face, the older ones will carry the title (and probably the glory) while the younger ones will work on the practical solutions to business problems: we recall the confusion of the US American negotiator (Chapter 1) who was trying to identify 'the main man' in the Japanese negotiation group. A current problem is the surplus of general managers at middle rank and in mid-career, promoted during the years of growth in order to avoid loss of face. We address this problem in detail in Chapters 6 and 7.

Fear of exclusion

Feeling safe and warm inside the boundaries of *ie* suggests an appreciation of the alternative: feeling cold and excluded on the outside. Both Mead (2001 – personal communication) and Renshaw (1999) recount how, in western cultures, when a child is naughty he or she is usually threatened with being locked in the house, meaning that he or she is not allowed out to play with friends. In Asian cultures the opposite tends to be the case: when a child is naughty he or she is threatened with being locked *out* of the house.

Outlaws?

We saw the practical importance attached to being considered an 'insider' or an 'outsider' in our discussion of face in Chapter 2. In the context of *ie*, Scher (in Bird, 2002: 184) states: 'Within the *ie*, the most important criterion by which to evaluate action and behavior was how well it served the group. In such a collectively oriented society, the individual hardly existed as a distinct entity, and failure to fulfill one's obligations was considered selfish, or even cowardly.'

Breaking the rules has potentially dire consequences. Individuals who do so can expect to be excluded, even 'outlawed'. This English term is borrowed from Old Norse and helps illustrate a point. Apart from major differences such as the social mobility of individuals and (not least) the social status of women, life in feudal Viking society was as insecure and probably as brutally short as in feudal Japan. To be 'outlawed' meant that individuals who broke the rules (e.g. who were being exceptionally 'selfish' or 'cowardly' in their behaviour) could expect to be excluded from the community, which itself sought harmony by referring to the common 'law'. The duration and nature of exclusion were laid down and made public by a democratic meeting of lawgivers. Exclusion meant that the law-breaker was put beyond the protection of the law; hence, *out-lawed*. Consequently, any 'in-law' could threaten him or her with little fear of sanction from the community. Some Viking outlaws went on to fame if not fortune, discovering for western societies lands that became Iceland, Greenland and the North American continent.

Mutual obligations

Guidance to individuals on how to 'fulfil one's obligations' (cf. Scher, cited above) is given by reference to concepts of *giri* and *on*. In Confucian philosophy, the inevitable tension between un-equals (i.e. un-equal in respect of age, gender, education, or knowledge, or other qualities) should be resolved within the family unit such that broader social order or 'harmony' (in Japanese *wa*) should ensue. In the context of *ie*, the mutuality of obligations and interests is expressed in terms of *giri* and *on*. Scher (in Bird, 2002: 184) defines *giri* as 'obligations and duties [owed by inferiors] to superiors' and *on* as 'benevolence [by superiors] towards inferiors'.

This mutuality of interest and obligation can be translated into Japanese HRM practice and general management behaviour:

- the organization (represented by senior managers) offers worthy subordinates (junior managers) lifetime employment, security of income, and training: in return, each subordinate offers lifetime loyalty and commitment to the organization;
- the organization offers (usually male) senior managers job rotation and automatic promotion: senior and line managers teach and monitor the deference shown by subordinates towards their superiors and towards organizational values and norms; subordinates who fulfil their obligations are promoted;
- senior managers adopt a paternalistic attitude towards their juniors, showing concern for their well-being and progress within the organizational 'family', and perhaps even helping to arrange a suitable marriage and accommodation for them; junior managers are expected to show due gratitude.

This last example illustrates how, in the culture-specific context of *ie*, expectations associated with *giri* and *on* further reinforce the 'diffuseness' of Japanese management culture: in the TH-T model, the extent to which 'the whole person' is involved in business or employment relationships.

Overall, *giri* and *on* indicate the type of mutual obligations that senior and junior managers are expected to fulfil if they are to avoid appearing individually 'selfish or even cowardly'. Senior managers – or other sources of authority such as tradition – tend to define the context for decisions, while more expert or energetic juniors will work out the decisions. In this way, adherence to *giri* and *on* can be seen to reinforce what the TH-T model terms 'particularism' whereby 'certain values (e.g. loyalty to friends or family) need to be prioritized according to circumstances' (Trompenaars and Hampden-Turner, 1998: 9).

SECTION 4: SOCIALIZATION – HOME AND SCHOOL

Based on their own experience, Japanese parents know what children need to succeed in the established structures and cultures of the Japanese education system. The system has changed only slowly in the past three generations. Referring back to the context given by *ie*, parents must have sufficient independent resources (money, determination, luck, and so on) to take the risk of allowing their children not to fit in. Consider the following comment of a Japanese mother:

> When my husband and I came back to Japan from living abroad, our first concern was to get our young daughter into one of the 'elevator schools'. These are private schools which prepare children from kindergarten onwards for the entrance exams to one of the high-ranking private universities. I'm hopeful we can get her in as I'm a graduate of that university myself.

This mother (now in her late forties) completed graduate study at a 'high-ranking' UK university and is currently the manager of an international education consultancy in Japan. She is able, she says, to convince her clients (parents and students) of the advantages of gaining an international education in preparation for a future international career environment. When in Japan, though, she focuses on making the Japanese system work for her daughter. A pragmatic expression of particularism: one would expect nothing less from a mother ambitious for her children's success. 'Ideally', she told us 'our children would have something of both: the solid skills training that a Japanese education gives [e.g. in terms of numeracy, literacy and teamwork skills], but with something more of the self-confidence and flexibility that an international education can give' (cf. Boxes 3.4 and 3.5).

Early-years schooling as preparation for work

Japanese children are expected to be able to read and write and be numerate to some degree before they enter elementary school. This is the

Box 3.4 Successes and failures of Japanese education

Dore and Sako (1998) identify two key roles for the Japanese state or government: 'to ensure the [vocational] trainability of all its citizens' (1998: xii) and 'to provide a [standardized] testing and certification system' (1998: xiv). The Japanese education system has been designed to develop sufficient 'human capital' so as to achieve 'the collectivist objective of national competitiveness' (1998: xvii) – an outcome which can also be interpreted as giving and sustaining national *face*.

By global comparison (e.g. World Bank Development Index), Japan spends a much lower proportion of GDP (less than 1 per cent, though this is now rising) on education than do most other OECD nations. Traditionally, the outcomes of Japan's national education system can be presented as a sustained and overwhelming success; not least, as a preparation for the world of work. However, as with any national education system there are advantages and disadvantages in terms of the relative and perceived quality of educational outcomes (cf. Bird, 2002; Rohlen and Björk, 1998; Dore and Sako, 1998). In the case of Japan, *advantages* include: the achievement of high rates of literacy, numeracy and teamworking skills; a developed sense for individual and collective commitment and perseverance; standardization of provision allowing for economies of scale; a testing system which is commonly perceived as being meritocratic and fair.

Perceived *disadvantages* include: emphasis on a uniform pace of learning and rote learning of 'facts'; marginalization of students at extreme high and low levels of learning ability; a system of testing which, though perceived as 'valid' (i.e. in relation to the purpose it is designed for – drawing up rankings) is of questionable 'reliability' (i.e. in relation to testing knowledge or quality of education, at least against non-national or non-insider criteria).

Box 3.5 *Kikokushijo*

Kikokushijo, or 'returnee children' are children who return to the national education system in Japan after living and studying for periods overseas, usually when accompanying their parents on an expatriate business assignment. They used to be regarded as 'problem cases' within Japanese society, but in the emerging employment and career environments their experience is increasingly perceived as a source of personal and professional advantage.

Some *kikokushijo* may have been able to visit a Japanese school overseas (perhaps at weekends) and so have been able to keep up with their peers in Japan: for example, in terms of learning *kanji* (see below). Others who did not have this opportunity, or whose parents chose to ignore it, often have severe problems re-integrating into Japanese school cultures. In addition, their presence in classes can be perceived as a threat to the authority of teachers, particularly in subjects such as foreign languages and geography.

continued

We heard of several cases where *kikokushijo* become cast as disruptive 'outsiders' by the established reference groups in schools.

Times are changing. High-ranking Japanese universities and internationally oriented companies routinely court applications from *kikokushijo*, assuming (understandably) that these individuals have developed higher levels of maturity, diverse experience and intercultural flexibility than the majority of their 'stay-at-home' Japanese counterparts. *Kikokushijo* may be offered more open-ended forms of entrance assessment to certain universities and companies in contrast to the rather rigid multiple-choice format offered to 'home' applicants: this also is an attempt to be fair to them. As career structures become increasingly diversified and internationalized in Japan (as elsewhere), trends in career opportunities in Japan appear to be shifting in favour of the erstwhile *kikokushijo* 'outsiders'.

family's responsibility. Classes are generally not 'streamed' according to ability: age and time of entry are the deciding factors – a reference group known as *doki* ('contemporaries' or 'same-time entrants') and a process mirrored in the recruitment and induction of new staff in business organizations.

As within the family, the teacher is not addressed by name but as *sensei* – the '*sen-*' prefix used to denote someone who is older and (by implication) wiser. Correspondingly, each child may be allocated or seek out a *senpai* (older individual) to guide them (*kohai* – the younger members of the dyad) in what is and what is not expected behaviour: *giri* and *on*. The role of the *sensei* is a precursor of the role of line-manager at work, the *senpai* that of the knowledgeable or experienced senior who can induct the newcomer and 'teach him/her the ropes'.

Until the age of twelve, most Japanese kindergarten and elementary schoolchildren do not need to wear a school uniform: this requirement comes later, perhaps in an attempt to reinforce 'uniformity' of social behaviour and expectations. In terms of space, elementary schoolchildren usually remain in one classroom with one class teacher. With each other they learn to refer to 'our teacher' (*uchi no sensei*) and 'our classroom' – much later 'our company' will roll off the tongue. The children serve and eat lunch in 'their' classroom; they tidy the room and the surrounding areas of 'their' school each day. Thus explicit diffusion of school as a place of both work and study is a discipline that is taught early on.

The curriculum is highly centralized by the Japanese Ministry of Education, though reforms based on international (above all, European) models are currently being trialled. In working through the curriculum the children are organized into mixed ability task groups called *han*. The *han* is a task- and context-specific reference group and presages the more specialized work section or group of the business organization.

Time and space

The amount of homework given to children and the amount of cramming required to progress through the school assessment system reinforces the 'diffuseness' of individual identity both inside and outside the home: children spend most of their time being schoolchildren or students. As the children get older, or when the homework becomes too specialized for family members to help, the teaching and drilling may be 'outsourced' – usually at considerable expense – to cramming schools (*juku*) or to private tutors who may visit the home, thus further reinforcing the home as a place of study. According to Dore and Sako (1998), up to 50 per cent of all 'city families' routinely try to 'buy extra chances' for their children in this way. Studying 'overtime' is therefore normal. As the mother/manager (cited above) explained to us: 'The attraction of getting a child into an "elevator school" is that, assuming she does ok there, they [i.e. the school's staff] will get her there [i.e. to the university and so choice of career she and her parents hope for]. She'll have to work hard, but at least we'll know that when we're together at home we can relax together and not worry about arranging extra classes for her.'

In the context of East Asian cultures, Bae and Rowley (2001) distinguish between the teaching or transmission of *self-regulatory* and *normative* behaviours. From early on Japanese children are taught normative behaviours such as how to speak and bow to people of differing social status. A key form of self-regulatory behaviour is the aforementioned communicative value of *silence*: 'children should be seen and not heard' as in the Victorian British tradition. On the other hand, children are very much indulged, perhaps in view of the competitive pressures that await them. Silence expresses a shared submission to the obligations of *giri* and *on*. It also expresses a sense of personal security (as in *ie*). If there is harmony (*wa*), what more is there to say?

SECTION 5: HOW JAPANESE MANAGERS LEARN

> Foreigners have often stood in amaze [*sic*] at Japan's
> ability to swallow so many new ideas and institutions
> whole. They have dubbed her superficial, and questioned
> the permanence of her conversion to European methods.
> This is because they fail to realize two things – the innate
> strength of the Japanese character, and the continuous
> process of schooling which has enabled this particular race
> to face the new light without being blinded.
>
> (Hall Chamberlain, 1905)

Basil Hall Chamberlain was British and arrived in Japan in 1873. He was
an instructor of English language at the navy academy and later became
Professor of Japanese at Tokyo University, retiring in 1911. He pioneered
the study of Japanese history and language in the west.

How Japanese managers learn to learn

Rote learning – or learning by heart – is at the core of the traditional
Japanese approach to learning. This is as true at elementary school as it is
at university. According to Dore and Sako, 'university teaching . . . tends
to be school-like in its reliance on bucket theories of pedagogy – the
student as receptacle into which knowledge and ideas have to be poured –
though a lot of the pouring has to be done by the student himself, sitting
down with his books in private study' (1998: 9).

Getting the right wrong answer

Unsurprisingly, the way that student learning is subsequently assessed
reflects this approach: tests and examinations tend to require the
memorization of 'facts' or stock answers to what – in real-life contexts –
are highly complex questions. We found this example in an English
language examination: *What is the opposite of 'must?'* Four alternative
(multiple-choice) answers were suggested, only one of which was deemed
'correct'. Well, 'the' opposite of 'must' in English might be: 'must not',
'mustn't', 'needn't', 'don't have to', 'can't', 'cannot' – or none of these,
depending on the context. This approach to learning and testing is still
widespread in Japan. Given its careless regard for real-life contexts (in our
experience, a common fault with multiple choice questions (MCQs) and
other closed forms of assessment) in such a context-sensitive culture

(cf. Chapter 1), the adherence to this form of testing suggests an exercise in power: the teacher/tester has the 'correct' answer; the student must jump through hoops to learn what answer is expected, not what answer might or might not be appropriate in real life. This form of assessment is also efficient to administer: MCQs can be scored electronically.

The cramming/testing industry in Japan is massive: at school level serviced by *juku* and (for university entrance) by *yobiko* cramming schools. Given the pressure to succeed (i.e. pass the test in order to enter the next stage or selective school) these schools profit enormously from parental worries and individual student ambitions. It is normal to see children coming home from extra classes late on weekday evenings and at weekends: learning to work indeed! To pass the national and university tests is an act of perseverance and (for the less able or willing students) endurance. Each student's score can be calculated against a national scale to generate 'T-scores' (*hensachi*). In turn these 'T-scores' can be used to rank various institutions together with the levels of the students who succeed or fail to enter them (Sugimoto, 1997).

There is a common view that the eyesight of so many young people deteriorates because of the type and intensity of study and testing they have to endure in order to 'get on' in society. Despite moves to more open-ended (or humane?) forms of assessment, the staple form of rote learning and testing persists and keeps cramming schools in good business and parents and their children in an ongoing cycle of stress and 'examination hell'. The trend is, however, towards more individualized and flexible forms of testing, significantly in university entrance and company recruitment procedures, described in Chapter 4.

Learning *kanji*

Rote learning or memorization is essential to becoming 'Japanese'. We have already stated how the learning of our 'mother' or 'native' tongue is inextricably associated with our learning of culture-specific core assumptions. This basis in language and associated assumptions and values allows us to take part in the communication of information which is essential to being accepted in our culture-specific reference groups, be they national, organizational, departmental, or centred on family, school or friends.

Distinctive in the socialization experience of young Japanese people is the effort given to learning to read and write (cf. Box 3.6). To do this effectively they have to be remarkably flexible, thorough, persistent, and patient. Japanese people learn to read and write in five forms of script: *hiragana* (the curvy Japanese phonetic script); *katakana* (the angular script for transliterating foreign or loan words or names); *romaji* (the roman script you are reading now); *furigana* (small *hiragana* to help learners pronounce unfamiliar *kanji*); and *kanji* or the 'Chinese characters' themselves. The character *ie* which was presented earlier in this chapter is an example of *kanji*.

Box 3.6 The sanctity of the written text

Japanese people are frequently shocked (and confused) by the readiness with which many westerners write important information using careless handwriting. Japanese students are initially reluctant to scrawl over authoritative texts. In Japan, a neatly and clearly presented text has authority and deserves respect. Training manuals in Japanese companies tend to be highly detailed and are designed to be memorized by new intakes of employees as part of their induction and initial training. Specifications and other product-related documents tend to be equally clear and detailed, obviating doubt and assumptions.

In absolute contrast, commercial and employment contracts and job descriptions tend *not* to be detailed. This is because this type of linear text represents a poor (if tangible and explicit) imitation of the complex and decidedly non-linear process that gives the essence of meaning to any contract: namely, a relationship based on mutual obligation and trust (see Chapter 6). To offer Japanese business partners a lengthy and highly detailed business contract – one that 'covers every angle', as the company lawyers might say – is an explicit indication that there is little or no basis of trust between the partners involved. Usual result: the collaboration fails.

In further contrast stands the *manga* phenomenon. *Manga* are cartoons or comics popular among all ages and social groups in Japan. The stories vary from the luridly violent and sexist to the instructively critical and argumentative. Others are highly informative about national and international political and economic issues. A recent *manga* series celebrates the thoughts and achievements of Nissan boss Carlos Ghosn.

Why do Japanese managers read *manga*? Common answers are: 'escapism', 'humour', 'easy on the eyes' or 'kills time during commuting'. The western world is catching up: today even non-Japanese executives might be relaxed about being caught with a Scott Adams comic book wrapped in their *Financial Times* or *Wall Street Journal*.

A major task facing all Japanese students is the need to learn (i.e. memorize and be able to write correctly) more than 2,500 *kanji* in order to be to function effectively – and without fear of exclusion – in the highly educated Japanese working population. The Japanese *kanji* denoting 'learning' (pronounced variously as *gaku* or *mannabu*) derives from the image or idea of children who, protected under a roof (similar to the roof suggested in *ie*), learn by emulating or imitating adult behaviour; for example, by learning to use their hands in writing, eating, or working. The emphasis given to patient imitation and practice derives in part from Confucian philosophy: the teacher (*sensei*) as an older and wiser expert whose behaviour should be emulated.

Managers and students who have been living or working in non-Japanese cultures for a while admit they 'forget' some *kanji*. They have to refresh their memory when they return to Japan or 'keep in practice' while they are away. Being able to read and write a number of *kanji* far exceeding the basic few thousand draws great respect. Calligraphy has the status of an art form rather than a hobby. The whole learning and practising process is unending and mirrors the search for quality perfection enshrined in *kai-zen* philosophy (Box 5.3).

SECTION 6: CASE STUDIES REVIEWED

In this chapter we have discussed how young Japanese people are socialized and so groomed for work. As in our discussion of reference groups in Chapter 2, the emphasis has been on learning how to 'fit in'; how to become an 'insider'; how to 'be Japanese'. Looking towards adult life, the socialization process should guide individuals on how to manage problems and dilemmas.

Having been born and socialized as a Japanese, *not* being Japanese is no longer an option. However, choosing *not* to fit in with expected norms in terms of education and career path is always a strategic option. But what are the incentives? What are the likely consequences? Consider this warning:

> Alienation worries everyone, if it happens. Children at the more individualistic end of the Japanese personality spectrum learn how difficult life is for those not spiritually integrated into the group. Japanese schools provide lessons not only in the horrors of isolation, but also in the inadmissible cruelty of letting others feel isolated. This training in groupishness is reinforced by, for example, the total absence of cleaning staff, the fact that it is the children's responsibility to clean 'our' classroom and 'our' school playground – a practice

designed to inculcate, also, a sense of responsibility for one's environment, as well as drawing on older traditions which emphasize cleanliness, the dignity of manual work and the dangers of pride.

(Dore and Sako, 1998: 8)

Pride and Kimura-san

Returning to our case studies of Chapter 2, it is our view that Kimura-san felt snubbed by his employer over the MBA awards: a degree of emotion is evident in his decision to quit. In contrast, he admits to feeling flattered by the company that eventually 'poached' him. A sense of pride may have sparked his decision, but probably did not cause it to be implemented. Given his background, his ascribed status as a graduate from a highly regarded university and as a manager in an important ministry, he should be expected to develop his career in time-honoured fashion, probably returning to his former university at some point to meet his professor and guide suitable new recruits towards a ministry post, thereby fulfilling obligations of *on* and *giri*.

However, something appears to have gone awry. Kimura-san began to find fault and lose patience with the tasks he was assigned. He began to lose trust in the structures of promotion; or perhaps he began to doubt his own ability to negotiate them.

Achievement and Takeda-san

Takeda-san's status is based more on 'achievement' rather than 'ascription'. According to the TH-T model, 'achievement means that you are judged on what you have recently accomplished and on your record' (Trompenaars and Hampden-Turner, 1998: 9). She worked hard, and felt exploited. In an understated way we inferred that she sensed her line-manager had failed to fulfil his obligations defined by *on*. Or perhaps he only interpreted this obligation in a different way, as evinced in his promise to 'see her right' in future. Either she had lost patience or she no longer trusted her boss's ability to deliver on his promises, giving us a further illustration of how time, information, confidence and not least opportunity are key elements in strategic decision-making.

Takeda-san appears to have taken herself by surprise with her decision to quit. The decision also took her family by surprise, one reason being that she and they lack sufficient 'role models' against which to evaluate her decision. She was open in expressing her worries: an emotional response, but after the event; for her decision to quit was measured and informed.

A key difference in our interviews with both was Kimura-san's relative silence about the background to his decision to quit (emotion masked by silence?) and Takeda-san's self-effacing openness about her decision. Perhaps this suggests a difference in male versus female attitudes? We suggested previously that silence relates to avoiding – or causing – further loss of face. In Japan's overtly 'masculine' management culture – at least according to Hofstede and colleagues – Kimura-san probably felt he (potentially) had more face to lose. The male/female dichotomy among Japanese managers is a theme we develop in Chapter 4.

Summary

In this chapter we have looked at common experiences of the socialization process in Japan, focusing on the learning of culture-specific assumptions and core values during the early formative years of family upbringing and education. Our purpose in this chapter has been to show how managers such as Kimura-san and Takeda-san – cases we introduced in Chapter 2 – and other Japanese managers we have spoken to learn to learn and learn to work. Specifically we have looked at how they approach problems and dilemmas, using a framework for analysis devised by Trompenaars and Hampden-Turner (1998). This model enables us to explain and predict more about Japanese management culture and about being Japanese.

Reflect on your own experiences and expectations in response to the following questions:

● To what extent do you recognize the influence of your upbringing and your early-years education on your subsequent choice and changes of career?

● Imagine you have been asked to address a class of ten-year-olds in your local school. What careers advice would you give them, and why? Imagine you have been asked to address a class of twenty-year-olds in your local university or college on the same topic. What careers advice would you give them, and why?

4 Starting a career

Introduction

> Men make their own lives, but they do not make them just
> as they please, they do not make them under circumstances
> chosen by themselves, but under circumstances directly
> encountered, given and transmitted from the past.
>
> (Karl Marx)

In Chapter 3 we looked at how Japanese children learn to 'fit in' to
Japanese culture and society and, in doing this, how they learn to work.
In this chapter we look at common experiences of higher and further
education, focusing on how these experiences impact on individual
choices of job or career. By use of case studies we illustrate how Japanese
men and women tend to experience recruitment, selection and
organizational induction processes differently.

Compulsory school education in Japan finishes at age fifteen, after which
students compete for places at schools, colleges and universities. Thus

each individual's experience of education, testing and training from the age of fifteen normally determines their subsequent career: i.e. a linear or (in Japan, often) cyclical sequence of jobs and responsibilities that, over time, should describe a pathway of professional experience. In Japan, only the exceptional manage to re-determine this path. In this chapter we highlight the characteristics of some exceptional managers.

Our objectives for this chapter are:

- to give an insight into how Japanese managers generally experience education in terms of preparing for a career;

- to show how individual Japanese managers commonly experience recruitment, selection and induction as initial steps on a career path;

- to illustrate how and why the experience of a career traditionally tends to differ for men and women managers in Japan.

SECTION 1: *LES JEUX SONT FAITS*

> Given that 40 per cent of the age group go through [the] university entrance process, and probably another 20 per cent contemplate doing so, and given that they are the brighter ones in whose success the teachers have a considerable stake, it is not surprising that the whole of the primary and secondary span of education should be dominated by the university selection system in which it culminates.
>
> (Dore and Sako, 1998: 4)

Entering university

In Japan, getting into a 'top-ranking' or 'famous' university is a key that opens the door to a successful lifetime career. Twenty per cent or more secondary-school students miss out in the tests for entry into their first choice university each year (Dore and Sako, 1998: 21), failing to get the necessary 'T-score'. Such is the pressure to succeed, these first-time failures (known as *ronin*) will delay for another year or more and dedicate themselves to self-study and/or enter a cram school (known as *yobiko*) designed to drill them in preparation for a repeat of their preferred university's entrance examination. The term *ronin* traditionally refers to a samurai warrior who, having lost his original master or warlord, must compete to find employment and protection elsewhere. Unlike the official state schools, *yobiko* 'stream' students according to their T-score. Accordingly, each individual is given a clear (if opaque, given the arcane nature of the tests) indication of where he or she stands in the competitive rankings.

Failure to get into the first-choice university is likely to be a great personal disappointment; and the aspirant's families and teachers suffer too. However, the potential for loss of face is diminished if the effort of the individual concerned was genuine and consistent – if the student 'did his/her best' (*ganbaru*). Like a direct 'no', open reference to personal 'failure' (i.e. loss of face) is avoided (see Box 2.1). Those who 'fail' are expected to 'get on with it' (*ganbatte*) and apply their energies towards finding a productive niche elsewhere, and the sooner the better in order to avoid a protracted loss of face.

Methods of university selection are generally perceived to be 'fair' (cf. Cummings, 1980; Kariya, 1995). The common perception is that the testing and selection regime is 'open to everyone' and so all children have a chance to succeed 'if this is the right thing for them'. Most Japanese managers we spoke to recognized that the 'game was up' at age fifteen when the selective examinations are held for entry into high schools: the common assumption being that entry to a 'good' high school facilitates entry to a 'good' university and hence entry to a 'good' career. 'Good' in this context is a value judgement and a culture-specific perception, widely shared and adhered to in society. One challenge facing Japanese managers who decide to re-determine the course of their career is to re-evaluate what constitutes a 'good' education and whether what they have experienced hitherto is sufficient for shaping a future career.

Who goes to university?

Approximately 47 per cent of all boys and 33 per cent of all girls in the year 2001 entered university, approximately three-quarters of both groups in private institutions. There is a common perception that 'the best places are reserved for men' (i.e. rather than women). The overall higher and further education Age Participation Rate (APR) in Japan is high by global standards: France and the USA are near to achieving similar APRs, while (in 2003) the UK government still dreams of such figures.

Currently, many private Japanese universities are suffering from a recruitment crisis. This comes as a delayed result of a rapidly declining national birth rate. It is the 'national' universities which demand much lower fees (if any at all), which are consequently highly selective, and which traditionally head the university rankings. 'In Japan, if you pass the test, you're in' was one manager's view. Tokyo and Kyoto (national) universities both have the reputation of offering graduates a passport into high-ranking public or private sector jobs.

Given the recruitment crisis, high-ranking private sector universities such as Keio and Waseda have begun consciously to internationalize and differentiate their 'product'. In response to the crisis in mid-career development opportunities (discussed in Chapter 5) these and other universities have begun offering executive-style MBA programmes (note: in both Japanese and in English) and other career-relevant qualifications. Most managers who have a job cannot afford to give it up and risk failing an MBA. Correspondingly, there is also growth in distance learning opportunities. In this field the Japanese University of the Air has a long and established pedigree.

This emerging trend in MBA study in Japan is paralleled in Germany. As we saw in Chapter 3, both countries have some similar industrial traditions. According to Goffee and Hunt (in Pitman/FT, 1997: 632) 'Germany and Japan have integrated managerial and technical functions much more closely [than US and UK management styles and traditions] and have not, until recently, developed an infrastructure of "management development" institutions external to the workplace.' The argument here is that in both Japan and Germany, managers have generally risen through the ranks of a company or industry on the basis of technical qualifications and experience and that it is only recently that both countries are seeing the development of 'general management' qualifications (e.g. MBAs, as opposed to company- or industry-specific qualifications). Both prestigious and cash-strapped Japanese universities are beginning to respond to this demand.

Many more managers decide to further their education, experience and qualifications abroad: the USA remains the most popular destination. Takeda-san, whose case we discussed in Chapter 2, decided to take an MBA in the UK because she wanted 'to differentiate' herself from the mass of USA graduates. Tradition being what it is, growing interest in

MBA-style programmes has prompted a significant expansion in cram schools preparing students for TOEIC ®, TOEFL®, GMAT® and other career-oriented English language examinations.

Experiencing university

The Japanese academic year runs from April to March. As in other countries, the standard of university education varies. There is a common perception inside and outside Japan that, having survived the obstacle course of gaining university entry, the four years of undergraduate 'study' is a chance to relax and enjoy the teenage pleasures one missed during years of cramming. The reality increasingly is that university study is perceived as 'just another obstacle course' on the way to 'getting into a good job/company'. Accountancy and finance are sought after subjects, thus matching a global trend. Fear of exam failure drives many students (again!) into a 'double school' syndrome of cramming *yobiko*-style courses in with standard university courses: 'examination hell' revisited!

Social networking is also important. The student and his or her *doki* provide the context for learning how to interact and prosper in more adult and ambitious reference groups than those in high schools. Cliques and societies and informal study-groups supplant the *han* groups of school education. A lot of beer is drunk, generating a very Japanese contradiction. By Japanese law, people under the age of twenty are not allowed to buy alcohol. A Japanese-style solution to this problem is public vending machines, discreetly hidden so no one need publicly lose face: CCTV eyes? In Japan as elsewhere, drinking and networking are time consuming but recommended in preparation for the next big challenge – securing a 'good' job (but see Box 4.1).

Box 4.1 *Freeters*

A typically Japanese coinage, *freeter* combines English 'free' with German 'Arbeiter' (worker) and refers to university graduates who choose a series of part-time jobs and live with their parents, thus saving time, money and effort in order to pursue an individualized form of lifestyle.

Hijino (2001) cites the experiences and expectations of several *freeters*. One woman quit her job at a trading company because of the stress of commuting and the hours and conditions of her work. She says: 'I wanted to have less stress and more time. I wanted to live a fully human life.' Hijino also cites one resolute thirty-year-old: 'I'd rather have time than money. That is an absolute.' This apparent shift in values is supported by current trends in the employment market. As we explain in Chapter 7, in order to cut costs Japanese organizations increasingly are outsourcing work (e.g. IT and call centre services). Others are slashing graduate recruitment. In Chapter 8 we describe how redundancies even among managers are becoming more common and (significantly) more public.

For this reason we say that the recent *freeter* phenomenon represents an *apparent* shift in employment and career values. In fact, the majority of university graduates in Japan traditionally had a rather tenuous hold on a steady career job. Figures from the Japanese Institute of Labour (available online) show that around 30 per cent of graduates routinely quit their first job after three years (without great social fanfare) and as few as 20 per cent of the 'bubble economy' generation expect to stay with one company from graduation to retirement. It is, however, this latter 20 per cent whose example has traditionally been the benchmark for employment values and expectations in Japanese society (cf. Box 4.2).

The social significance of the *freeter* phenomenon is to broadcast that other sets of work-related values are both valid and viable. Thus, these values stand as an alternative point of reference to Japanese managers who sense that the established values are increasingly becoming a constraint to their individual career and lifestyle ambitions. This is a theme we develop in Chapter 8.

SECTION 2: ENTERING THE WORLD OF WORK

Recruitment and selection

In HRM terms, recruitment can be defined as 'the first stage in filling a vacancy' (Hannagan, 1998: 307). Companies match their requirements and current staff resources with current and future (strategic) need. They then advertise their needs – independently or through agencies – and await a response from job seekers. In Japanese companies, the perception of 'future need' is traditionally long-term. New recruits are seldom expected to enter with specialized or immediately transferable skills. Rather, they should show evidence of general learning abilities and qualities such conscientiousness, personal motivation, and (not least) reliability.

Selection is the second stage of the vacancy filling process and can be defined as 'the assessment of candidates for vacant jobs and the choice of the most suitable people [for these jobs]' (Hannagan, 1998: 316). The assessment can take the form of sorting by quality of application documents, interviews, tests, or the strength of recommendations from people who claim to know the candidate's qualities. The outcome of selection is a job offer or a rejection.

Recruiting potential

From an HRM perspective, recruitment and selection processes are time consuming and costly. However, and because Japanese HR managers tend to have an intimate insight into the national education system, these processes in Japan tend to be more straightforward than more diversified or internationalized contexts. In Japan, HR managers traditionally know what to expect from applicants who have had a 'good' Japanese education, interpreted on the basis of shared values, assumptions and (until recently, perhaps) experiences. High-ranking Japanese organizations have traditionally recruited management-track candidates based on their learning potential and culture-specific fit rather than on their specific skills. For this reason they prefer to recruit graduates from high-ranking universities, thereby showing trust not only in the ranking system itself (cf. Box 3.2), but also in the long-term potential that graduates from these universities will bring. Thus the tradition for graduate recruitment and selection dovetails with the traditional experience of high school and university education.

However, the emerging strategic environment is challenging the ability of Japanese HR managers to predict what types of staff skills and qualities their organization will need in the near to mid-term. The recruitment and selection processes thus become more complex. Current trends show that large companies are becoming more discerning and less general in their recruitment processes: quite simply, there are fewer management-track jobs for graduates. Correspondingly, there is an increasing reluctance to offer new entrants a firm prospect of lifetime employment and career progression. The environment for graduate recruitment and selection in Japan is thus undergoing a fundamental shift in values and priorities (cf. Bird, 2002; Kono and Clegg, 2001; JETRO, 2002).

Traditional experiences of recruitment and selection

Yoshimura and Anderson (1997: 19–21) give a vivid account of a traditional experience of graduate recruitment and selection. Hiro, an archetypal *salaryman* figure (cf. Box 8.1), was nearing graduation when, unexpectedly, he was contacted by a graduate from the same university. This alumnus was now working for a bank. Hiro was asked whether he had thought of working in banking. Hiro said he had. The alumnus then arranged to meet Hiro 'for dinner' to talk, among other things, about careers in banking. The evening went well. Contact was maintained. Hiro found himself drawn into a *senpai/kohai* (i.e. senior/junior) relationship.

Hiro then started getting invitations from alumni who were working at other banks and financial institutions. In Yoshimura and Anderson's story, Hiro actually wanted to move abroad after graduation, but the prospect of a job from a prestigious bank put him in a dilemma. He was given time to consider the first bank's offer together with any other job offers he might receive. However, his experience of socialization told him that 'the game had changed. Japanese banks do not want to be compared and only a fool would try to attract as many offers as possible before picking one, as a Westerner might. Dodging the [first bank's] offer would show the wrong attitude and embarrass the bank' (1997: 20). All sides knew that 'this was a decision expected to last for decades' – a reference to the 'lifetime employment' expectation. Hiro chose the first bank that had contacted him because by this time he felt that 'he had a trusted friend senior to him there' (1997: 21). We can therefore recognize the *emotional* (i.e. as opposed to the 'neutral') dimension to this individually very important decision. We discuss in detail the power of 'trust' in Chapter 6.

Aotagai

Hiro's experience of recruitment is commonly known as *aotagai* or 'buying (the green rice) before it is harvested'. We can compare Hiro's experience of recruitment with that of Kimura-san, introduced in Chapter 2. Kimura-san's entry into the ministry was facilitated by a personal recommendation from his then university professor. Other professors in the same university department would recommend their students to other employers, each apparently conscious of his or her role as member of a reference group whose purpose was to improve Japanese society, and (probably) sustain their own insider status as reliable judges of human character and potential.

Kimura-san's professor informed him one day that an alumnus, now working at the ministry, was keen to meet him and talk about his studies and his future career plans. Kimura-san was assured that this was 'normal procedure'. Realizing what was in prospect, Kimura-san told his family and all were excited about the possibility of him being offered a job in the ministry. Similar to Hiro, Kimura-san 'passed' a series of informal and then formal recruitment and selection interviews and was offered the job.

We should recognize the influence of face in these two cases of Hiro and of Kimura-san. Hiro 'felt' obliged to take the job in the bank because a powerful reference group had evolved around his choice. Of course, they could have declined, but a continuing sense that the 'eyes' are everywhere would probably have undermined their confidence in committing to another career path or another employer. Japan is a big country; but a relatively small world in terms of recruitment among a perceived elite (cf. Box 4.2).

Box 4.2 The '20:80' rule

In our research we were surprised how often there was reference to '20 per cent of this' or to '80 per cent of that'. We developed an impressionistic '20:80' rule, modelled on the '80: 20 rule' used in Pareto analysis and named after Vilfredo Pareto, an Italian economist and sociologist. The purpose of Pareto analysis is to rank items (products, sales activities, etc.) in terms relative to the value they add to an organization. The 'rule' states that the 'top' 20 per cent of items usually generates 80 per cent of the total value. Describing a Pareto curve (where the vertical axis records a qualitative value and the horizontal a quantitative or percentage value) managers can identify which 20 per cent of activities or products generates 80 per cent of the organization's business value and, consequently, which 20 per cent of their business they should concentrate on developing.

Using Pareto analysis terminology, and taking *Japan Inc.* as a metaphorical company with its national education system as a core business activity, potential managers become 'items' of the national inventory. Through various testing systems the top 20 per cent of 'items' are identified. This top 20 per cent can be assumed to generate 80 per cent of Japan Inc.'s added value.

Accordingly, HR managers are encouraged to concentrate their attention on this top 20 per cent, offering them incentives such as lifetime employment, guaranteed promotion and other expressions of social status. However, 80 per cent of companies in Japan can be classed as small and medium-sized enterprises (SMEs) or family companies: they cannot offer 'lifetime employment', so the struggle is to offer 'secure employment' to the most value-generating staff (cf. Box 5.1).

It is therefore the top 20 per cent of companies – the large corporations – and their managers whose experience and expectations tended to generate and sustain the 'lifetime employment' totem broadcast within and outside Japan. Simultaneously, the 'top 20 per cent' management group sets the benchmarks for career ambition in society as a whole: they form the 'significant minority' that stands as a benchmark for educational achievement (Dore and Sako, 1998).

With the expectation of continued economic growth now removed, the benchmark of 'lifetime employment' is challenged. Some managers see this challenge as an opportunity, others may see it as a threat. This is a theme we develop in Chapter 5.

Current experiences of recruitment

The vast majority of university and college graduates seeking jobs scour magazines and websites for companies they like. Discrimination is embedded in tradition. Soon-to-be-graduates from 'top-ranking' universities receive thicker booklets listing career opportunities than their counterparts at lower-ranking universities. Male students are sent more information than females. Both male and female students can contact the companies directly for information packs and some of the larger companies organize mass information sessions. Tapping into the advice and experience of former school and university colleagues is vital. There are also many recruitment agencies – many named using variations on the term 'recruit' – who will sort and advise soon-to-be-graduates for companies which on cost grounds prefer to outsource this function.

Renshaw (1999) describes a uniform 'recruit style' of dress and behaviour evolved for both men and women: dark-coloured suit, white shirt or blouse, carefully groomed hair, no jewellery or accessories; a serious and purposeful demeanour for men; a smiling expression for women. Respondents in our sample found this look very old fashioned: 'look at our current Prime Minister', suggested one, referring to Koizumi's relatively relaxed hairstyle and demeanour. Nevertheless, the 'recruit look' is alive and well, judging by the groups of nervous young men and women to be seen making the seasonal rounds of company interviews.

The companies in each industrial sector routinely agree a 'recruitment season'. However, larger and higher-ranking companies also routinely indulge in *aotagai*. During the selection stage most applicants will need to sit a company-specific examination and a series of interviews – a process known as *naitei shiki*. As one university graduate told us, forlornly: 'tests, tests, and more tests – finally getting down to work will be a relief after all these tests!' If all goes well, the company will send out an individualized acceptance letter, though probably not yet specifying which job the successful applicant will be asked to do. Applicants who do not get an offer from their preferred company may delay graduation for another year in order to be more successful in the following year's recruitment season in a repeat of the pre-university *ronin* experience.

Current trends in graduate recruitment

In Japan as in other developed economies, the service sector is growing in importance as a mass employer of graduates. Approximately 70 per cent of all graduates currently find jobs in this sector. Increasingly, international companies such as investment banks, business consultancies and media-related enterprises are becoming increasingly sought after. As one student counsellor at a high-ranking university told us (2001): 'Goldman Sachs is this year's favourite. It used to be BOJ [The Bank of Japan] or Mitsubishi Corporation.' According to recent JETRO figures (2002), in Japan's export-oriented economy over half of recruits to foreign-owned firms find jobs in the manufacturing sector. A little over one million out of a total of forty-three million employees nationwide choose to work for international companies. According to Selmer (2003), both male and female managers in Japan are breaking with in-group expectations and instead choosing to offer their talents and commitment 'at a higher level of market-oriented flexibility than previously existed'. As information flows across borders (e.g. via the internet) the perception is that the 'market' referred to by Selmer and others is becoming increasingly internationalized (cf. Chapter 7).

Traditional recruitment and selection procedures in Japan are becoming (i.e. from the supply side) increasingly internationalized. English titles for jobs routinely appear in recruitment journals, though the job may be 'for Japanese nationals only'. Many sought-after organizations now require university graduates to apply in English and/or show a recent TOEIC® exam score – more business for the cram school industry! Why? As one Japanese HR manager told us: 'Because our major competitors are doing it'. Another explained how in his company 'money [for selection and recruitment] is getting tighter, the openings fewer, and so competition for management-track jobs is increasing. The number of applicants is increasing so we have to make the selection process more efficient, concentrating our time on applicants who are serious about working with our company and who have a certain level of [foreign language] skills. The English language component [of the application procedure] is designed to discourage time-wasters.' 'And no-hopers?' we asked. He smiled faintly, but said nothing. The egalitarian Japanese education system is (to its credit) not yet willing to condemn genuine aspirants as 'no-hopers'.

Traditionally, over 20 per cent of graduates find employment in family businesses: few become self-employed, though the *freeter* phenomenon is gaining in social credibility (Box 4.1). Only 15 to 20 per cent work in large companies and public institutions such as ministries, universities and other public sector enterprises. The majority of these employees are four-year university or college graduates. We say 'only' 15 to 20 per cent because it is the managers in these organizations who commonly represent the image or (in Japan) the career aspiration of 'the Japanese manager' or *salaryman* (cf. Box 8.1). The traditional 'top jobs' for *salaryman* would be in a ministry, a top-ranking company, or a public/private sector hybrid such as one of the county's main banks; although, as we discuss in Chapter 7, the status of banks in Japan is currently in something of a trough.

SECTION 3: CONSTRAINTS TO WOMEN'S CAREER CHOICES

> Submissive and chaste Japanese women no longer exist.
> More precisely, they never did.
>
> (Ueno, cited in Yoshino, 2002)

Consider the following scene:

A talented young woman who, being about to graduate from a respected university with a degree in a subject where there are still skill shortages in Japan, found herself being 'courted' by a number of prestigious Japanese and international companies in Tokyo. In response to her general enquiry they were sending her recruitment literature. Some, having got her address from her university, were sending direct mail-shots promoting themselves and trying to attract her application. This was *aotagai*.

She showed us one prospectus from a leading Japanese securities company. It presented a series of expensively produced images of how three recent recruits (called 'players') were enjoying their new lifestyle as individuals and team members in this company. It depicted these individuals at work and at play (e.g. surfboarding). They were all male. The young woman hadn't noticed this at first and looked again at the brochure in surprise. We asked ourselves: is this the power of socialization in Japan? We all looked through the prospectus for a female face. We found one, in the background of a sweeping office-wide photograph, doing what was clearly a clerical job. What was this company thinking about? They send a recruitment mail-shot trying to attract a talented woman recruit, but in their prospectus they only show upwardly mobile men. Did they choose to ignore the obvious irony? Or did they not even realize it? The image of Japanese women, as the quote above suggests, continues to be projected through the eyes of Japanese men.

Good wives, wise mothers

Women in Japan make up more than half the total population and, by living longer than men, give Japan the highest longevity ranking of almost any nation on earth. Approximately 60 per cent of Japan's workforce is over sixty years old, the oldest active workforce in the world. Women currently make up nearly half of this workforce. Female employment has more than tripled since the 1960s, prompting the introduction of equal opportunities legislation in April 1986. Nevertheless, deserving the label 'good wife, wise mother' (*ryosei kenbo*) has long summed up, from a dominantly male perspective, the benchmark for success among women in Japanese society.

Since the social and economic reconstruction after World War Two women have been expected to fulfil three distinct roles: as complementary breadwinner to the socio-economic family unit (*ie*); as a 'wise mother', monitoring and promoting her children's education; and as a 'good' and loyal wife who supports her husband's career development. From the national perspective, a woman's role as breadwinner has tended to mean either restricting her choice to certain low-skilled trades and professions or standing by as a pool of reserve labour during times of national economic growth. According to Renshaw (1999), Japanese women are Japan Inc.'s 'hidden assets'.

The rapid progress of post-war reconstruction saw the emergence of a strong if vaguely defined middle-class consciousness (cf. Odaka, 1966) and with it a general perception of widespread social and economic affluence that had been unknown at any time in Japanese history. It could therefore appear somehow ungrateful, even shameful, if married couples did not take advantage of this and allow women to concentrate on tending the home and the family (comprising children and grandparents). Usui (in Bird 2002: 475) talks about the 'ideology of the middle-class housewife' that, until the 1980s, appeared to provoke general consensus among Japanese men and women and so determine how each expected the other to behave (cf. Box 4.3).

Box 4.3 Being middle class in Japan

When asking Japanese people which 'social class' they feel they belong to, they will probably give the accommodatingly vague reply: 'middle class'. A minority of Japanese believe they are *not* 'middle class'. The middle class thus takes on the status of a society-wide 'reference group'.

Ishida (1993) identified three types of Japanese middle-class identity: *chusan*, meaning middle-class in terms of economic status and visible in terms of disposable income and ownership of property and other material goods; *churyu*, meaning middle-class in terms of ascribed social status (e.g. having attended a 'famous' university or having a 'famous' family name); and *chukan*, meaning an indeterminate and anxious status of being 'in the middle' and therefore not belonging to the other two groups.

The most reliable indicators of career success are regarded as: occupational prestige (e.g. who you work for), educational qualifications and background (e.g. which university you attended), income (e.g. basic salary, bonuses and perks), visible assets (e.g. property and/or car), lifestyle (e.g. number of foreign holidays per year) and power (e.g. who you know) (cf. Ishida, 1993). The reliance on education as a key factor in affirming middle-class status has led to a system of 'educational credentialism' whereby Japanese families invest massive amounts of money and effort into getting their children into the highest-ranking institutions (Ishida, 1998). The *freeter* attitude (Box 4.1) challenges these established values.

As an expression of face this is not unique to Japan. We interviewed a Swiss colleague who works (unsurprisingly, perhaps!) for a private bank. One day he was called in to see his boss because word had got around that his wife had a part-time job. They also had two school-age children. Was our colleague's 'salary not high enough'? Did our colleague 'have a problem' (e.g. gambling, drinking or some other expensive vice)? 'No' was the answer. The truth was that his wife *wanted* to work. She stopped (for a while) when it was suggested she might be 'embarrassing the bank' and simultaneously undermining her husband's promotion chances.

Career expectations of Japanese women

Rising prosperity and national confidence created a 'baby boom' in the 1970s. This caused a rapid expansion of the education system, largely catered for by private education institutions – the same institutions now facing financial crises and fiercer competition in response to the collapsed national birth rate.

The larger proportion of our respondent sample was 'baby-boomers' (i.e. born in the early 1970s). They experienced the competition for selective places in education. They remember how mothers were expected to take on an important role in the management of their children's education. The economic burden of funding their children's education became immense. Large companies recognized this and staggered their managerial salary scales and bonus awards accordingly. The pressure on children to succeed – and, by extension, on their mothers to see that they did succeed – created the common family experience of 'examination hell'. Figures show that during the 'baby-boom' period 55 per cent of women aged between twenty-five and thirty-four were not in employment. This was a reverse position to that of the early 1950s during the post-war reconstruction. Not until the 1990s did the proportion of women in employment in Japan again approach the 50 per cent mark (Bird, 2002: 475).

In Japan as elsewhere, the true participation of women in work tends to be overlooked by the dominant masculine voices in society and politics. In Japan, this can in part be explained by the '20: 80 rule' (Box 4.2). The majority of women in Japan traditionally worked in industries 'unfashionable' to the emerging urbanized post-war social majority (cf. Clammer, 1997). These include agriculture, forestry and fishing. Women also tended to work in socially 'low profile' companies such as family businesses and other small and medium-sized enterprises.

Until the 1980s women generally expected to be married by the age of twenty-five: any woman still available after this age could be referred to as 'left-over Christmas cake' (i.e. cake unattractive after 25 December). In our sample we met many women anxious about being a 'thirty-something' single (cf. Takeda-san in Chapter 2). Accordingly, major companies have been reluctant to invest in training up women employees, offering even university graduates jobs as tea-making, photocopying and ever-smiling 'office ladies' (OLs) or (euphemistically) 'office flowers' until their expected departure soon after marriage. One female respondent claimed to have worked for an SME where 'the owner had a reputation for hiring pretty young women mainly in order to attract the best male [graduate] talent'.

In Japan as elsewhere, women with a higher education are more likely to marry men with a higher education background: one of the 'top 20 per cent'. Having 'got her man' (very often from the same company as herself), the pressure is on to have and raise children who themselves should join the top 20 per cent. This consensus view of the woman's role still appears to dominate social perception. However, the figures show that housewives are now a minority among Japanese women (Yoshino, 2002). Takeda-san represents a transitional generation of 'career women' (*kyaria woman*, a female alter-ego to *salaryman* – Box 8.1) who is struggling to shake off the career 'shackles' of normative social thinking.

Ippanshoku and *sogoshoku*

The Equal Employment Opportunity Law (EEOL) of 1986 stands as a important socio-cultural signpost. In response to this social and political initiative, some larger companies made the effort to formalize separate career tracks open to women: *ippanshoku* and *sogoshoku*. In reality, women were usually recruited to follow the *ippanshoku* (general clerical) track rather than the *sogoshoku* (managerial) track. From the organization's point of view, these women could be easily replaced if they left to have families, or removed when economic or business performance slumped. Furthermore, these women could easily be re-recruited and re-integrated when their children had grown up or when family finances were stretched: 'Japan's hidden assets'. Based on what we have been told, the EEOL barely dented existing HR policies and practices. In 1999 an amendment law was passed which stipulated sanctions against employers found to discriminate against women at work. One interpretation of the timing of this amendment suggests that, as the national workforce shrinks, women become perceived as more valuable (Kambayashi and Rutledge, 2002).

The introduction of *sogoshoku* in 1986 was a genuine attempt to set up a formalized managerial track for women. Women on this path were basically expected to behave and perform on a par with their male counterparts in order to succeed. This meant committing themselves to the same open-ended working hours, with little or no support in terms of childcare facilities or other measures designed to counterbalance the burden of traditional social expectations. Conditions have improved dramatically in some of the more enlightened Japanese organizations. However, 'by 1990, women still held only 2.2 per cent of the managerial positions in large firms' (Usui, in Bird 2002: 476).

Accordingly, *sogoshoku* exists in the context of traditional masculine values (cf. Chapter 1). We elicited views from male HR practitioners. One said, '*sogoshoku* gives women a fair chance to succeed and so it's up to them to take it if they want a managerial career' – the Japanese meritocratic view, and an expression of '[visible] performance is everything' masculine values (cf. Chapter 1). Another's view was: 'it's difficult for women to get promoted [to senior management positions] because they don't know how to drink [alcohol]'. In other words, they miss out on the informal politicking and bonding ('nomination') that smoothes the career paths for junior (male) managers in Japanese organizations (cf. Chapter 1). We would class these two respondents as relatively modern thinking.

Learning from the experience of others

One of our colleagues used to work on a business programme for radio. She told us about a show she had helped to produce on the topic of what women see as abuses of the Japan's two-track career system (Shimizuishi, 2002 – personal communication).

Twenty lost years

The first speaker was a woman in her early fifties who had worked for over thirty years for one of Japan's major electric supply companies. She is a trained accountant, but complains that she has never had the same opportunities for job rotation – and so promotion and salary increases – as her male colleagues who joined the company at the same time as her. She sees men with exactly the same educational qualifications as her earning up to US$2,000 more than her each month. She claims to be one of the victims of the 1986 EEOL legislation that gave her company the opportunity to define her career track as *ippanshoku* and thereby 'trap' her into a present position which suppressed any salary and promotion aspirations she might have had.

She had no proper job title, no business card, and claims she was still sometimes asked by younger male colleagues to make tea for them. She claims not to have been informed of the change in law (i.e. EEOL) and found out only later that the company had allowed equally qualified male members of staff to switch to *sogoshoku*. She finally lost patience in 1995 when she decided to sue the company on grounds of sexual discrimination. The court rejected her case in 2000, reasoning that the discrimination law had not been in place when she joined the company. However, and perhaps in order to fend off the potential loss of corporate face that her law suit threatened, the company did finally let her sit a promotion examination. She passed and now, at the age of fifty-one, she holds a job normally taken by thirty-year-old men. Understandably, after a long fight she has made progress, but she still feels she has been cheated of more than twenty-years of her career potential.

Only a joke

The second speaker was a younger woman: twenty-nine years old. Bright and confident, she recognized that she was one of the very few women to go straight into *sogoshoku* of one of Japan's major brewing companies aged twenty-three, just after graduation. She left the company only three years later. She explains why: 'one day my boss suggested we had a business meeting together with other managers in a sauna. I knew I couldn't do this, even though I knew that something important might be decided at that meeting. I questioned my boss about it and he said "it's ok, you can wear a swimming suit if you wish" '. She claims that she recognized that her boss's comments were 'only a joke', but it made her realize that the company just 'had not matured enough' to cater for women – and she might have said women with self-esteem – on the *sogoshoku* path. Finally she left the brewing company to become a flight attendant with a European airline, taking a 20 per cent cut in salary for the privilege. As recompense she claims now to have no more health-endangering stress of 'conflict with male workers'.

Learning from exceptions

We should be wary of over-generalizing the obstacles faced by ambitious career women in Japan. For every rule there are exceptions. Renshaw (1999) made a comprehensive study of such exceptions.

Renshaw's account of the career paths followed by successful women managers, executives and entrepreneurs in Japan appeared at a time when the sense of cumulative economic crisis in Japan had become palpable. Looking at the almost exclusively male unemployed (unemployable?) sleeping rough but with remarkable dignity in the public parks of Tokyo and other big cities, it is dawning on increasing numbers of Japanese that the 'old' (i.e. male-oriented) ways of management have led Japan to economic and (perhaps) social stagnation.

Renshaw's study focuses on exceptions, the top 2 per cent or so of women who have made it to senior managerial or executive positions. The largest single sample of the women managers she interviewed (34 per cent) was born before the end of the Second World War. Another half of her sample was born in the twenty years following the end of the war, and 15 per cent in the 1960s and 1970s. It is this latter group which overlaps most in terms of age and outlook with our own sample in researching for this book.

Renshaw's basic research question was: 'What helped you to succeed?' (1999: 38). The responses can be categorized as follows.

Time

'Being born at the right time' was the common response. This implies entering the workforce at 'the right time' – for example, in times of social and economic crisis (e.g. after 1945) when many social constraints are put in abeyance. Interestingly, 'now' (i.e. the new millennium) is also suggested as a promising time for women to embark on a successful high-profile career.

Place

Age, opportunity and other common success factors identified by Renshaw are impossible for today's ambitious women to replicate because they are past and immutable. They include: being born into a family which itself runs a business and/or where the father and mother are seen to share managerial responsibility; getting a 'good education' – a predictable response, but easier said than done when most places at 'good' universities in Japan are traditionally reserved for men. Families thus tended to invest most resources in getting a good education for sons. This perhaps explains why the 'absence of [near-aged] brothers' was given as the most commonly shared career success factor among Renshaw's sample.

Role models

According to Renshaw's research the most immediate role model for young Japanese women was the mother and/or the grandmother. These two figures may influence and inspire the ambition of daughters in at least three ways. First, in that the daughter strives to match her mother's educational achievements – making use of the 'map and compass' already at hand. Second, by compensating in terms of her own study and career success what her mother or grandmother were unable to achieve. And third, by the daughter vowing never to find herself in a position of dependency or serial abuse (e.g. in an unhappy marriage) that the mother or grandmother endured. Within the context of *ie* and the dominance of male/masculine values in Japanese society, the patterns of female dependence are held to be so distinctive that they have spawned a dedicated term of reference (*amae*) and a distinguished and established field of research and (albeit muted) public debate (cf. Doi, 1971/2002; Yoshino, 2002).

Good news for women managers

We have referred extensively in this section to Renshaw's study for two main reasons: it remains a ground-breaking work; and because many aspiring Japanese women managers we spoke to find some conclusions 'old-fashioned'. We take this as encouraging evidence of change in the perceptions that have developed since the turn of the century.

The norm for increasing numbers of aspiring women managers tends to be contained less within the family and more within the wider context of emerging trends. Global information flow (e.g. via the internet) far outpaces developments in local tradition. In our sample, mothers tended to be recognized more for their moral support than as role models. Grandmothers have almost negligible influence except in terms of serving as a source of moral or financial support and as a reminder of core values. Far more significant than 'the absence of brothers' in our sample was the presence of a 'kind' or supportive husband.

Other good news is that more Japanese women today recognize they have the resources and horizons to look beyond the constraints set by one social system. For example, a 'good' (i.e. relevant) education may come later, as in the case of Takeda-san who completed her MBA study overseas. Better news might be that more women are seen to achieve higher starting salaries and career prospects in international or more modern-thinking Japanese companies. We profile some of these in Chapters 7 and 8.

The best news is that some of the keys to career success that Renshaw identified are accessible to both women *and* men. These are personal qualities such as 'self-confidence' and 'strong sense of self', and the power these give individuals to 'alleviate the loneliness of being an outsider' (Renshaw, 1999: 49) – qualities we translate into a notion of enhanced 'self-esteem' and the determination of individuals to measure their own ability and social worth against either their own criteria or against the standards set by those people they choose voluntarily to respect. This is not the same as being 'selfish' (cf. Chapter 2). But it does represent a significant shift in attention away from established notions of face and therefore of career development in Japanese society.

SECTION 4: THE FIRST STEPS ON A CAREER PATH

The HRM cycle

Studies of human resource management tend to list five or six key function areas or processes: *recruitment and selection*; *organizational induction*; *socialization, training and development*; *performance appraisal*; *compensation, rewards and promotion*; and finally, redundancy, resignation or dismissal, often termed somewhat abruptly *organizational exit* (cf. Devanna *et al.*, 1984; Storey, 1989; 1992). In this chapter so far we have discussed common experiences of *recruitment and selection* in Japan. In this final section we illustrate common experiences of *organizational induction* or what happens when men and women join a

Japanese organization and start their career. Note that the 'HRM cycle' is complete when, at some point along their career path, an employee leaves an organization – a process called *organizational exit*, discussed in Chapter 8.

HRM and culture

We should recognize that HRM policies and procedures are culture-specific artefacts (Schneider and Barsoux, 1997: 128). In similar fashion to language, their interpretation and implementation serves to define culture-specific barriers: for example, the values and norms informing an employee's induction into different organizations and the culture-specific boundaries of one industry (e.g. banking as opposed to chemicals) and of one department (e.g. Sales as opposed to R&D).

In discussing HRM in the context of Japanese management culture, Takeda (in Bird, 2002) emphasizes human *relations* management. In her analysis:

> The human relations approach relies on the assumption that an employee enters the company as a 'clean slate'. Thus, human relations management focuses upon interpersonal skill development, teamwork, flexibility and generalist knowledge.
>
> (Takeda, in Bird, 2002: 181)

Correspondingly, graduates (called *shinsotsu* when recruited as a group) are not expected to have any organization-specific skills when they join the organization as reference group. They rely on each other to make sense of their new context. With the emphasis being given to interpersonal relations and communication rather than 'facts', the *emotional* tenor of Japanese employment relations are established from the beginning of a person's employment (cf. the 'TH-T model' discussed in Chapter 3).

The role of HR managers

The experts in the strategic management of organization-specific human relations are (in larger organizations) the HR managers. Their decision to advertise a vacancy and recruit a potential manager (who arrives with the expectation of lifetime employment) thus represents a major resource investment. As we shall see, Japanese HR managers play a key role in shaping each new recruit's experience of culture in that they formulate and communicate the norms and values which will inform a would-be manager's experience of working and of 'getting on' in a given organization. Japanese HR staff thus play a key strategic role – an observation which promoted the development of 'strategic human resource management' (SHRM) paradigms in western management thinking (cf. Storey, 1992; Mabey *et al.*, 1998a).

The first stage of induction in Japan tends to be at the level of organization: i.e. an HR department responsibility. Subsequently, new recruits are allocated to departments or sections and with them the responsibility for guiding and monitoring each recruit's context-specific development in terms of 'interpersonal skills, teamwork, flexibility and generalist knowledge', as outlined by Takeda (cited above). We discuss this role of line-managers in the context of performance appraisal in Chapter 6.

All new recruits are offered similar contracts and similar starting levels of salary, thus emphasizing the requirement to build up an employment relationship on non-quantifiable or on 'integrative' rather than 'instrumental' terms. Overall, the induction process is important not only for providing a number of relevant and company-specific skill- and knowledge-oriented activities, but also for demonstrating to new entrants what is and what is not expected in the specific work culture that new recruits are entering: i.e. they learn about the culture-specific context for avoiding loss of face.

The experience of organizational induction

Consider the example of Miura-san. At the time of the interview Miura-san was thirty-five years old and had been introduced to a company through a university professor. The professor had introduced Miura-san to a visiting former graduate – 'an excellent research student' – who had since become a senior manager in one Japan's top-ranking pharmaceutical companies. They got talking, and Miura-san was invited to visit the senior manager and other managers at the company headquarters in Tokyo. The visit went well. A job offer followed in due course and was accepted. Miura-san told us about the induction process into the company. As you read, you might try to work out whether Miura-san is a man or a woman.

Miura-san

This is what Miura-san told us: 'On the first day we were about 200 new recruits in a large hall. Various directors and senior managers gave speeches, welcoming us and informing us about the company, its history, and the vision of its future role in the industry and in society generally. What I remember most is the mixture of people there. Among the recruits there were people from all classes of society and with very different educational backgrounds: some similar to mine [high-ranking national university], some very different. I had never been together with such a mix of people before.

'We then had three months of training. We lived in a hostel outside Tokyo. We had to study manuals giving specifications of the company's many products. Occasionally managers and specialists would travel out from the company headquarters to give us lectures about various things – sales, product development and so on. We would be tested regularly on what we had learned. Staff from the human resources department also came out to talk to us. More and more frequently we would be divided into different groups, usually mixed, but also with men and women separated.

'We began to make regular visits to the Tokyo headquarters and other plants. I was introduced to the people in the section where I would be working (product development). There were eight people in each section, and a supervisor (*kakaricho*) for each section. I began to spend more time talking and working with them. The atmosphere in the group was good. I think this was because the manager (*kacho*) of this area of product development was a kind man (*shinsetsu na hito*). I looked forward to working as a "proper" employee together with him and with the others in the section.'

Comments

To what extent does the experience differ between male and female recruits? This raises the question asked at the beginning of this account: is Miura-san male or female? And how can one tell from this short account?

The reference to a 'kind' manager may suggest to some readers that the speaker is a female – given the assumption (discussed in Chapter 1) that 'masculine' values dominate in Japanese management cultures. However, we have seen in Chapters 2 and 3 how Japanese employees in general tend to have an emotional and diffuse attitude towards their job and place of work and recognize a strong dependence on the consideration of influential figures in whatever reference group they encounter (cf. the 'TH-T model' discussed in Chapter 3). A Japanese man could just as easily describe his future line-manager in this way.

The clearest indicator that Miura-san is a woman is perhaps the reference to that stage in the induction process where groups of men and women were being separated and, as it transpired, being given different types of tasks to do. In fact, Miura-san is a woman and, according to her own memories of induction, 'talking together in the evening about what had happened each day [during induction] we began to realize that the men were probably being "groomed" for management positions in the company'. An educated male recruit may not have made particular mention of this; out of modesty or (more likely) socialized indifference.

What happened next?

Miura-san duly became a 'proper' employee in the pharmaceuticals company: 'proper' being a word which has been borrowed into Japanese to denote an employee who is trained and established within the company – in other words, an 'insider'. Over the years that followed Miura-san worked in various sections of the product development department. Promotion was slow. However, she and her various teams were so successful that some years later she was transferred from this department to another department (clinical trials) where (it was rumoured) performance was not so good and, as a result, the company was losing ground to competitors. This decision was made by HR managers and their justification was perhaps to use the introduction of Miura-san and others to bolster the performance in this failing department: 'perhaps' because HR staff seldom need to give clear reasons for their decisions, as Takeda-san learned (Chapter 2). The decision pleased neither Miura-san nor her former line-manager, who was losing a valued and experienced member of his team. Some years later Miura-san was transferred overseas. She quit after eleven years of service and is now back in Tokyo working for an international company. We return to illustrate Miura-san's indirect experience of organizational exit at this company in Chapter 8.

What about loyalty?

In the context of assumptions about 'lifetime employment' in Japan
(Box 5.1), there is a corresponding assumption of the primacy of each
employee's loyalty towards their company: the 'company as family', as
discussed in Chapter 3. In this chapter we have suggested reasons why
ambitious women and men might choose to leave their first company and
re-determine their career path. For example, they might see their career
ambitions blocked or may eventually lose patience with the weight of
negative discrimination they perceive. Alternatively, women may leave
to marry and set up a family – a traditional enough reason and, one
assumes, a positive and independent choice. In fact, a significant number
of employees leave their first company on average three years after
induction. The reasons vary between 'disappointment' (including
'boredom') and in response to 'a better offer' from elsewhere. Making
too much of company 'loyalty' among Japanese employees is perhaps to
over-generalize the reality. Japanese women, it appears, 'often admit they
are less loyal to a company, but in these times, that's becoming an asset'
(Kambayashi and Rutledge, 2002). But this applies not only to women, as
we discuss in Chapter 8.

Ikemura-san

Ikemura-san was just graduating from a first degree in Economics.
She spoke to us in November, just after she had received a job offer from
her preferred company. She held one other firm offer. Her employment
was to start formally the following April but already in October she had
spent two days at the company headquarters and met her company *doki*
and HR staff. A contract had been signed, but no job had been specified.
The group were told what jobs were likely to become available in April.
Each member submitted a form saying which department they preferred.
Ikemura-san had a clear preference (HRM). However, the conditions of
the contract stated that she was bound to accept any job the company
might give her.

'It was important for me to get into the department I wanted from the
beginning' she said, 'because I probably wouldn't be able to change later.
That's one reason why I chose this company: they don't automatically
rotate people to different departments. Some of the men in our *doki* group
also chose this company for the same reason. We wanted to specialize in

one field. We were also told that the promotion system would be the same for men and for women. This is all very different from my father's generation.'

An unofficial discussion within the group revealed that Ikemura-san probably had only one rival for a job in 'her' HRM department. All others (about twenty-five in total) were interested in different departments. She therefore knew two things: first, if only one job was available in HRM come April, she would probably have only one 'competitor'. She began to think back (and worry!) about things she had said or not said in her selection interview and during discussion on the induction days that might prove detrimental to her case. Second, she knew that whichever department she ended up being assigned to, she would need to be there for at least three and probably five years before she gained enough skills and experience to ask for a transfer within the company or, if necessary, move to another company.

'Why not resign if you don't get the job you want?' we asked. 'If I do that I will find it very hard to get a job in a similar company. As it's a famous [i.e. high-ranking] company, my family and any other company I apply to would not understand why I left: I would be seen as unreliable. Also, I need the skills they can teach. I know I will do a different job in future, so the experience is good for me. But the thought of five or seven years in a job I don't like – the company people say we need at least seven years to really understand the job and the company – frightens me a little. No, it frightens me a lot.'

Summary

In this chapter we have outlined the systems of secondary and higher education in Japan in terms of how common experience of these dovetails with common expectations of recruitment, selection and induction into a first job and a subsequent career path. We have paid particular attention to the extent to which men and women tend to be socialized in different ways such that their career expectations differ.

Career pathways – like HRM policies and procedures generally – can be perceived as culture-specific artefacts, analogous to the structures of language and communication in specific national, industrial and organizational contexts. One of the most important choices that we as individuals make in our lifetime is the first step on a career. Later we can reflect on how much choice we actually had in taking this step. In Chapter 2 we saw how attention to face informs how individuals make and don't make choices in a Japanese contexts. In this chapter we have given voice to Japanese managers who have confronted and executed this choice with varying degrees of confidence and success, focusing on the particular experiences of women in Japanese management.

Questions for reflection:

- How relevant was your experience of education for your current choice of career path? What or who set you off along your current career path? Do you believe that men and women tend to have different career expectations? Why should this (not) be the case?

5 Losing patience

Introduction

> 'Organization' means 'people' in Japan.
>
> (Ohmae, 1982)

In Chapter 1 we recounted the impressions and experiences of non-Japanese managers when they had their first encounters with Japanese management culture. We also took a critical look at some of the distinctive features of Japanese management culture as identified by researchers such as Hofstede and Hall: for example, that this culture is overtly 'masculine' in terms of the values its members learn to emphasize and express such as 'strong' or 'corrective' behaviour (Hofstede, 1991/94); or that this culture is diffuse in that individual experiences of space and social status at work and at home tend to overlap, that use of language for communication tends to be 'high-context' – meaning is 'in the person' and consequently often opaque to outsiders who have not experienced socialization as a 'Japanese person' and subsequently as a 'Japanese' employee or (later) manager, processes we described in Chapters 3 and 4.

In this chapter we illustrate common experiences of skills training and professional development in Japanese organizations. We have all been new to an organization at some stage in our life. We all recognize the need to learn quickly 'how things are done around here' – a process that for many Japanese managers is expected to be a lifetime endeavour. We also recognize the need to learn new skills (training) and qualities (development) in order not only to keep up with what appears to be expected of us, but also to 'get on' in this organization or, if needs be, in other organizations.

Our objectives for this chapter are:

- to illustrate how and why the traditional structures of Japanese-style HRM are coming under strain, and why ambitious managers are losing patience with them;

- to explore how Japanese managers commonly experience training and development, making reference to the notion of 'organizational learning'.

SECTION 1: THE CLASSICAL MODEL OF JAPANESE-STYLE MANAGEMENT

> Japanese management is not some outcrop of a distinctive cultural universe or a relic of the feudal past. Japanese managers eagerly learnt US theories and implemented them, initially under US tutelage during the occupation but freely thereafter. As more than one American professor of management has remarked to us, 'why didn't American managers learn our theories when the Japanese did?'
>
> (Kono and Clegg, 2001)

The roots of patience: lifetime employment

On the basis of what they learned at school and university, at home and in society generally, managerial recruits to Japanese organizations traditionally expect a lifetime of secure employment. The induction and subsequent training and development structures tend to be geared to fulfil this expectation in a manner that enhances the long-term strategic potential of the organization (Box 5.1).

Given the strategically integrated nature of HRM traditional in Japanese organizations, the expectation of lifetime of secure employment has a direct impact on the structures and cultures informing *training* and

Box 5.1 Lifetime employment

Of the so-called 'three sacred treasures' of Japanese-style HRM, the one that tends to attract most attention is 'lifetime employment' – understandably, for the notion that a private sector/profit-making organization should commit to employ a member of staff for a tenure of forty-five years or more is striking to western ears; as (increasingly) is the suggestion that an employee would want to trust or commit his/her career to one organization for so long. Indeed, the term 'lifelong employment' was originally emphasized as lifetime 'commitment' and this more value-based connotation probably expresses its significance more clearly in a Japanese context (cf. Abegglen, 1958).

The HRM emphasis is on regarding selected or 'core' (i.e. strategically valuable) staff as strategic assets (cf. Mueller, 1998). Since the 1950s core staff could expect a level of job security that, though seldom formalized, became an expectation and (until recently) an experience of lifetime employment. The rapid economic expansion and business growth during the 1960s and 1970s tended to blur the expectation between 'lifetime' and (merely) secure employment for most employees. As a result, employees who were loyal and did a decent job could expect a lifetime of career development within one company, if that was their preference (cf. Inohara, 2000). Traditional structures of promotion and reward are based on this assumption (cf. Chapter 7).

The emergent 'lifetime employment' tradition not only supports the long-term orientation of corporate and HRM strategy in Japan, it also serves the interests of governments fearful of mass unemployment and social unrest. Accordingly, it tended to be the privilege of core staff in large public and private sector organizations: i.e. those with close relationships to national governments and with the resources to deliver such a long-term commitment. Security of employment for managers in SMEs, start-ups and family businesses was more subject to business cycles and to less powerful personal contacts, as were the career paths of women and 'non-core' employees (cf. Box 4.2). Given the nature, extent and tradition of interests involved, the assumption or expectation of lifetime employment is hard to shake off. Some experts see this as a drag on innovation and necessary industrial reform (cf. Porter *et al.*, 2000).

development. This degree of strategic integration of training and long-term staff development was considered so 'normal' that a paradigm was developed by management experts specifically to describe the traditional Japanese organization as a 'learning organization' (cf. Nonaka, 1994; Nonaka *et al.*, 1997; Nonaka and Takeuchi, 1998). The strategic potential of learning organizations/organizational learning had been developed by western experts (cf. Argyris and Schon, 1978; Senge, 1990). However, and not for the first time, Japanese management researchers and practitioners appeared more adept at adapting and operationalizing 'common-sense virtues' of western 'scientific management' theory than their western counterparts (cf. Kono and Clegg, 2001; Tsutsui, 1998). It is possible to explain this by highlighting the extraordinarily high levels of cultural cohesion in Japanese organizations that make the collective pursuit of strategic objectives (e.g. in the form 'organizational learning') more realizable. Given time (i.e. a lifetime of employment), managers in Japanese organizations could learn how to exploit this level of cohesion.

The classical model of Japanese management

Lifetime employment is a key component of what Smith and Misumi (in Hickson, 1997) refer to as the classical model of Japanese management. With this model they explain some of the management structures and processes that readily came to be regarded inside and outside of Japan as distinctive or even 'unique'. These 'unique' traditions of Japanese HRM developed into modern and comparable form after the Second World War. They also add 'with irony' that several aspects of Japanese-style management that had been 'discovered' subsequently by western companies had 'their roots in the West as much as they do in the East'. For example, the highest-ranking award for quality management in Japanese industry (the 'Deming Prize') is named after the American quality management expert W. Edwards Deming, who was drafted in to assist in the economic and industrial reconstruction of Japan after World War Two (cf. Deming, 1982).

Of primary interest in our current discussion is the extent to which many of these 'classical' structures and processes of Japanese-style HRM, until recently commonly regarded as distinctive strengths, have become – in the experience of numbers of individual managers – sources of frustration and loss of patience. From an organizational perspective therefore these classical structures and processes are becoming a source of vulnerability and weakness.

Smith and Misumi's classical model outlines four key 'attributes': namely, *lifetime employment, collective orientation, seniority system,* and *influence processes* (1994/1997: 378). The first three of these have already been referred to in this and previous chapters. The fourth, 'influence processes', we equate to the channels and processes for management communication and decision-making within the organization. In the context of Japanese-style HRM these four attributes reinforce culture-specific interpretations of notions such as self-regulation, managerial control, trust, 'groupishness' and shared perceptions of power and authority: i.e. notions related to face and the reference group, as developed in previous chapters. Distinctively Japanese HRM outcomes include values such as long-term (strategic) stability and loyalty and commitment in the employment relationship between individual and organization.

Following Smith and Misumi (1994/1997), the interaction between these HRM attributes and outcomes generates sources of 'vitality'. These are the sources of competitive advantage commonly ascribed to Japanese organizations in comparison with their non-Japanese counterparts. Applying Hofstede *et al.*'s terminology, certain expressions of this 'vitality' appear overtly 'masculine'. For example:

- the expectation of a 'whole-person contribution' and 'devotion' to work: this expectation connects both with the notion of the 'diffuseness' of Japanese work culture and the emphasis given to performance and personal/professional commitment to the organization as a whole and to reference groups within the organization structure (cf. Chapter 1);
- the sense of 'belonging' and 'wishing to contribute to the group', 'collective morale', and a recognition of the 'power of the group': these images evoke a rather macho interpretation of the reference group and the required attention given to face (cf. Chapter 2);
- the sense of 'all being in the same boat': this image evokes the notion of national face and the effort required to survive and prosper against the odds (cf. Chapter 3);
- the experience of organizational induction as a form of initiation into a closed circle or reference group (cf. Chapter 4).

The 'classical model' under strain

However, Smith and Misumi's model also identifies a number of 'difficulties' that these sources of 'vitality' 'effect' (1994/1997: 378). Our recent discussions with Japanese managers suggest that these 'difficulties' correspond to sources of individual frustration. For example, the 'attribute' *lifetime employment* is becoming associated by both managers and those they are managing as offering low job mobility, limited career prospects and therefore small incentives to develop oneself and/or to perform well. Kimura-san (Chapter 2) represents this view.

Similar transformations are evident in perceptions and experiences of *collective orientation*. Smith and Misumi refer to 'stress from the suppression of "ego needs" and a requirement for individuals to tolerate "unclear powers and duties" ' (1994/1997: 378). We re-interpret the first tension as 'suppression' of 'self-esteem needs' in relation to the attention given to face. The second we recognize as a primary factor in the frustration experienced by Takeda-san (Chapter 2), whose decision no longer to 'suppress' her self-esteem needs nor tolerate 'unclear powers and duties' we interpret as representative of a shift in attention given to face.

Mention of Takeda-san and other women managers we spoke to highlights the frustrations arising out of the traditional combination of *collective orientation* and the largely inflexible and male-oriented *seniority system*. The criterion of physical *age* is one that no individual can control or redress. Thus the effectiveness of the seniority system relies on the generosity of individual *patience* or (less positively) a passive acceptance of 'take-it-or-leave-it' senior managerial control.

In reality the classical structure benefits (as previously mentioned) male employees ahead of female employees. However, this is more than a gender issue. Where the perception arises that the system facilitates the 'promotion of low ability persons to management' a 'loss of morale' among what Smith and Misumi (1994/1997) term the 'elite' is likely to generate a mood of growing frustration with established HRM structures – for example, in respect of reward and promotion, and particularly when compared with what might be available in other organizations or contexts. As one manager (a credit analyst, aged early thirties) explained to us:

> I felt I needed more skills to improve my career. Of course, within the company I could learn many things about management and maybe I could experience many things. But I wanted a job in which I could integrate my knowledge and experience. I wanted to go abroad and know more about international management.

When the trendsetting 'top' 10 or 20 per cent (Box 4.2) become restless, a loss of patience in established HRM structures and a searching out of alternative contexts becomes more 'normal'.

SECTION 2: THE EXPERIENCE OF TRAINING

Offering relevant training is one way in which organizations can work to dampen core staff impatience in addition to striving towards improved operational efficiency and effectiveness. Generally speaking, 'the purpose of training is to improve employees' performance in their current jobs and/or equip them for more demanding roles. It is expensive . . . Moreover, there is no guarantee that trainees will actually benefit from participating in [training] programmes' (Hannagan, 1998: 319).

We saw in Chapter 4 how there is a traditional expectation in Japanese organizations that new recruits will enter as a 'clean slate' for training and development purposes, initiated by HR staff and monitored and fine-tuned by line-managers. There is a further assumption that 'employees, having a strong (lifetime) stake in the firm and its success, are also emotionally identified with it and so can be motivated to make extra effort as may be necessary to improve their existing skills and acquire new ones, not only by the prospect that they will gain personal advantage' (Dore and Sako, 1998: 97).

OTJ

The standard form of training in Japanese organizations can be characterized as 'On-The-Job' (OTJ). OTJ training is 'learning by observing and doing, with little or no systematic measurement or evaluation' (Takeda, in Bird, 2002: 181). Dore and Sako vividly contrast the western convention of informal training whereby the new recruit 'sits with Nelly' [the 'old hand' at this particular job or function] and watches how she does it with the Japanese preference for detailed learning manuals and texts so that 'you do not just stand by Nelly; you read what Nelly has thoughtfully and meticulously written about what she knows' (1998: 98). Dore and Sako's comments also explain their further observation, corroborated by many years of our own personal experience, that the 'Japanese are great note-takers' (1998: 100). From our own experience of working with Japanese management students and trainees, we wish that more of them would be more often critical, confident and discriminate note-takers; Japanese students in lectures and seminars tend to take copious notes first and then discuss and reduce them in study group discussion later. We see this as a residue reaction to the training students receive in order to negotiate the testing systems outlined in Chapters 3 and 4 (cf. Box 5.2).

Informally, among the subordinates there are also the *senpai/kohai* relationships where knowledge and skills necessary for 'fitting in' and 'getting on' in the company can be learnt over time. In this relationship, older and more experienced employees (*senpai*) who both 'know the

Box 5.2 Football training

Football ('soccer' in Japan and the USA) is the world's most popular sport. Its popularity in Japan received a boost during the country's highly successful co-organizing of the FIFA World Cup in 2002. In time football is likely to supplant the nation's current number one sport: baseball.

Both the Japanese and co-host South Korea's national football teams rose to international prominence under foreign managers: in Japan Philippe Troussier of France. Troussier's successor is another foreigner: Zico, a Brazilian and world footballing legend. Zico had helped to develop Japanese football to world standards, and became a legendary figure in Japanese sport.

An article in *The Japan Times* (8 November 2002) describes Zico's early attempts to train individual creativity and tactical flexibility into his players. Zico was dismayed by how his players arrived at pre-match meetings with notepads, took notes, and then tried to memorize the notes before going on to field. 'No, stop it. Soccer is not like that' he proclaimed. While recognizing his players' strengths in terms of tactical discipline and team cohesion and spirit, he struggled to make clear how 'the game changes according to the flow of the play, not exactly in the way that your manager told you beforehand.' In his role as national team manager, Zico concludes that: 'Players need to make decisions on the field by themselves, not by trying to do only what their manager told them.' He goes on: 'One thing I want them to remove from their game is the fear of making mistakes. They seem to be obsessed with the idea that they shouldn't make a mistake. But I want them to understand that if they try things and make a mistake, they can try again and try to do better next time . . . The important thing is that they take on challenges. I want them to be more positive and creative.'

ropes' in addition to what the immediate line-managers expect, can guide the new recruit and so help him or her avoid losing face. Accordingly, the members of each year of intake will, as time passes and the unfolding of the seniority system becomes visible in terms of promotion and other favours, compete fiercely and/or harbour hopes and frustrations about their individual progress. We are reminded of Takeda-san's sense of being let down or even led on by her line-manager: even 'Nelly' can have career ambitions.

Language training

As an illustration of the challenge facing Japanese organizations trying to negotiate an increasingly globalized strategic environment, we spoke to one HR manager about provision made in his company for English language training. To explain the context, this pharmaceuticals company was in the process of negotiating an R&D alliance with a US American MNC. What did the company now offer its managers? 'One hour of TOEIC training per week – on a voluntary basis, though most weeks managers were too busy to attend or do their homework.' The TOEIC® is an English-language test popular among Japanese employers. It drills and tests an understanding (listening, reading and writing) of the structures of English language rather than the use of the language (e.g. speaking) in critical communicative contexts. In this sense it emphasizes the view of language as a 'product' and that learners can improve their knowledge of this 'product' by memorizing certain structures rather than developing confidence in applying whatever language they know in intercultural business communication and relationship building in (for example) business negotiations together with the social 'small talk' which can oil the wheels of such negotiations.

So, why did this particular HR manager choose to offer his staff TOEIC® classes? 'Because it's known – our competitors use it – and our employees expect us to choose it.' 'Will it work?' we asked, knowing that this HR manager had learnt his English on a three-year overseas assignment for the company. 'Maybe not, but it's the best we can do at the moment.'

Kanban

However, we should not get the impression that training in Japanese organizations is limited to functional rote learning. A high degree of individual flexibility and critical judgement is required to operationalize some of the distinctive features of Japanese production and information management. One notable example is *kanban*. Developed by Taiichi Ono, former vice-president of Toyota, *kanban* are small cards which carry information about the parts used in, for example, the assembly-line manufacture of automobiles. All staff involved can see immediately which parts are required, or have been used and therefore need replenishing from stock, at each stage in the assembly process. One result is reduction in waste time and materials, tying in with the Just-In-Time system of inventory control (Fujimoto, 1999; Bird, 2002).

Another result of *kanban* is the explicit and efficient sharing of information, forming a context and multi-layered and multi-skilled reference group around the assembly process. As within culturally cohesive reference groups, costly or disruptive information asymmetries are avoided. With *kanban*, each member of the assembly reference group is trained to exercise critical judgment in terms of quality control. If a fault is detected, any level of employee is empowered to stop the assembly process. At first glance this empowerment appears to represent an opportunity to experience a massive loss of face: imagine being responsible for suddenly and mistakenly stopping production in an entire Toyota plant! However, and given the focus on quality and the trust and responsibility awarded to individual employees critically to recognize and act on it, the potential for individual loss of face can be contextualized away.

Kai-zen

This focus on quality (however defined) and the commitment to improve oneself and the effectiveness of the work processes one is involved in has a philosophical basis in the notion of *kai-zen* – the virtue of being modest in respect of what one already knows, and of seeking out possibilities for continuous learning and improvement (Box 5.3). However, the expected commitment to the various formal and informal training opportunities offered and to observable individual self-improvement can have instrumental motives: 'a higher performance rating by their pleased superiors carries the possibility of a better bonus or faster promotion to a more interesting job [and furthermore] if everybody expects frequently to be a learner, so everybody expects frequently to have to be a teacher' (Dore and Sako, 1998: 97) and further: 'it is the managers who have more learning to do' (1998: 98).

Mercer (1996) generalizes on this culture-specific propensity and, picking up on one of Smith and Misumi's themes alluded to above, concludes that: 'Japan's secret is that they thoroughly understand and apply the existing textbook principles. The Japanese came to the United States to study marketing and went home understanding its principles better than most US companies did' (1996: 13). As we discuss in Chapter 8, times have changed and Japanese companies are again sending staff overseas to study techniques relevant for organizational survival in today's more globalized markets.

Japanese organizations as learning organizations

Learning is central in defining the middle-management role. Japanese line-managers stand as culture-specific models of behaviour: they monitor the learning of subordinates. As mentors they act as an immediately accessible source of guidance into 'how things are done around here'. As coaches they intervene to guide subordinates along a path that should ensure them a lifetime of employment, and contribute towards creating a 'winning team' – or, at least a team that doesn't lose too often.

Line-managers play a central role in what experts have termed the Japanese-style 'learning organization'. Nonaka and Takeuchi (cf. 1995; 1998) and colleagues have been prominent in this field of research and practice. According to their analysis, Japanese organizations have been able to gain competitive advantage on the strength of how they engage their line- or 'middle-managers' in strategic HRM structures and processes: 'Middle-managers mediate between the "what should be" mindset of the top and the "what is" mindset of the front-line employees by creating mid-level business and product concepts . . . [they] are in a position to remake reality according to the company's vision . . . [they] play a key role in the knowledge-creation process. They synthesize the tacit knowledge of both front-line employees and senior executives, make it explicit, and incorporate it into new products and technologies' (Nonaka and Takeuchi, 1998: 317–318). We see similar patterns in the information 'architecture' (cf. Kay, 1993) attending distinctive techniques and philosophies such as *kanban* and *kai-zen* (Box 5.3).

Box 5.3 *Kai-zen*

The term *kai-zen* is composed of two *kanji*: the first denotes 'change for the better' while the second denotes 'positive improvement'. The search for perfection is incremental, achieved by taking small and detailed steps; or, in Herbig's ballpark terms, 'hitting for singles and doubles, but not homeruns' (1995: 110). The systematic application of *kai-zen* philosophy reflects distinctive features of Japanese management culture such as:

- reducing or avoiding waste in terms of time, effort, emotion and other limited resources (evinced in techniques such as Total Quality Control);
- improving correctively on what already exists (e.g. the product) rather than speculating on what might be a new 'winner' idea or product;
- collective efforts towards gradual and reliable (even predictable) improvement (evinced in techniques such as quality control circles) rather than giving individuals licence to 'break' established 'rules' and perhaps fail and so lose – or cause loss of – face (cf. reference to *kanban* in this chapter).

Kai-zen differs from *innovation* in that *kai-zen* emphasizes process (e.g. the value of learning and creating new knowledge), whereas innovation focuses on a desired outcome: the 'homerun' (cf. Nonaka *et al.*, 1997). Innovation suggests a bolder leap by choosing not to focus on an existing product but rather work towards a vision of what might be. Herbig characterizes innovation as 'a pervasive attitude that allows businesses to see beyond the present and create a future vision' (1995: 114). Sony's 'Walkman' is a much-quoted example of Japanese innovation in that it *created* rather than developed on an existing niche or product. Such successful business innovations are rare, in Japan as elsewhere. A culture-specific aversion to uncertainty (cf. Chapter 1), to 'dramatic effects' (Herbig, 1995) and even 'creative conflict' (Nonaka, 1994), together with a propensity for avoiding loss of face combined with pervasive structures of management control and caution at both corporate and individual levels (cf. Chapter 2), are factors which explain why *kai-zen* rather than 'innovation' is the preferred model for business performance improvement. Nevertheless, Goto and Odagiri (1997) illustrate examples of innovation and innovation processes in Japan. Cole (1991) discusses difficulties in getting Japanese managers to embrace innovation with confidence.

In Nonaka and Takeuchi's model of a learning organization, middle- or line-managers act as 'shock-absorbers' for change. As mentors for the creation of new knowledge they enable the organization to interpret and respond to change cohesively. Effectively co-ordinated by middle-management, staff of large Japanese organizations achieved global admiration for their ability to respond, collectively and cohesively, to simply-stated strategic visions or challenges. For example, the *kanban* technique described above allowed Toyota to produce many different versions of their cars simultaneously while assembly lines at their rival western plants tended to focus on the mass production of one car model.

Komatsu

The learning organization expresses a vision of the value of learning and striving to improve. This can be expressed aggressively, as in the much-quoted example of *Komatsu*, a construction machinery manufacturer, whose deceptively simple 'battle cry' (communicated in English) of 'Beating Caterpillar' (i.e. the US American manufacturer who set global standards during the early 1980s) encouraged members of the organization to concentrate their efforts and, in fact, effectively and efficiently take substantial market share away from Caterpillar. In the 'battle cry' we should note the emphasis given to the process: i.e. 'beating' – suggesting a learning or formative process – rather than 'beat', which emphasizes the proposed outcome. We suppose that western organizations would be inclined to choose the latter form: 'beat'.

Commitment and skills

The learning organization paradigm highlights some of the distinctive features of skills training in Japanese organizational culture. For example, and appropriately for a 'high-context' communication culture, members of a learning organization specialize in 'converting' tacit into explicit knowledge and thus can operate (in key strategic terms) a form of communication which appears essentially opaque to outsiders and essentially non-transferable to rivals. Also, the learning organization suggests a conceptual fit with the structures and processes of the 'classical model' (discussed above) and culture-specific features such as power/distance relationships, long-term commitment and collective acceptance of vertical lines of ascribed authority based on assumed expertise (age) or accumulated knowledge (culture-specific learning). As with the expectation of 'lifetime employment' (Box 5.1), commitment is key. As Nonaka and Takeuchi explain: 'The personal commitment [and] . . . identity within the company and its mission become indispensable. In this respect the creation of new knowledge is as much about ideals as it is about ideas' (1998: 312).

However, and as we suggested in the introduction to this book, to what extent are established or even 'classical' HRM structures and organizational learning processes in Japan able to keep up with global developments? We spoke to one HR manager (in his late forties) who made this analogy:

> I used to coach a local rugby team. I knew the skills I had to try to get across to the players. [This HR manager had, before injury cut short his career, played rugby at international level.] The challenge was to put this knowledge into to words [i.e. what Nonaka (1994) termed the 'verbalization' or 'externalization' of knowledge] and I was happy when I felt I could carry over this skill to my job as an HR manager and kind of *coach* to our company's junior staff. But the skills that our junior staff need now [e.g foreign language skills and other intercultural competencies] go beyond what I feel I can give them. It's like the rules of rugby have changed and the game has become so much faster.

Consistently being a model for expertly skilled behaviour can be tough. A frustration we encountered among many HR and line-managers was: 'Where and when can I find time to update my skills and experience?'

SECTION 3: THE EXPERIENCE OF CAREER DEVELOPMENT

According to Hannagan (1998: 321), 'staff development seeks to improve a person's overall career prospects rather than train him or her to perform duties necessary for the present job. Hence it normally comprises a series of planned training activities and work experiences designed to improve a manager's performance and equip him or her for higher level work.'

A key factor therefore in distinguishing interpretations of training and development in the context of HRM is by reference to time and space: development should generate a stronger sense and experience of future potential (e.g. in dealing with new technologies or more sophisticated strategic imperatives) than training, which will tend to be focused on immediate needs (e.g. learning how to operate a new software programme). Culture-specific perceptions of time and space are also relevant in highlighting this distinction in the context of Japanese organizations. We have seen how recruitment into large-scale Japanese corporations is normally expected to be for life. Accordingly, managers and employees who for whatever reason 'fail' to acquire certain job-specific skills (training) can be transferred to other areas of activity rather than excluded completely from the organization. Similarly, with 'time on their side', the experience of development takes on a different emphasis, the context being given by the 'parent' organization rather than by the wider employment market.

Job rotation

The job rotation approach underpins the classical or traditional structure of staff development in Japanese organizations. The experience of rotation emphasizes 'the learning–teaching process' and the sustenance of the 'learning community' (Dore and Sako, 1998: 100–111). It therefore generates the shared experience of contributing towards sustaining a 'learning organization'. In practical terms, having a cadre of 'shop floor' workers and junior managers with experience of the rotation between functions within one department gives line-managers and other HRM staff a ready source of cover for when one worker drops out (e.g. through illness, transfer or maternity leave). However, it also generates and sustains the culture of the reference group whereby the formal lines (hierarchy) of communication and control tend to be vertical: 'experience + age = authority'.

Rotation encourages knowledge sharing and the establishment of long-lasting intra-organizational relationships and therefore of culture-specific cohesion within the organization. From an individual manager perspective the experience of job rotation affords insights into all major strategic functions of the organization and therefore lends credibility and authority to a future role in higher-level decision-making. Rotation also reminds managers of how much they still have to learn, thus sustaining a *kai-zen* attitude and the notion of the 'learning organization' generally. Rotation as a form of development is, in a Japanese context, a core element in managerial expectations of promotion and reward, themes we discuss in more detail in Chapter 7. Job rotation also emphasizes the expectation that patience is required before an individual can achieve sufficient status as an organizational 'all-rounder'/'insider' and on this basis aspire to a senior management position.

Constraints to innovation

From the organizational HRM perspective, staff development is likely to be emphasized in strategic terms; i.e. what is of use to the organization in helping it achieve its objectives. Ordinarily, and given the emphasis placed on individual commitment and the diffuse nature of Japanese work cultures, this perspective would be readily adopted by individual staff members also. However, and as the nature of face among individual managers shifts towards a greater sense of self-esteem (as we maintain in this book), then the perspective of individual managers will turn towards interpreting (collective) staff development in terms of (individual) career development – within the organization (if possible) or outside the organization (if necessary). This is a process that can be termed *individualization* and is discussed in Chapter 6.

The traditional paths of staff development (i.e. the seniority-based training and promotion system) in part explains why managers who for various reasons drop out of the system find it very difficult to re-enter at a level commensurate with their age and experience. The traditional employment market in Japan reflects the interests of the major institutions (i.e. the influential elite of educational establishments and major corporations) and so 'horizontal' or mid-career labour mobility between traditional Japanese organizations has been (until recently) difficult. We saw an example of this dilemma in the case of Kawaguchi-san in Chapter 2. However, and as the requirement for a quicker and more diversified strategic response to globalized markets becomes the norm, Japanese companies are becoming more used to buying in specialist expertise. Traditionally minded line-managers have problems in asserting their authority over these interloping (and often younger) experts in 'new' (i.e. 'extra-organizational') learning.

Consider the experience of this line-manager:

Hori-san

Hori-san tried to introduce an (outside) innovation into his (internal) operational context. At the time he was in his mid-thirties and worked for a Japanese airline. Being unmarried he devoted much of his free time to charitable work. He took part as a relief group leader during the aftermath of the Kobe earthquake in 1995. In his own words: 'the logistical task was clear, rapid and accurate communications [were] very important, but [these] had to be effective across different relief and rescue groups because the needs of the victims were so diverse'. Returning to his airline company, and after consultation with his divisional head (*bucho*), he set up a 'forum' for operational groups to share logistical information horizontally – in effect, meaning 'they didn't have to go through their line-managers to get the information they need'. Soon he had created (and begun to satisfy) the need for an intra-net communications system. The project was, however, soon stopped 'from above'. This was despite the potential for operational cost-savings in the company – a strategic imperative at the time and since. Hori-san was never told why his project was stopped, although he suspects that the intra-net idea may have appeared to undermine the status of one or other *bucho* or more senior manager. He has since left the airline.

'Outside the box'

Hori-san's experience illustrates what Smith and Misumi in their model identified as 'group process problems' (1994/1997: 378). We could also choose to recognize other difficulties such as 'tepid' management and 'elite morale low'. We would adjudge Hori-san's initiative and ability to 'think outside the box' (i.e. innovate) should qualify him as one of the strategic elite in this or any other business organization. Certainly his commitment cannot be questioned. However, we should also recognize the politics of innovation or new knowledge and the understandable resistance by members who have an established (career or status) interest in keeping things as they are. Was Hori-san being politically naïve? Certainly his experience is not unique to Japanese organizations. We perhaps all have first-hand experience of the ironic insight common among junior managers that 'I can get away with anything that my boss can take the credit for.'

More significantly Hori-san's story may represent an example of an endemic and ultimately self-defeating approach to HRM: an aversion to this type of 'rule-breaking' innovation – and particularly in the area of intra-organizational and electronic communications – that is likely to result in more and more Japanese organizations risking business failure and loss of talented staff in the context of emerging strategic environments (cf. Porter *et al.*, 2000; Box 5.4).

Box 5.4 Career development in Japanese organizations

Sparrow and Hiltrop (1994: 432) list critical events and experiences that tend to shape an individual's experience of career development in the context of organizations. They are: organizational entry and induction; transition from being a generalist to becoming a specialist; transition from operations or technical work to spending more time fulfilling management or supervisory responsibilities; balancing the incursion of family or other outside responsibilities with work; recognition that one is no longer 'on the way up' but rather that one's career progression is 'levelling off'; transition from being fully employed to part-time employment or retirement (*organizational exit*).

Time and other personal resources (including patience) are key in providing individuals with these development opportunities. The traditional Japanese expectation of lifetime employment is geared towards encouraging individual managers to seek and find these opportunities within the context of one organization. Accordingly, crucial are the size of the organization and the diversity of opportunity offered within the confines of established career paths. Unsurprisingly, managers in SMEs and family businesses, in addition to entrepreneurial start-up companies, tend to have a very different experience of career development. However, we have seen how and why their experiences have (until recently) not informed general perceptions of 'Japanese-style' management (cf. Box 4.2).

Kono and Clegg (2001: 274) list the specialist career paths available at Toyota as follows: *general management*; *marketing*; *technical development*; *production engineering*; *production control*; and *new business development*. Toyota is distinctive in that high-performing managers have the possibility of switching between career paths – i.e. over and above the traditional rotation across paths or fields of specialism for training and/or staff development/promotion purposes. Generally, there is no differentiation in pay or compensation between career paths, thus reinforcing the individual and collective experience of the Japanese organization as a learning community. We have seen, however, that there is scope for pay differentiation *within* career paths (cf. Box 2.2).

Interestingly, Kono and Clegg (2001) take a less pessimistic tack by emphasizing the virtues of certain 'big name companies' where 'the dynamics [of] excessive egoism [and] heroic individualism . . . are the exceptions rather than the rule'. In positive cases these dynamics are 'embedded in disciplinary practices that inscribe action that is fluid, committed and exceptionally well-managed from the perspective of innovative organizations' (2001: 286). Hori-san, perhaps, was just unlucky.

SECTION 4: PATIENCE AS A CORE VALUE IN JAPANESE HRM

> Matsushita creates respectable personnel before the production of goods.
>> (a slogan from the Matsushita company 'creed')

A comparative study by Sato (2000) highlighted how Japanese employees who are considered eligible for internal promotion can expect to experience their first substantial rise in status within the organization after seven years or more: the figures given for their US American and German counterparts are (respectively) three-and-a-half and just under four years. Work by Ariga *et al.* (2000) further suggests that this is a period sufficiently long for the organization to manage and reward differences of ability and potential within any one year's graduate intake without causing severe loss of face or demoralization among staff. According to Sato's study, it takes US American and German managers about ten years before they have to realize that they belong to the half of all simultaneous entrants who have no meaningful promotion prospects within the one organization. In contrast, Japanese employees have to wait (on average) more than twenty-two years to reach this moment of truth. By this time, of course, the 'non-promotable' Japanese employees will be virtually unemployable in another organization where human resources are managed along similar lines. They therefore rely on the lifetime employment expectation of their current company.

However, both the talented and ambitious and the (perhaps) less talented and complacent managers will require considerable patience in order to prosper and/or achieve some significant degree of job satisfaction in the traditional Japanese organization. What is the alternative? We have seen that horizontal mobility beyond the boundaries of the 'home' organization is barely catered for in the traditional employment markets. And the longer a managers stays within the culture-specific bounds of one organization, the less easy it is to transfer his or her reputation to another organizational context. As one manager suggested to us, it is akin to buying and amassing postage stamps in a currency which is only valid in one small country (e.g. Monaco) while the opportunity for more expansive correspondence and career opportunities is located in the much larger and more diversified 'Eurozone' countries.

Matsushita

One qualitative solution to such individual dilemmas is *patience*: in other words, the tradition-bound hope or expectation that 'things will get better' or that 'the company will see me right'. Patience has firm roots in the traditions of Japanese-style management, largely due to the towering legacy of Konosuke Matsushita.

Matsushita is known in Japan as a 'god of management' (Craig, in Bird, 2002: 295) and, by adapting Charles Handy's (1991) play on this theme, Matsushita correspondingly represents one of the pillars of 'classical' Japanese management. In the pre-war years he founded the now giant Matsushita Electrical Industrial Co. Ltd by dint of filling his 'idle hours' with hard work, product and marketing innovation, and a 'relentless pursuit of manufacturing efficiency' (2002: 296). One of the company's high-profile achievements has been winning (under its JVC label) the VHS versus the Betamax video format war with Sony in the 1970s and 1980s, the source of several case study discussions on MBA programmes in western business schools. Today's the Matsushita organization also owns the Panasonic and National labels and is Japan's largest manufacturer of consumer electronics. Matsushita himself is seen as pioneer among Japanese entrepreneurs; indeed, as an example for entrepreneurs of all nationalities (Matsushita, 1988; Kotter, 1997).

The reverential status accorded to Konosuke Matsushita the manager and business leader (he died in 1989 aged ninety-five) derives mainly from his spiritual and practical input into traditions and procedures of

Japanese-style HRM. For example, he was a workaholic who popularized the five-day working week in Japan. He led by 'hands-on' management example, espousing vertical lines of management responsibility and commitment to the prosperity of staff, customers and society in general. He emphasized the social responsibilities of business, regarding profit as evidence of customer and social confidence and performing good work as a means of enhancing the quality of life throughout the world. He introduced company songs, promoted the notion of a simple and unifying corporate and/or strategic vision, and a company-specific code of values (the 'Seven Principles') which promoted 'national service through industry, fairness, harmony and cooperation, struggle for betterment, courtesy and humility, adjustment and assimilation, and gratitude' (Craig, in Bird, 2002: 298). As a reward for upholding these principles, staff members at all levels could expect lifetime employment.

Troubled times

Currently, Matsushita Electric is, like many Japanese giants, in economic difficulties: the potential of the founder's innovations appears to have expired. Since its foundation in 1918, Matsushita Electric had become synonymous in Japan with innovation in product development and marketing, but in recent years the company has sought in vain for 'hit products'. Its image appears to have become rather conservative in comparison with its more nimble Japanese and international competitors.

Desperate times call for desperate measures. In an article entitled 'Matsushita shows tradition the door', Minoru Naito in *Nikkei Net Interactive* (accessed 3 June 2002) explains how the company is breaking its tradition of vertical structures of management in order to create horizontally structured project teams 'by reaching out to far-flung areas of the group to gather the best talent'. This very Japanese company is also engaging overseas partners (e.g. Leica Camera AG of Germany and Fuore Design International of Spain) in order to speed up new product development and position its products and its global brand identity more effectively and (specifically) 'in order to stand up to fiercer competition from . . . Asian rivals'. According to Naito, 'the company has closed plants and – in a reversal of the founder's fervent belief in lifetime employment – axed over 10,000 employees through an early retirement programme'. Such drastic measures fall very hard indeed for long-serving managers in an organization where one of the founder's core values was 'Matsushita puts respect for personnel before the production of goods'.

Losing patience

In our research we frequently interviewed managers who had already made the decision to quit their intended 'lifetime' company. We asked them what it was in general that was inducing them to look for a change in career prospects beyond what their current or previous employer either wasn't able or willing to offer them in terms of training and development. The sources of frustration or loss of patience with their current or former employment conditions can be summarized as follows:

Long working hours

As companies cut jobs, those who remain get more work to do. As many existing operational procedures are perceived as 'inefficient' (i.e. relying heavily on high context communication and 'face time'), the necessary work takes longer. According to a recent survey (July 2002) conducted by the Ministry of Public Management, Home Affairs, Post and Telecommunications, between a fifth and a quarter of male Japanese workers work more than eighty hours of (usually unpaid) overtime per month. This is on top of a standard fifty- to sixty-hour working week. In comparison, the recommended working week regulated by the EU is forty-eight hours per week, although also in the UK 30 per cent of managers regularly work significantly more hours per week (*The Guardian* newspaper, online edition, accessed 24 September 2002). Many respondents would prefer to work flexi-time and (for parents) spend more time with their families and enhance their 'quality of life' – a phrase that, as we discuss in Chapter 8, is gaining currency in Japan.

Shortened working hours

Perhaps unsurprisingly in the context of Japanese culture, there is a contradictory element to the previous complaint. One manager in a major Japanese broadcasting company told us how he was initially at a loss as his company started sending staff home early in order to reduce operation costs and avoid the obligation (not always honoured) to recompense overtime in the twice yearly bonus payments. He lived with his wife in a suburb of Tokyo. When he began to arrive home earlier than usual he began to receive anxious enquiries from his parents who lived nearby. 'Was there a problem at work?' The neighbours were beginning to talk!'

In traditional expectations, 'not being there' (i.e. at work) means 'not getting on' (i.e. career-wise). For the following two weeks, and until his parents got used to the situation, he used to spend a few hours in a *pachinko* parlour [a type of amusement arcade] before taking the train home. He now spends his 'spare time' looking for a new job.

Loss of benefits

Also unsurprisingly (from a western perspective), one of the first targets for cost-cutting in Japanese organizations was expenses for business entertainment and travel, above all at middle-management level. Accommodation subsidies and bonuses to pay for children's education are particularly valuable in major conurbations such as Tokyo and Osaka. Benefits or 'perks' can make 'the long commuting time' seem worthwhile. It can be argued that such subsidies and benefits are hardly the responsibility of companies to provide – certainly western managers would argue this. This is, however, to underestimate the tradition of *ie* (Chapter 3) and the embedded nature of large-scale employers in Japanese social and political life. As one Japanese trade union official told us: 'It's usual in industrial relations – in Japan or in the west – that taking away an existing benefit causes more distress and dissatisfaction among employees than appeals for a benefit which by rights should be theirs, but isn't.'

Few holidays

The average (paid) holiday allowance of managers we spoke to was ten days per year. There is a tradition of middle-managers declining to take their full allowance – an overtly masculine value. The phrase *wagamama* has been coined in this context to describe the kind of 'selfishness' that should be avoided: i.e. by not allowing leisure time to eat into time necessary to complete work. Given *kai-zen* philosophy, 'work' is never completed. One alternative is to opt out of this entire holiday structure and/or make a conscious choice of personal 'quality of life' over work (cf. Box. 4.1). However, most managers we spoke to see this approach as too radical and (anyway) infeasible within the career structures offered by their current organizations. Teleworking and other more flexible work structures are still relatively rare in Japan – one reason being the continued reliance on informal communication and career development processes such as 'nominication' referred to in Chapter 1. There is a common misconception that managers in non-Japanese companies enjoy shorter working hours and longer holidays.

Health

Embedded in the type of masculine values espoused in Japanese *samurai* legend is perseverance until death. *Karoshi* is the term given to the much-feared 'death from overworking'. Compounding this pressure is the expectation that days off sick are compensated for by forfeit of days of holiday leave. We were told by industry insiders that the per capita consumption of 'over-the-counter' pharmaceutical products in Japan is rivalled only by the USA: Japanese drug and convenience stores sell a wide range of 'quick fix' vitamin drinks and preparations. As one French manager told us: 'one of the first things you learn about working in Japan is how to sleep standing up [i.e. on commuter trains]'. Having said this, Japanese society has one of the highest longevity rates in the world. 'But it's the individual perception which counts', as the union official reminded us.

When asked about specific barriers to their career development ambitions, the managers intending to quit their current job tended to mention the following and in this order of frustration: ageism; sexism; educational elitism (i.e. which ranking of university a manager graduated from). As discussed in Chapter 4, these are sources of personal and professional frustration because they cannot be changed by the individuals concerned; although, one escape from the experience of educational elitism can be found by choosing to undertake graduate study abroad.

Individual perceptions of discrimination by 'ageism' suggest a direct challenge to traditional seniority promotion structure. 'Sexism' is an issue we discussed (from a female perspective) in Chapter 4. However, the preponderance of masculine values also weighs heavily on gay employees. There is still tremendous pressure put on both male and female employees to marry: indeed, the traditional view is that marriage is evidence of an individual's long-term reliability and willingness to commit and so a prerequisite for a smooth career path within the traditional structures and cultures of Japanese organizations.

SECTION 5: TRENDS IN CAREER DEVELOPMENT

Sparrow and Hiltrop (1994) discuss 'career development' in terms of progress as measured, for example, against indicators such as starting salary compared to present salary and starting job status compared to current job status. These indicators can be measured 'externally' (i.e. in our terms by reference groups such as the organization and its HR staff, peers or work colleagues, family and society generally). These reference groups tend to lend authority and credibility to what a 'career' is or should be as expressed in culture-specific norms and values.

Not all managers will experience careers or career progress in the same way: indeed, not all managers want a 'career' as defined by collectively-generated norms and values. According to Sparrow and Hiltrop's analysis, the key trend in reshaping both 'internal' (i.e. individual) and 'external' (i.e. social) perceptions of career development among managers in Europe during the 1990s has been their experience of *internationalization*. This means, for example, not only the recognition by individual managers of the need for their work to appeal to an increasingly international customer base and (perhaps more significantly) a more international or multi-cultural senior management structure. It also signifies recognition on their part of the opportunities offered by an increasingly internationalized employment or career market, contextualized and illuminated by their access to global information technology.

We can find parallels for these now established European trends in career development among Japanese managers. For example, one of our colleagues interviewed a group of Japanese managers who had quit their companies in Japan in order to pursue graduate studies at a management school in the UK (Kasai, 1999). The average age of these former managers was thirty-six. There was a fifty-fifty split in terms of male/female respondents. Their responses show a clear level of dissatisfaction with the training, development and career development prospects they had perceived before quitting their last job in Japan. The following comments were typical:

> To tell you the truth I lost interest in my job. With the changes in the [Japanese] economic system I thought my job would change too. But the company didn't change [and so] I decided to change [my skills and qualifications] so that I could change my job in future (male, DOB 1966, asset portfolio manager).

> I wanted to work in a foreign branch but [the bank] closed its foreign operation. [Overall] the sector I worked in was chaotic, changing all the time. I could not imagine my future [with the bank] clearly. I wanted to keep my future [and my ability to change] with me (male, DOB 1969, customer accounts manager in commercial bank).

> I became bored. After ten years [in the job] it became easy for me to predict what was going to happen in our company. The company is not so sensitive to the outside world. The company is very conservative and not very dynamic. It's very slow to respond to [for example] e-business. I could see that I would not be able to improve myself. I also wondered whether the company [itself] had a future (male, DOB 1965, sales associate in heavy machinery industry).

> If my last company had had a system for training people abroad I would have stayed. One female employee took one year off and went abroad but she didn't return to the company. Since then, top management decided not to allow any employees to study abroad (female, DOB 1958, trading company specialist).

In these comments we can recognize individuals who have decided to take more direct control over their future career development by investing in paths of development outside and beyond the existing HRM structures and processes of the organizations they had left one year previously: i.e. 1998 – the year when for many prescient observers the Japanese economic slump became adjudged to be chronic. Their testimony suggests that they had lost patience with the career development opportunities that their former organization either could or appeared willing to offer them.

Kasai (1999) identifies a sense of 'psychological contract violation' among her sample of respondents: a feeling that 'things didn't turn out as we were led to expect' (cf. Morrison and Robinson, 1997). We discuss the nature of the 'psychological contract' in Chapter 6. It is significant that two thirds of Kasai-san's respondents had a background in banking or other sectors of the financial services industry. As one respondent suggested, managers in this industry in Japan are coming under particular strain to respond to the competitive pressures of globalization (cf. Chapter 7). Unfortunately (for them), the Japanese banking industry is also one of the most conservative – and as some managers vehemently express to us – 'complacent' in terms of updating its HRM structures and cultures in Japan (cf. Box 7.1).

Loyalty: a core value

To what extent are the managers in Kasai-san's sample 'typical'? We believe they are not typical, but that they do represent an increasingly significant and influential minority. As we noted in Chapter 1, culture-specific norms may change with the speed of fashion, but culture-specific values change much more slowly, perhaps with the speed of human generations. Core culture-specific values include patience (discussed in this chapter) and trust (discussed in the following chapter). Another such is loyalty, as illustrated in the case of this manager.

Mikimura-san

Mikimura-san is in her mid-thirties and heads a laboratory research team just outside Tokyo for a top ranking Japanese pharmaceutical company. She studied chemistry at university, and is also highly talented as a musician and as a speaker of foreign languages (English and German). When we spoke to her she was on maternity leave: 'one year at 30 per cent of salary'. But her real problems were soon to begin. During her maternity leave the laboratory team she headed had been moved – as a cost-cutting measure – to a plant further away from her and her husband's flat. Mikimura-san now faces a three to four hour commute each day, in addition to finding a nursery place for her child. Her husband's company is 'very old-fashioned' and so they are unlikely to make allowance for him to take time out to look after the child. Her and her husband's parents live too far away to help out. Moving flat is too expensive and would anyway only make life more difficult for her husband – he would have to commute further and is already committed to an extended period of increased overtime.

We asked Mikimura-san whether she felt the need to look for another job. She discounted this, even though she felt confident she could find one. The reasons she gave were:

- 'I enjoy my present job and my career prospects in the company, for a woman, are very good. I have good contacts with the other women managers in the company [six out a total workforce of 7,000 employees]. Also my salary and bonuses are good.'
- 'If I went to another company now I would lose salary and slow down my career chances. Anyway, we need the money now to continue paying off the flat.'

- 'During my maternity leave my colleagues have been covering for me. I couldn't leave the company after what they have done for me. My loyalty is to them: not to the company.'

Looking ahead, Mikimura-san believes that her knowledge of the company's products and strong R&D, her skills in foreign languages, and her skills of endurance and flexibility in juggling career and family life will stand her in good stead, one reason being that her company is likely soon to be merged with or acquired by a rival US American company. 'Perhaps then the company will think of bringing in some child caring facilities for staff!'

There was no mistaking the sense of loyalty and trust she felt in her work colleagues and the debt she felt she owed them. The practical and logistical problems she was about to face 'would get solved somehow': she remains patient for now. We discuss changes in the experience and expectation of trust in Japanese management culture in Chapter 6.

Summary

In this chapter we have discussed the structures and cultural values that give shape to the traditional or 'classical' model of Japanese-style management, taking Matsushita (the business leader) and Matsushita (the organization) as examples. We have illustrated ways in which this 'classical' model is increasingly coming under strain and why. We also outlined culture-specific notions such as 'lifetime employment/ commitment', *kanban* and *kai-zen* and examined their relationship to staff training and development within the paradigm of the (Japanese) 'learning organization'. In this context we again illustrated the key role played by line- and middle-managers and other practitioners with HRM responsibilities in Japanese organizations.

Overall we identified and contextualized some of the main sources of frustrations that Japanese managers currently appear to experience and suggested that these frustrations are eroding the credibility of HRM policies and structures which are based in large part on the core value or assumption of patience. We concluded that most Japanese managers (from our sample, at least) are still willing to 'wait and see', but suggested that increasing numbers are likely to seek more meaningful career prospects outside their current organizations.

Consider the following questions:

1 To what extent has your experience of company or 'in-house' training prepared you for emerging developments in:

- your current job?
- the particular industry or business sector you work in?

2 Do you feel that the structures for training and development in your current organization are actively addressing your individual career development and self-esteem needs? Do you believe that what your current organization offers is matched by (a) what is available in other similar organizations or (b) what is happening in the employment market generally?

6 Losing trust?

Introduction

> The first lesson is . . . trust.
>
> (Ouchi, 1981)

Ouchi identified 'trust' as one of the key features defining the relationship between managers and their subordinates in Japanese organizations. He regarded this relationship not only as one of the key drivers informing how Japanese organizations operated and were managed. Trust also formed one of the key sources of competitive advantage that (at the time) Japanese organizations appeared to have over their western rivals.

The subtitle to Ouchi's study – *How American Business Can Meet the Japanese Challenge* – reflects the mood among western managers at a time when organizations in many established industries (e.g. automobile and steel manufacture, coal-mining) were undergoing a series of industrial relations conflicts generated by processes of strategic restructuring. Ouchi did not propose that western organizations became more 'Japanese': the culture-specific contexts were too diverse. However, he did conclude that the one 'lesson' to learn from Japanese-style HRM was about the advantages of managing people based on a relationship informed by a dynamic of mutual trust.

In this chapter we explore various perceptions and experiences of trust among Japanese managers, focusing on their experiences of performance review or appraisal.

Our objectives for this chapter are:

- to explore how and why the experience and expectation of trust in Japanese management culture is changing;

- to illustrate how Japanese managers typically experience processes of performance appraisals and explain how and why they may be losing trust in how these processes are managed.

SECTION 1: MANAGING TRUST IN JAPANESE ORGANIZATIONS

'My door is always open'

From the perspective of many Japanese managers, HRM in western organizations tends to operate based on a shared acceptance of the bureaucratization or formalization of trust and control. This mechanistic view characterizes the Personnel Management (PM) paradigm as opposed to a strategic human resources or relations management (SHRM) culture said to distinguish Japanese organizations (cf. Mabey *et al.*, 1998). As a result, Japanese managers who have worked in western organizations tell us about their perception that trust and control in western organizations tends to be formalized: the French organizations with their very strict and explicit ('snobbish') hierarchies of status and authority; German organizations and their 'obsession' with individual office or work space. As one Japanese manager (who had worked in a UK company) asked us: 'When my [British] line-manager says "my door is always open" is he offering me trust? Or is he just looking for information which he or other people can later use against me [e.g. in performance appraisals or behind-doors discussion of my promotion prospects]?' And a further question, recalling images of the UK as a global showplace for industrial relations strife and conflict over 'job demarcations': 'Why do employees in the UK so often complain like "but that's not in my contract" or "that's not in my job description" when they're asked to do something unexpected or in an emergency?'

Trust and control

This is because management is also about control. In Chapter 2 we suggested that ways in which 'control' tends to be managed in Japanese organizations can be explained and understood with reference to individual and collective attention to face. The way in which attention to face serves to generate a shared experience of trust can be read from Kono and Clegg's definition of 'trust' as something 'built up over time and means that one can predict others' behaviour and expect that others will treat one well in difficult situations' (2001: 280). Thus, giving attention to face and thereby (predictably and reliably) meeting the expectations of the reference groups is central to shaping and guiding the normative behaviour of Japanese employees. The reserve of trust that members of the reference group have accumulated among themselves means that no one need fear being abandoned in times of crisis. Given the 'diffuse' nature of Japanese management culture, we can understand that a helping hand is made available irrespective of whether the crisis is professional or personal.

There is a different tradition of management control – and thereby of managing trust – in western organizations. For example, much that is still written about HRM in western organizations tends to emphasize the 'functional' control aspects of HRM processes (cf. Golding and Currie, 2000). Examples include detailed job descriptions, strict demarcations in terms of responsibilities, and even parking spaces and dining areas in the works canteen: i.e. those non-essential aspects of western HRM which can baffle many Japanese managers. To detect the difference of emphasis between Japanese and western HRM traditions we can take a glance through the index of management theory compendiums such as Pugh, Hickson and Hinings (1983). Here we find various definitions of managerial 'control', whereas 'trust' scarcely receives mention as an aspect of effective management. In the Ouchi (1981) text cited in the introduction to this chapter, the exact opposite is true. Interestingly, this imbalance appears to be rectified later in 'post-crisis' HRM texts such as a Sparrow and Marchington (1998).

Trust and the reference group

Our discussion of organizational induction (Chapter 4) and training and development (Chapter 5) noted the central the role taken in Japanese organizations by HR staff in setting policy – 'setting the mood' for management relations – while line-managers took a more immediate hands-on approach to monitoring and guiding staff on an individual basis. In the typically open-plan Japanese office or work group there is no requirement for the line-manager to announce that 'my door is always open'. Rather, the unspoken understanding is that 'I'm sitting just a few metres away from you. Through your induction and training – together with your education and other experiences of socialization – you know what I/we expect of you, I/we know what you expect of us, and (through your experience of induction and ongoing experience of learning in this particular organization) I/we know that you know what I/we expect.'

Consequently, the managers and the managed tend to share the same space – physically and (as a reference group) relatively in terms of the expression of culture-specific norms and values. As we saw in the example of *kanban* (Chapter 5), both managers and the managed share much of the information vital for working effectively. This information is furthermore available to all members in real time. The managers and the managed also visibly share the same time: both in terms of daily work-time (who comes and goes when) and taking a longer-term perspective who gets promoted when, who gets married to whom and when, all over the course of a lifetime of employment (cf. Box 5.1).

As we discussed in Chapter 5, what line-managers and their HRM colleagues expect above all of their subordinates is a personal 'commitment' to the shared purpose of the reference group, be this the immediate group formed by the line-manager and work colleagues, or the larger group described by the organization. From an individual perspective, the parallel to the experience of education and *'ganbaru'* (i.e. 'doing one's best') is marked. This emphasis on diffuse individual commitment also serves to reconcile some of the messier overlapping of complex and controversial notions such as power, authority, influence and control. As Etzioni (1975; 1988) explains: 'the more employees are committed, the less formal control mechanisms are needed'.

The harmonious office?

However, we should be wary of assuming that the mood within the Japanese office is 'harmonious'. As new recruits learn the ropes and how to get on in the section, department or organization, internal competition for promotion becomes fierce, particularly now as, through restructuring, meaningful promotion opportunities are becoming fewer. Traditionally, however, competition for promotion is understated and channelled into the achievements of the group. Overt individualistic behaviour within the group is usually frowned upon while conflict generated by external circumstances tends, over time, to be managed away collectively. As we shall see, this traditional view informs the traditional Japanese-style approach to performance appraisal.

Consider this scene:

At Tokyo Station around 08.30, commuters are streaming towards the exits of what is one of the busiest railway stations in the world and one which is integrated into an extensive and highly efficient network of commuter trains. Unusually today, one of the lines has experienced a 15-minute delay. A queue of commuters stands near the exit turnstile to be handed a note of apology from the rail company responsible. The commuters will later hand this note to their line-manager as an explanation for their late arrival at work. They may have to wait more than 15 minutes in the queue.

We asked one of our respondents whether he had ever waited for a late note to present to his line-manager (*kacho*). He said he had. And now, as a line-manager himself, what did he expect from his subordinates? He answered that the situation had now changed in his organization and that these late notes are not expected anymore. How did this change come about? One of his subordinates had arrived late one day and brought a note, but he [the *kacho*] had needed the subordinate earlier to deal promptly with a fax message from overseas: i.e. the *kacho* would have preferred him to be at work earlier rather than arrive with an excuse for being late. The *kacho* later spoke about this situation with his line-manager (*bucho*) one evening after work. Later it became apparent that other *bucho* in the organization had questioned the need to require late notes. Over time it became routine that anyone arriving late should make an apology to the work group and make clear that any 'lost' time or work would be made up subsequently. In this informal way, the organizational policy on late notes changed.

In Chapter 2 we saw how the mechanisms for communication and control in Japanese organizations/reference groups tend to be highly regulated. However, where relationships are based on trust the self-regulatory commitment of all individuals involved can be subtle and highly flexible insofar as each member of the group remains consistently aware of his/her responsibility and what it takes to become a 'trusted' insider (cf. Box 6.1). We saw the operational expression of this relationship in discussion of *kanban* and *kai-zen* in Chapter 5.

Box 6.1 *Nemawashi*

Nemawashi literally means 'preparing the roots of a (mature) plant or tree before replanting it'. It explains how managers in Japanese organizations manage and communication change. It also explains how these managers effect horizontal communication and (when it comes to processes of staff appraisal, discussed in this chapter) assess the extent to which individuals are coping and fitting in with expectations and thereby gaining the trust of their superiors, peers and (where relevant) subordinates. *Nemawashi* can operate like this. Senior or middle-level managers identify and suggest a need for change: e.g. in terms of product development or strategic focus. The suggestion is then communicated downwards within the organizational hierarchy. The junior members of staff in different departments confer (horizontal communication), work on the idea, and report upwards (vertical communication) on the practicalities of implementing the change. The recommendations make their way upwards and are amended or commented on by different levels of management until the proposal is back with the senior managers. These may then decide to go ahead, abandon the idea, or send it back down the line for further consultation. One obvious purpose of *nemawashi* is to draw maximum benefit from the organization's human assets. However, it is also a mechanism for sharing ownership – and thereby trust – in change or new ideas. Conversely, it also serves to minimize loss of face should the idea fail (cf. Box 2.5).

Shared ownership/responsibility is more explicit with the related *ringi-sho* or *ringi seido* process. Here a proposal is circulated in hard-copy form and each manager writes comments on or marks with his/her personal 'chop' or seal to show approval.

Both processes characterize the Japanese 'learning organization' (Nonaka and Takeuchi, 1995; 1998). In sharing information and criticism, participants affirm their 'insider' status, loyalty towards the organization's strategic purpose and thereby their trustworthiness (cf. Lu, 1987). Unsurprisingly, perhaps, neither process has been a success with non-Japanese staff in subsidiaries overseas. Even in Japan, several respondents suggested that *nemawashi* and *ringi-sho* should not automatically be regarded as 'democratic' decision-making processes given that few subordinates are likely to 'stick their neck out' and contradict a suggestion made by their superiors.

SECTION 2: EXPERIENCING TRUST IN JAPANESE ORGANIZATIONS

Consider the following scene:

Towards the end of another working day, Suzuki-san kacho stands up from his desk to leave the office space he shares with 24 other colleagues. It is around 6.20 in the evening and Suzuki-san kacho has an appointment to meet some of his former university colleagues (*doki*) now working in the same organization (though in different departments) and in other companies. He had already cleared this need to leave early with his line-manager, who is still working at his desk. As Suzuki-san kacho leaves the office he says: *O-saki ni shitsurei shimasu* (literally: Excuse me for leaving ahead of you). His colleagues (still working) reply: *O-tsukare sama deshita* (literally: Thank you for your hard work).

Several Japan managers talk about the difficulty in the evening of leaving the office 'before the boss': overtime can thus take on the nature of 'face time' or being seen to be working 'hard and long' as expected by superiors. Of course, this occurs in western organizations also. But in Japanese organizations 'hanging around' at the workplace is normal and not obviously (to outsiders) productive. For example, a manager may have taken responsibility for finishing a detailed or drawn-out task before leaving the office. Alternatively, he or she may need to confer with colleagues as part of a *nemawashi* exercise (Box 6.1) or on less formally focused matters where the primary objective is to avoid causing loss of face to oneself or others. A cliché used to do the rounds among western managers that Japanese office buildings were full of windows 'so that the big boss can check from the outside who's still working and who's already left'. In fact, this task may be performed by reception staff or uniformed officials in the lobby area (usually male retirees receiving a nominal salary). More likely, the task is performed by staff members individually by relying on their and their colleagues' sincerity and willingness to regulate their behaviour appropriately: an effective combination of 'CCTV eyes' (cf. Chapter 2) and trust.

Collective trust

In the scene described above, Suzuki-san kacho can leave the office with a clear conscience, first, because he has already cleared it with his line-manager and, second, because his colleagues *trust* (and anyway almost certainly have seen enough to know) that he has done his share of work that day. If for any reason they think he has not, they can trust him to make it up at a future date.

When we ask ourselves what we each understand by 'trusting someone' we should recognize that our core values or assumptions come to the fore: our expectations of trust are shaped by socialization into believing how people should behave. These socialized assumptions become qualified by individual experience (good and bad) of who to trust and why. This dual nature of trust (i.e. both highly individualized *and* highly collectivized) explains why we struggle to communicate and interpret mechanisms and processes of trust in other cultures: it is very much like trying to be naturally fluent in a foreign language. *Apropos*, in trying to define notions such as trust and respect in the context of Japanese management culture Kono and Clegg (2001) reach for a German notion (*Gemeinschaft*) and use this to compare Japan to other more explicitly task-oriented *Gesellschaft* cultures. The dualism is itself derived from Tonnies (1922/1987). Next step: ask a native German speaker what he or she understands by *Gemeinschaft*!

Defining collective trust

Francis Fukuyama came to global prominence for announcing 'the end of history'. He has also worked intensively with the definition of 'trust' (cf. Fukuyama, 1995; 2000), which he defines as 'a key by-product of the cooperative social norms that constitute social capital. If people can be counted on to keep commitments, honor norms of reciprocity, and avoid opportunistic behavior, then groups will form more readily, and those that do form will be able to achieve common purposes more efficiently' (2000: 49).

In this definition we recognize the collective and collectively binding effect of trust. Thus Suzuki-san kacho's behaviour can on the face of it be interpreted as generating trust among his colleagues or immediate reference group while simultaneously generating trust among his related but more distant *doki* reference group – the people he has arranged to meet that evening. From the perspective of both groups, Suzuki-san can be 'counted on'.

In Fukuyama's definition we can also recognize some distinctive and overlapping elements of Japanese working culture: the emphasis on developing human or 'social capital' (cf. Chapter 3); the emphasis on developing human relationships (cf. Chapters 4 and 5); and the emphasis given self-regulatory convergence of norms of behaviour and purpose which define each individual's role and status within a reference group (cf. Chapter 2). We can equate Fukuyama's emphasis on 'avoiding opportunistic behaviour' to the culturally ingrained need to 'avoiding breaking the rules' and thereby avoid causing loss of face. Thus, and over time, *and* according to context, we learn to trust other people by the extent to which they behave predictably, reliably, meet our expectations and thereby help us to avoid loss of face.

Trust and co-operation

From a practical HRM perspective, the shared experience of trust among staff members should motivate them individually and collectively to make and express personal commitment to the section, the department or, where the impact of HRM is strategically cohesive, the organization. The presence of trust should mean that managers can fulfil their 'control' tasks much less contentiously and abruptly than in western contexts: doors, whether open or shut, need not define boundaries of trust. This is a situation we can all empathise with, both in our role as managers of employees and as employees being managed. Just as attention to face is negotiated according to context, so the boundaries of trust in Japanese organizations tend to be subtle, informal, and thereby 'organic' and flexible according to context (cf. Mintzberg, 1979; 1983; Morgan, 1989; 1997). This is a co-operative 'win-win' HRM strategy of choice and recalls Takeguchi-san's conviction (cited in Chapter 3) that the 'Japanese way' based on collective effort and collaborative trust will prevail even against current economic adversity, and that the trains in Japan will 'run on time' – as, indeed, they still do, spectacularly.

Box 6.2 Motivation

The title of the Ouchi (1981) text cited at the beginning of this chapter is 'Theory Z'. This is a conscious play on McGregor's Theories 'X' and 'Y' (cf. Bennis, 1968). These theories refer to the two generalized assumptions that managers and business leaders have about what motivates their workforce. Namely: 'Theory X managers tend to believe that people have an inherent dislike of work, regarding it as necessary for survival, and will avoid it wherever possible . . . They have to be coerced, controlled and directed to make them work towards organizational goals' (Hannagan, 1998: 39). In contrast: 'Theory Y managers believe that people see work as a natural phenomenon, that they accept responsibility . . . They will help to achieve organizational objectives provided that they both understand them and are rewarded for their efforts' (Hannagan, 1998: 40). McGregor's model emphasizes the dangers of 'self-fulfilling prophecies': i.e. managers will tend to assume that their subordinates are motivated by the same norms and values that motivate the managers themselves (e.g. money, perks rather than job satisfaction) and probably over-generalize about what motivates individual staff members. A classic study by Kovach (1987) shows how often these managers are mistaken.

In Japanese organizations, the convergence and cohesion in terms of fundamental values is assumed to begin already during the recruitment and induction processes (cf. Chapter 4). In HRM terms, being recruited and offered lifetime employment is an expression of considerable trust. Being offered the prospect of promotion operates partly as an incentive and partly as an indication of trust. Offering responsibility – as in the *kanban* example cited in Chapter 5 and the *nemawashi* example cited in this chapter – is an effective means to both generate and channel employee effort and motivation.

A keystone in discussions of motivation is Maslow's 'hierarchy of relative propensity' or human needs and motivation (1942). At its base are human needs such as warmth and food. Once satisfied, human behaviour becomes driven by a higher-level need for a sense of security and then of belonging and acceptance (cf. by the reference group). Later come self-esteem and self-actualization needs (cf. the changing attention to face we develop throughout this book). Interestingly, 'Maslow's hierarchy' does not specify money as a motivating factor (cf. Chapter 7).

SECTION 3: PERFORMANCE APPRAISAL

> The hierarchy succeeds only to the extent that we trust it to
> yield equitable outcomes.
>
> (Ouchi, 1981)

Performance *appraisal* forms one of several performance management systems available to HR and other managers: some practitioners and texts distinguish between performance assessment, performance evaluation and performance appraisal. See Mabey *et al.* (1998a) for a fuller discussion of various forms of performance management systems.

In generic terms, performance appraisal refers to a manager's judgement about an employee's performance. In terms of specific and intended outcomes, 'appraisal is the analysis of employees' past successes and failures, and the assessment of their suitability for promotion or further training' (Hannagan, 1998: 323). Each side thus expects an outcome (e.g. a reward or benefit) from the process: i.e. further training (discussed in Chapter 5); or promotion; or pay (discussed in Chapter 7). What constitutes 'success' and 'failure' in terms of individual performance will depend on culture-specific perceptions and expectations, in addition to time and place: in other words, any appraisal judgement will perforce be relative and, when paired with individual (e.g. line-manager) authority, essentially subjective.

The 'psychological contract'

This perception of 'subjectivity' corresponds to the deliberate imprecision of standard Japanese employment contracts and job descriptions. In western employment contracts, Fukuyama's 'norms of reciprocity' tend to be formalized and explicit (e.g. in terms of a written contract or job description) whereas the culture of Japanese HRM tends to emphasize (and usually tacitly) more what can be referred to as the 'psychological contract' (cf. Sparrow, 1996; Makin *et al.*, 1996). This is defined as 'a rich and nuanced collection of shared understandings [between employer and employee] built up over time' (Mabey *et al.*, 1998: 133). Thus, a key element in making the 'psychological contract' effective is trust.

Lacking tangible form, the psychological contract is realized through human behaviour and, in a management context, by the nature of human relations. We saw (in Chapter 4) how HRM in the context of Japanese organizations tends to emphasize the structuring and management of complex interpersonal relations, focusing as a strategic imperative on developing 'teamwork, flexibility and generalist knowledge' (Takeda, in Bird, 2002: 181) rather than emphasizing the achievement of specified tasks or objectives. In this way core staff become emotionally bound to the organization that offers them secure employment and (almost) guaranteed promotion.

The emotional bond is attached from day one. We recall (from Chapter 4) Miura-san's and Ikemura-san's experiences of the induction process. We saw how the initial training in the respective organizations assumed no prior knowledge of the company and its products and that members of the *shinsotsu* (new recruits) group had to rely on each other to complete the initial tasks. We recall Miura-san's gradual introduction to her designated work/reference group and the line-manager who was 'kind' and therefore probably perceived as someone to be trusted. The working relationship between line-manager and recruit will develop until Miura-san (for example) had acquired sufficient insider information to be able fluently to regulate her behaviour and thus prove herself a useful and reliable (or 'proper') group member. She was later transferred against her line-manager's wishes. Senior HR managers overruled his wishes. The HR department learned about Miura-san's progress and apparent suitability for a new set of tasks on the strength of her own line-manager's appraisal of her performance.

Accordingly, new recruits and aspiring managers are expected at least as much to fit in with a prevailing and context-specific attitude (i.e. matching the strategic priorities of HR and senior managers) as satisfactorily to perform specific tasks. The attitude required to complete the tasks (for there must be some measurable output from work or performance) is expressed as self-regulation, co-operation and mutual support, all given substance over time. This is the essence of the Japanese-style 'psychological contract'.

Trust and performance

Thus, the predominant expectation in Japanese organizational culture is that individuals will work long and hard and show sustained commitment towards co-operating with the work group and by extension help the organization realize its strategic vision or objectives. The outcome for this effort is specified by senior managers, as they are expected to focus on the long-term strategic well-being of the organization and so should specify what rewards the organization can or should afford at any one time. From the individual employee's perspective, access to these rewards is interpreted in the first instance by the line-manager. Without 'going over the line-manager's head', the employee needs to trust that his/her line-managers communicate upwards accurate reports on his/her performance and effort. This moment of trust becomes critically highlighted during the performance appraisal process.

Many Japanese managers we spoke to experienced performance appraisal as formulaic – 'just going through the motions' – and as a distraction rather than as an opportunity to progress their career. This is common to Japanese and non-Japanese employment contexts (cf. Butcher, 2002). However, and given the convergence of values between HR and line-managers (the *appraisers*) and the employee being appraised (the *appraisee*) expected in Japanese organizations, the formal appraisal event should fit a pattern established in experiences of ongoing informal assessments and other forms of intra-organizational communication and feedback. Accordingly, formal performance appraisals should offer few unexpected or surprise outcomes, thus reinforcing their basis in trust. As such, the event becomes almost forgettable, as indeed most of our respondents admitted to us, so vague were their memories of the process.

Best practice?

There can be no one 'best' system of performance appraisal: the perceived or effective value of each system will depend on the strategic and cultural context of the organization – but each system normally tries to link the following features:

- the setting and communication of performance objectives or goals;
- the measurement of outcomes in working to achieve these objectives;
- giving feedback on efforts in achieving these outcomes (e.g. to what extent they coincide with performance objectives);
- giving rewards according to efforts and achievement of objectives;
- suggesting or making changes to objectives and future individual behaviour.

Performance management systems should provide what is perceived as a valid and reliable framework for managing these. Ideally they should also motivate (Box 6.2).

We saw in Chapter 5 how Konosuke Matsushita was a pioneer in terms of informing HRM practice with notions of strategic vision and core organizational values. His consistent expression of vision was designed to set benchmarks for formal and individual performance appraisal throughout the organization (cf. Tanner Pascale and Athos, 1981). This benchmark expresses what value individual employees can add to the organization and its operations in the long term. Distinctive about Matsushita (and, typically, inspirational managers in other Japanese organizations) is the attention given to what the organization can or should give back to the individual employee. In this context, Kono and Clegg (2001) talk about 'respect', whereas in our current discussion we are focusing on trust. Together they can be said to inform the 'psychological contract' outlined above (cf. Box 6.3).

It is useful at this point to recall the scene cited from Yoshimura and Anderson (1997) and presented in Chapter 2. Those Japanese sales associates were being subject to a 'performance appraisal' of the crudest kind. Sales staff in Japan work to numerical targets as do sales people in other national cultural contexts; although, as Usunier points out, 'in high

Box 6.3 Performance appraisal in Japanese organizations

Kono and Clegg (2001) outline performance appraisal processes at Toyota. All employees are appraised 'three times per year: once for promotion and wage increases, and twice for bonus payments' (2001: 262). Bonus payments in Japan are normally awarded in winter and in summer, while salary increases normally take effect from April of each year, coinciding with the university graduation and organization induction schedules. 'The employee's duties, goals and required skills are defined in April, taking into consideration the department's goals. Performance evaluation [or appraisal] against the set standards is conducted in October (and used for the winter bonus) and again in April (when it is used for the summer bonus)' (2001: 262). The 'supervisor' or line-manager conducts the first appraisal, the supervisor's line-manager the second, and the head of another department or member of the HR department might conduct the third. Initially, the appraisee is asked to 'explain' his or her performance [i.e. self-appraisal] before receiving feedback and advice on how to improve. To complete the process the appraisee fills out a questionnaire.

The criteria used for appraising 'managerial' and 'core professional' staff are differently weighted: for example, managerial staff are expected to show high levels of 'conceptual skills' while for 'core professionals' the emphasis is more on 'technical skills'. Fifty per cent of the appraisal of managers is given to 'people skills': specifically, 'management of groups' (20 per cent); 'encouragement of subordinates' (20 per cent); and 'respect from others' (10 per cent). Respect in the context of Japanese organization and human relations management is a key theme in Kono and Clegg's study.

Pucik (in Bird, 2002: 27) takes a slightly different approach. He explains how the initial experience of appraisal tends to be one where each individual is compared to an employee with his or her *doki* or 'core peer group': i.e. those of similar background and assumed potential who enter the organization at the same time. We recall from Chapter 4 that graduates from 'good' universities are recruited on the basis of their perceived potential rather than demonstrable skills. One outcome of 'peer group' appraisal is a set of comparative *rankings* (cf. Box 3.2).

Later appraisals 'are more complex' as the reference group for comparison is extended to cover all staff at the same grade or employed under the same conditions or 'tenure'. Appraisals usually assess four areas of competence: 'human relations skills'; 'attributes' such as 'creativity, leadership and reliability'; 'personality-related attributes such as sociability, flexibility [and] confidence'; and one overall achievement score (Pucik, in Bird, 2002: 27). Scoring these multiple dimensions of 'good' performance should remind the appraisee that individual improvement is always possible (cf. Box 5.3).

context societies [such as Japan], numbers are considered as efficient, but oversimplified' (1996: 467). We recall that the sales staff in Yoshimura and Anderson's example were ritually reminded of what they '*hadn't* achieved' that day. As a performance appraisal event, the logical question is thus: what should they have achieved? In a Japanese context, the positive – and complex – answer is expected to come from the sales associates themselves, based on their general understanding of *kai-zen* (Box 5.3) and other work-related values and attitudes. In addition comes their specific understanding of what level and (probably more significantly) what *quality* of performance is expected in this department, this organization, and indeed in this particular industry. Against this culture-specific background, the emphasis given to qualitative performance measures by inspirational business leaders such as Matsushita become more operationally transparent.

Process and outcomes

In Japanese organizations formal appraisal discussions usually take place three times per year (cf. Box 6.3), whereas informal peer and line-manager appraisal (referring back to our definition of the psychological contract) is 'nuanced' and continuous. The process of combining peer and self-appraisal in addition to formal 'top-down' communication has become formalized in western HRM contexts as '360-degree feedback': i.e. a fully rounded picture of the individual employee's efforts and achievements should emerge. In a Japanese context, communicating a rounded view of individual behaviour and performance is a key function of the 'reference group'. Correspondingly, the process of 'self-appraisal' should not be separated from the notion of 'self-regulation', as outlined in Chapter 2.

The outcome of both formal and informal performance appraisals essentially relies on the quality of information available to both the appraisers and the appraisee. How line-managers as appraisers collate and interpret this information will depend on what is understood of organizational standards (probably set by HR staff), their own experience, and their expectations based on their perception and opportunity to observe key aspects of the appraisee's performance. The perceived quality of the appraisal outcome also depends on how the appraiser is disposed towards the appraisee, so social influences and notions of power cannot be divorced from the appraisal process (cf. Townley, 1991). Paraphrasing Ouchi (cited at the beginning of this section): 'fair' outcomes lend credibility to existing hierarchies of power.

Essentially, the appraisal focuses on contextual skills: in other words, the extent to which the appraisee 'fits in' with expectations (first encountered during organizational induction) and accordingly – and without wishing to over-dramatize the event – how far the appraisee can be trusted. We have seen how the proximity of communication and observation of behaviour in the work context facilitates an ongoing monitoring of individual employee behaviour by both line-managers and work colleagues: the reference group. This behaviour might be recognized informally and qualitatively as 'effort' (e.g. 'x tries really hard') and formally and more quantitatively as 'performance' (e.g. your performance over these past six months qualifies you for a bonus'). From our discussions with Japanese managers we concluded that these two observations are commonly confused: i.e. effort equals performance.

Fearing a negative outcome from appraisal (i.e. being caught 'breaking the rules'), many managers we spoke to appeared content for appraisals to be conducted on vague terms. Other more ambitious managers, or those who had 'stuck their neck out' with startling behaviour or interventions and suggestions for innovation relied more on the line-manager or (at a higher level of authority in the appraisal process) senior members of the HR department to recognize the strategic value-added of any non-conformist behaviour. Depending on the time and the place (e.g. senior management perceptions of the current strategic position of the organization), what we are calling 'non-conformist' appraisee behaviour may or may not be rewarded positively. We saw a negative experience of reward in the case of Hori-san in Chapter 5. He confesses to have lost trust in the appraisal procedures at his former company. Using Ouchi's terms (cited at the beginning of this section), Hori-san felt the outcome of subsequent appraisals was neither 'fair' nor commensurate (i.e. equitable) with the imaginative and constructive commitment he had shown towards the organization. He felt let down and exploited.

The line-manager/appraiser's view

As one respondent told us: 'If something needs saying, we can say it anytime, we don't need to arrange a special appraisal meeting. The real function of these formal meetings is to inform – but then this usually means confirm – to the HR department or other "higher ups" what bonuses a particular individual should get next time round.'

In more positive terms, performance appraisals were seen as an opportunity to praise and sing the praises (to other 'upstairs' managers) of particularly talented individuals. The danger in doing this, however, was that these talented individuals might then be relocated to another section or department, as happened to Miura-san soon after her induction (Chapter 4). Losing 'good' people in this way might weaken the line-manager group's ability to achieve their collective targets for the subsequent performance appraisal period. We did not hear evidence of appraisers deliberately downgrading their reports of employee performance in order to retain what they saw as key staff. However, we did hear the airing by some appraisees of suspicions that they had been treated in this way: Takeda-san (Chapter 2) was one such case.

Why did Takeda-san not ask for a transfer to another group? One reason is because her skills had become so specialized in one section that she would struggle to make (to her) satisfactory progress in another, particularly as a woman. Another reason is given by the inevitable dark side to trust: namely, loss of trust and (recalling the subjective aspect of performance appraisals) potential resentment on the part of the line-manager/appraiser and other members of the original group. In the context of lifetime employment, together with the traditional HRM techniques such as job rotation and *nemawashi*, there is considerable risk within the one organization of an individual appraisee disappointing or even making long-term 'enemies' of the line-manager and of the group members s/he leaves behind. In such circumstances it may be easier, as Takeda-san herself decided, to leave the organization and set off on new and unfamiliar career paths.

SECTION 4: THE 'TRUST DILEMMA'

One complaint among ambitious managers we interviewed was the extent to which they perceived that they as individuals could only progress by virtue of how well they could co-operate with their colleagues: 'People are different. Some people are lazy. Some people are ambitious. Why should the lazy ones slow down the talented ones?' We accept that such views are more likely to be aired with group outsiders than insiders (cf. Matsumoto, 2002; Box 1.2).

The most common complaint we heard from Japanese managers about appraisal was that 'we didn't get any direct feedback'. Another was 'we had the meeting and then maybe a long time later I would find out that I had done well or not well, but even then no specific details, just what was based on my appraisal record where (I was told) "I had made good progress". In the end it came down to the relationship between me and my line-manager' (Takeda-san).

Of course, such views and experiences are not limited to Japanese organizations. However, we did harbour an expectation that Japanese managers who had transferred from Japanese to international organizations would have a clearer view of their experience of performance appraisal and that they might find that the performance appraisal procedures they were experiencing now were more reliably 'objective'. Our expectation remained largely unfulfilled. What did generally appear more reliable and transparent was the nature of the outcome: the immediacy of a reward (e.g. in the next pay or bonus packet) and promotion (e.g. getting a higher position or being transferred to a more challenging and satisfying task); or, not least, in terms of organizational exit. As one business consultant told us: 'We know that there's a 10 per cent turnover of staff each year and we know that failing an appraisal (for performance) means the sack for about 5 per cent a year' though he couldn't specify how this figure became known – it was part of the folklore of this particular company or industry culture. The business consultant concluded: 'So, which 5 per cent goes because of a better job and which goes because they get sacked we don't know, unless they tell us.'

Trust and voice

We saw in Chapter 2 how high-context communication plays a key role in defining and sustaining the identity and authority of the reference group and so shaping each individual's experience of face. The Japanese equivalent of the English word 'trust' is formed by combining two *kanji*: one denoting 'human being' (person), and one for 'voice' or what a person says. Pronounced *shin*, this combined *kanji* appears in many company names, notably those in the financial sector – a kind of 'trust us' appeal that, as we discuss in Chapter 7, the Japanese financial sector currently badly needs. Accordingly, what people do or do not say is essential to understanding how far they should or should not be trusted. By this token, the performance appraisal process (like business negotiations discussed in Chapter 1) becomes significant at least as much for what is said – and not said – as for the discernible outcomes it generates.

Several managers we spoke to compared the context for performance appraisals to 'a kind of self-marketing exercise: you need to know who to impress, when, and how'. The recent emphasis given to self-appraisal identified by Kono and Clegg (2001; Box 6.3) adds further significance to this question, particularly in the current broader environment of increased job insecurity in Japan. Any informal definition of 'marketing' will make reference to the importance of effective communication, the perceived quality of information, the changing and fragile nature of image and perception. In the context of face and the reference group in a Japanese organization, 'self-marketing' becomes akin to self-regulation. By regulating one's behaviour – and not least what one says – one seeks to comply with expectations and so generate trust.

The typical open-plan office layout in Japanese organizations ensures that almost no personal or business communication is 'private'. This, over the long term, can be exhausting. Based on what managers tell us, the only sense of escape from this intense workplace monitoring and self-monitoring of communication may be found (in terms of space) at the coffee machine or water cooler, in the smokers' room or the rest rooms. Given the diffuse nature of Japanese work culture, the venue for 'off-the-record' talk is likely to be a local bar or restaurant with selected colleagues, and (in terms of time) usually late in the evening and after a ten- or twelve-hour working day and followed by a one- to three-hour commute.

The tradition of job-rotation for management track employees also generates a source of 'all-round' information about individual employees. For, although this form of promotion and development enhances the in-house career prospects of individuals while simultaneously advancing organizational learning (cf. Chapter 5), it also gives a series of line-managers in various departments the opportunity to view first-hand each management aspirant's potential and credentials. Their impressions will subsequently be communicated to HR staff.

A sense of crisis

A common individual response in times of crisis – corroborated by recent surveys (cf. Hakuhodo, 2000) – is increased reliance on the friendship and advice of close and trusted colleagues. Mikimura-san (cited at the end of Chapter 5) emphasized this point to us: her expressed loyalty was more towards her colleagues than her company. As another manager said to us in respect of formal performance appraisals: 'I know that our line-manager is himself under pressure. He's not sure where we're going. I appreciate his honesty in talking openly to us about the problems that our section and the organization are facing. But, in the end, this doesn't really encourage me in my own career prospects.'

In fact, in a period of heightened social and economic uncertainty, performance appraisals are becoming perceived as part of a process of job retention rather than performance improvement. We saw how, in generic terms, that performance appraisal should open up prospects of promotion. The current economic slowdown in Japan is stretching the credibility of this potential outcome. There is currently a 'backlog' of lower and middle-management incumbents from the growth years, meaningful promotion positions are becoming even more limited and so the balancing act for HR managers is becoming more precarious.

Some experts paint a fairly desolate picture. The numbers of 'phantom promotions' (i.e. fancy-sounding titles covering non-jobs) has probably been exhausted: there are estimates that 50 to 60 per cent of 'middle-manager' jobs in some firms are non-jobs (Pucik in Bird, 2002: 29), meaning a tremendous strain on resources of finance, and (not least) of trust in the system. Pucik further observes 'a culture in many Japanese firms today resembles more a mediocre and complacent planned economy bureaucracy than the fearless global competitor of the 1980s' (2002: 28).

Individualization

In the highly integrated structures of Japanese-style HRM, the impact goes further. The mood generated by many responses we received suggests a growing trend towards the *individualization* of views on performance appraisal and (by extension) other overlapping HRM processes such as organizational induction (Chapter 4), training and development (Chapter 5) and reward and promotion (Chapter 7). By 'individualization' we mean the growing emphasis given to individual (as opposed to collective) contexts for performance appraisal decisions (cf. Sparrow and Marchington, 1998).

Respondent comments quoted above such as 'I know our line-manager is himself under pressure' and 'Why should the lazy ones slow down the talented ones' illustrate (in our view) how 'individual differences come to the fore and HR practitioners become fixated with the lifestyle and personal motivation factors and the consequent need to realign and target HRM policies and practices to new realities of employee behaviour [. . .] Therefore we find a wider variety of [psychological] contracts' (Sparrow and Marchington, 1998: 133). As a result, established expectations and certainties are upset and a 'trust dilemma' arises.

In our research we registered how many managers were willing to admit asking themselves more frequently questions such as:

- What am I worth in comparison with my colleagues?
- What am I worth in comparison with managers on higher or lower salary scales to me?
- How do my bosses value my contribution? Do they think I 'fit in'?
- How do my friends and family really perceive my career progress and prospects?
- How do I perceive my own worth (i.e. self-esteem)?

Individual answers to these questions might emerge in discussion with trusted colleagues. Alternatively they may be gleaned by reference to organizational rumours or myths or what is reported in the media. Such sources of information – and often *mis*-information – form the context in which the individual makes a professional decision on whether to stay or go, feel good or despair. Overall, the fact that individuals are now concerning themselves more consistently with these questions suggest that trust in current promotion and reward systems and (by direct implication) performance appraisal systems is becoming challenged and probably also eroded.

In the broader context of Japanese-style HRM, the emergent trust dilemma puts traditional core values such as lifetime employment and seniority promotion in question. It also puts the third 'sacred treasure' of in-house or enterprise unions in a predicament. On the one hand, members of these unions are keen to be involved in sharing and supporting the positive outcomes for individual staff members. On the other they feel duty-bound to protect the interests of established members whose appraisal outcomes – over time – may worsen. As one union official confided to us: 'We find ourselves spending a lot more time protecting the interests of the lazy or inefficient employees [after appraisals] and so have less time to support the hard-working and ambitious ones.'

SECTION 5: REDEFINING TRUST

Cruise O'Brien (2001) gives a definition of 'trust' that emphasizes the individual as opposed to the social, collective or organizational perspective on trust, as outlined in Fukuyama's (2000) definition of trust cited above. For Cruise O'Brien 'trust' can be defined as an individual's 'confidence in the outcome of a situation'. In the context of face, individuals choose to behave in ways which they can confidently assume will match the expectations of the reference group. Based on feedback from members of the group (i.e. in a form of ongoing 'performance appraisal'), individuals learn over time to predict 'with confidence' what outcomes in which situations are preferred. By regulating his or her behaviour towards achieving predictable outcomes, the individual becomes 'trusted'. But what happens when the individual begins to lose confidence in the judgement of the group, or the means by which members of the group arrive at these judgements? What if the individual begins to recognize contexts or shifts in existing contexts which make the judgements and judgement-making procedures of the group or its dominant members appear increasingly redundant or irrelevant?

From an individual perspective, trust can be experienced not only as binding, but also as a *bind* on professional initiative and career development and expression, and for both the managers and the managed. In these terms it equates to attention to face acting as a constraint to individual choices of behaviour. The nature of face – and of trust – shifts when individuals themselves set criteria for a successful outcome: in other words, when they generate confidence by relying more on their sense of self-esteem than on the authoritative judgements of others.

Role models

The criteria for each individual's confidence in achieving successful outcomes (i.e. trust) will vary according to circumstances or to context. Consider and compare the following summaries of statements made recently by two leading Japanese sportsmen:

> You have to believe in yourself. You have to believe in your own skill and do what you think is right without paying too much attention to what other people think.

> This is a dream for me. But I hope that the people – the fans, my club, and my fellow team-members – will support me and not think that I have betrayed them. I need their support in 'pushing' me towards this decision. I have given ten years to this club [the Yomiuri Giants] but now it is time to fulfil my dream. I'm sorry.

The first summary of comments comes from Hidetoshi Nakata, the first Japanese footballer to make a lasting impact on European football (in Italy) in the mid-1990s. His comments were reported in an interview with

the UK *Financial Times* (18–19 May 2002) just before the summer FIFA
World Cup competition got underway. The second quote comes from
answers given by Hideki ('Godzilla') Matsui, star hitter of the Yomiuri
Giants baseball team, in response to questions reported in all Japanese
media at the weekend (1–2 November 2002) when he announced his
decision to leave the Giants and join a team in the US Major League.

When we compare the individuals involved we recognize that both are
men at the top of their respective sports in Japan. They are instantly
recognizable to all Japanese who follow sport (probably a majority) and
so feature in all forms of merchandising and endorsements. However, the
context for each individual's statement is very different. In an industrial
context (i.e. recognizing professional football as the massive and growing
global business it is), Nakata's decision in the mid-1990s to play football
in Europe was generally greeted with pride by Japanese football
supporters and public opinion: by his example, Nakata – the first Japanese
to rise to prominence overseas in 'the beautiful game' – could announce
to the world that Japanese football was coming of age (cf. Box 5.1).
He could act as role model and inspire other talented footballers and so
surely help the national team prepare for the forthcoming World Cup.
National pride (and face) was unbounded.

In contrast, Matsui already had a god-like status in Japanese baseball – a
sport in which the Yomiuri Giants are as good as it gets in terms of star
status and earnings or rewards. For him there was (in competitive sporting
terms) nowhere else to go in order to fulfil his dream – at least in the
context of Japanese baseball. As the story unfolded it appeared that his
supporters understood and vindicated his decision to leave for the North
American major leagues. Only his managers appeared dumbfounded and
resentful. Senior managers at the Giants said they spent long hours trying
to elicit from Matsui what it was he really wanted and so encourage or
persuade him to stay: 'What more could Matsui want?' they seemed to
ask.

Ironically, and a matter of days later, these same managers announced the
signing of a 'business agreement' with the New York Yankees. More
ironically, as Nakata's football star begins to wane the English footballer
David Beckham is beginning to supplant him in terms of advertising
exposure in Japan. Even more ironically, Beckham's football team in the
UK (Manchester United, a Yomiuri Giants equivalent in terms of recent
domestic dominance in their sport) arranged a business and
merchandising understanding with the New York Yankees earlier in 2002.

A large measure of face was saved all round when, subsequently, Matsui did in fact join the New York Yankees.

Looking at the social and industrial context, the industry that Nakata works/plays in (professional football) is already internationalized in the Japanese psyche: his move to Europe is seen as advancing national pride and face. In contrast, Matsui's comments display the doubt and nervousness of the first high-profile mover: his shift to the US Major League will diminish the domestic game and so in his comments he appears instinctively to seek collective approval for his decision to look for more than his industry in Japan can currently offer for his talents. Nakata appears confident in appealing to his own sense of self-esteem, while Matsui still seeks approval from the reference group. In this way the globalization of an industry (professional sport) can be seen to impact on the complexity of the motivations and aspirations of the players (i.e. individuals and organizations and teams) within it. Simultaneously, it can be seen how the media and the nebulous notion of 'popular opinion' operate in defining the context for interpreting and responding to the opportunities and challenges that globalization appears to generate. Individual Japanese managers in all industries are no less vulnerable to social and industrial trends, together with media-driven constructs of 'popular opinion' or 'success'.

'Individualistic management'

Watanabe (in Hasegawa and Hook, 1998) refers to the 'formation of individualistic management' in Japanese HRM to describe systems which aim 'to deal with employees according to their desire for personal growth' and 'satisfy their inclinations, independence, needs, aspirations, occupational consciousness and value systems' (1998: 174). One thinks of Matsui's 'dream', cited above. One is also struck by the contrast between individuals feeling bound to regulate their behaviour and their emotions 'to fit into the organization' [or reference group, as described in Chapter 2] to a 'system that acknowledges that people are different individuals and attempts to foster a wide range of independent individuals within it' (Watanabe, 1998: 174).

In our interviews, enlightened Japanese HR managers – who may or may not be working in enlightened Japanese organizations – recognize this and claim that this is what has made their organizations strong: in other words, a management of diversity which is based on a shared foundation in hard work and trust in one's fellow employees. We saw in Chapter 2 how 'reference groups', in order to be effective, rely on a combination of mixed attributes and talents (cf. Matsumoto, 2002). What appears to have changed, however, is the emphasis given to the individual in assessing what 'hard work' and 'trust' are rather than relying on received definitions of these (e.g. in the form of 'tradition' or the way things are/have always been done around here). The 'individual' in this case may be the manager; or may be the subordinate, regardless of ascribed authority according to age or rank. Increasingly, the priority is to get the job done; and the outcome that saves face is the job done effectively rather than done with obvious effort.

Box. 6.4 Corporate whistle-blowing in Japan

One act that throws into extreme and critical light Fukuyama's (2000) definition of trust as 'avoiding opportunistic behaviour' is the act of corporate whistle-blowing. It is still rare in Japan: to blow the whistle on fellow insiders makes one a company 'traitor'. Being rare, it is important to refer to context in explaining why it does (and doesn't) happen. Nakata (2002) writes about the 'courage' needed by employees who risk 'vulnerability to retaliatory mistreatment by their employers' in order to 'spill the beans' on corporate wrongdoing in Japan. Nakata cites the case of Horoaki Kushioka, 'a 56-year-old employee of a trucking firm [who] was moved to a small isolated room far from the headquarters [and] given neither specific tasks nor promotion for 28 years'. This was because he exposed a price-fixing cartel involving his company. According to Nakata's article, the company exerted pressure on Kushioka, his family and his relatives, but he refused to leave the firm. In his own words: 'I was confident that I had done nothing wrong. This gave me courage.'

Belatedly and just short of his retirement, Kushioka decided to sue his employers, demanding 'an official apology' and compensation. Nearing retirement, Kushioka's context has changed: he needs the money. Second, the opportunity to tell his story to the press has changed: these stories are now more widely regarded as news in Japan rather than something to be ignored or kept quiet.

The Japanese government and other civil society agencies are pushing for increased protection for corporate whistle-blowers, and companies have (formally, at least) begun to comply by setting up mechanisms for protecting corporate whistle-blowers from internal retaliation and discrimination. As Japanese organizations become more sensitive to external shareholder value and the threat of public loss of face and compensation costs (trends we discuss in Chapter 7), the context for corporate whistle-blowing is likely to change further.

Summary

In this chapter we have explored the central importance of trust in informing the human resources relationship and the 'psychological contract' in Japanese organizations. Specifically we have considered the role of trust in shaping the expected procedures and outcomes of performance appraisals. Within the context of a changing strategic environment for Japanese organizations we have identified a shift in expectations of performance appraisal and concomitantly, a shift in the emphasis given to the experience and expectations of trust from collective to more individualized perceptions. We have discussed this shift from an international perspective and in terms of 'individualization' and a 'trust dilemma' between organizations and ambitious managers, making a case study of leading figures from the Japanese sports industry. In Chapter 7 we continue to develop an understanding of changes in Japanese-style HRM from an international perspective.

Questions for reflection:

1 How relevant has your experience of performance appraisals been in:

- motivating and/or helping you to work more effectively?
- motivating you to trust your career development to your line-manager(s)/employer?

2 How do you account for the relative success/failure of performance appraisal to motivate you in these ways?

7 Regaining confidence

Introduction

> Japan has lost confidence in itself.
> (Japanese Prime Minister Koizumi to US President Bush
> cited in *The Economist* 23 February 2002))

At the end of the last millennium, Prime Minister Junichiro Koizumi was elected on a wave of popular desire for political and economic reform. From a broad international perspective, Koizumi's arrival on the ritually conservative political scene in Japan prompted comparisons with the 'third way' blend of social and economic reform popularized during the late 1990s by President Clinton in the USA and by Prime Minister Blair (UK) and Chancellor Schroeder (Germany). As we write, Koizumi's reform project appears to be stuttering against some entrenched opposition. Nonetheless, there is now an open public debate on what should and should not be changed, not least in comparison with international (i.e. non-Japanese) trends.

In Chapter 3 we looked at common experiences of the socialization process in Japan: essentially, we looked at what it meant to 'be Japanese'. In Chapters 5 and 6 we identified a number of significant shifts in values informing the employment or psychological contract between Japanese organizations and their more ambitious managers: e.g. *individualization*. We saw how these shifts in values have international (e.g. European) parallels. In this chapter we further examine the extent to which internationalization appears to be impacting on core values in Japanese-style HRM; specifically, on how individual managers experience performance-related rewards such as *pay* and *promotion*. We also explore the challenge of managing *diversity* in Japan, illustrating some current problems of linking rewards and promotion to the management of *research and development* (R&D).

Our objectives for this chapter are:

● to explore the impact of international practice and global standards on the experience of Japanese-style management, specifically on perceptions and expectations inherent in the management of rewards and promotion;

● to illustrate some of the constraining factors to reform of these HRM processes in Japan, and give examples of Japanese companies and individuals who have managed to overcome these constraints.

SECTION 1: REWARDS – PAY AND PROMOTION

> The younger generation [of Japanese managers] are increasingly less likely to accept certain current values, such as seniority-based promotion, and are equally likely to press for greater financial reward based on performance and merit.
>
> (Kakabadse *et al.*, 1996: 149)

Rewards (sometimes termed *compensation*) for work done can be experienced and implemented in many forms. Examples include: pay or remuneration (e.g. a cash bonus or a salary rise); praise (e.g. a 'thank you' from the boss or from colleagues); more interesting work (i.e. assuming senior managers know what you might find interesting);

promotion (e.g. a new job title); more responsibility (e.g. training new recruits, or having your own client portfolio); time off *in lieu* (e.g. extra holidays or permission to leave work earlier); or perhaps something symbolic such as a new 'internationalized' business card (e.g. with a translation on the back).

The perceived value of a reward is defined by the culture-specific context of the industry, the organization, or the relevant reference group: rewards distinguish themselves in having value *in comparison with* established norms and expectations. For example, some industries such as sales or brokering may tend to emphasize pay rewards while retail sectors may prefer to offer time off. In discussing rewards we also need to consider the systematic withholding of rewards: a situation sometimes referred to as *sanctions*. Sanctions emphasize the control function of managing rewards: 'Do as we expect and we will reward you accordingly.'

Pay

In terms of pay, most Japanese employees receive salaries in the form of regular monthly transfers of money to an individual bank account by the payroll section of the HRM department. Pay also includes the significant and usually twice-yearly bonuses. The level of salary is usually fixed according to rank. Bonuses are managed more flexibly and can be supplemented by other benefits, such as travel or accommodation subsidies, expense accounts (cf. Brown, Nakata and Ulman, 1997); and even gifts (cf. Herbig, 1998)

Kono and Clegg's (2001: 268) overview of a typical 'salary schedule' for employees in a Japanese organization shows that the year-on-year salary increments are predictable and encourage long-term commitment. In an organizational context, these increments are traditionally graded to facilitate the management of competition between *doki* group members: e.g. through appraisals where the outcome is a ranking (cf. Box 6.3). In a broader socio-cultural context, salary increments are phased or graded to reflect the 'normal' lifestyle choices of upwardly mobile and committed (predominantly male) employees: finding accommodation; buying suitable clothes; buying gifts; finding a wife or husband; getting married; having, bringing up and educating children; preparing for retirement.

Bonuses

The twice-yearly bonuses give managers and their organizations more scope to reward staff on an individualized basis. In Chapter 2 we illustrated how this dual pay/reward system allowed senior managers the flexibility in rewarding specific performance as opposed to tenure without *explicitly* upsetting the traditional expectations of seniority or causing loss of face (cf. Box 2.2). In this sense, bonus systems allow managers to reward staff not only for 'fitting in' but also for working productively, regardless of age or rank or relative status. Starting salaries in Japanese organizations tend to be relatively low – though 'relatively low' in Japan still means relatively high in a global comparison. The differentiation between highest and lowest earners is also relatively narrow, putting more emphasis on the bonus system. The Japan Institute of Labour regularly publishes data on average salary levels in Japan.

The pace of salary increments is slow but more or less assured. In times of low business growth, it is the bonuses and other reward perks (such as travelling and entertainment subsidies) which disappear first (as in western organizations) or overtime goes unpaid. Also, if employees join a company 'late' or in some other unorthodox way, they are likely to miss out initially on bonuses and other benefits. Recently (February 2003), unemployment in Japan has matched a post-war record high (5.5 per cent) while pay in 2001 fell on average by nearly 2 per cent. The situation is fluctuating and uncertain.

Exit bonuses

The real 'pay off' for years of loyal commitment comes in the form of exit bonuses. Depending on the industry and organization, the normal retirement age is fifty-five to sixty, but there are sufficient exceptions to these parameters that it makes more sense to take a case-by-case perspective. In view of rising unemployment, health and pension costs in a working population which is simultaneously ageing and shrinking rapidly, senior managers increasingly rely on massive (and tax efficient) 'exit bonuses' which constitute several years of final salary. The prospect of the exit bonus thus reinforces the benefits of staying loyal to one company (cf. Ito, 1992). However, near-retirement managers constitute (from an organizational perspective) a considerable financial burden.

The slow progress of salary increments tests the patience of younger and aspiring managers (i.e. those aged in their mid-twenties to mid-thirties) who have yet to accrue sufficient service or 'commitment points' to enjoy the high salaries of senior managers. These managers can resemble 'hostages' to a system structured for the benefit of seniors (cf. Kay, 1993). It is easier for organizations to 'off-load' ageing women employees as wives are traditionally expected to take on responsibility (giving up work and career, if necessary) for the husband's parents in old age. State-funded facilities for care of children and the elderly are still rare in Japan (Ohta, 1998).

The notion of a government-funded retirement pension (e.g. from age sixty-five) is not prominent in Japanese society – at least, not among the salaried 'elite' (cf. Box 4.2). State-funded pensions exist, but appear most commonly regarded as a last resort insurance: in other words, a potential loss of face after a lifetime of loyal commitment. We spoke to near-retirement managers who claimed they would rather rely on their family than on government 'hand-outs'. Against this background, we found that many older managers feared *risutora* – an imported term for 'organizational restructuring', and all the more threatening (it seems) because of its foreign origin. As in western organizations, 'restructuring' threatens enforced redundancy or early retirement. The dilemma for HR and senior line-managers is to decide whether to shed the least loyal or the least productive staff: the categories do not necessarily overlap.

Promotion

According to Hannagan (1998: 326): 'Apart from improvements in pay and conditions of work, the most immediate incentives available to employees are opportunities for promotion. If the organization has trained its staff adequately and ensured that employees' work experiences are sufficiently wide, internal promotion should be feasible . . . Prospects of promotion represent significant motivators.'

Promoting an employee is essentially an expression of trust. As with sanctions, a systematic withdrawal of promotion prospects is likely to represent a significant *de*-motivator for ambitious managers. Conversely, it is not usual for staff officially to 'skip' ranks on their way up the promotion ladder: it is easier to create a new job title for them (cf. Box 2.2). As outlined in Chapter 6, the years of steady business growth in Japan saw a concomitant inflation in staff promotions with the result that even today many Japanese companies still have a range of middle- and senior management positions (vice-'this' or deputy-'that') whose effective responsibility goes little further than carrying a *meishi* with the title (cf. Pucik, in Bird, 2002).

The relative value of rewards

In considering the perceived value of rewards (i.e. the question: 'what's it worth to me / us / them?') we need to consider a multiple of perspectives and expectations, including information about international comparisons (cf. Brown, Nakata and Ulman, 1997). Kovach (1987) presented a classic study in this field which showed how very often senior managers expected staff to want only more money when the staff members themselves preferred more interesting work or even just respect (cf. Box 6.2). Expectations based on culture-specific values are key variables; as is time. For example, a pay bonus may satisfy a manager who is facing severe short-term debt but who, in the long term, actually values enhanced promotion prospects more highly. We have seen how Japanese-style HRM traditionally prefers the longer-term option.

A mismatch between what employer and employees value in terms of reward usually reflects a lack of cultural cohesion within the organization and/or poor intra-organizational communications. The management and negotiation of the meaning of rewards thus becomes a key responsibility of HR managers and line-managers through formal or (given the significance of the time variable) ongoing and informal performance appraisal and feedback promotion systems (cf. Chapter 6). Reward management (and HRM generally) in Japanese organizations is assumed to operate informed by a remarkable degree of shared values. Kakabadse *et al.* (1996, cited above) suggest this cohesion may be increasingly challenged, above all from a younger generation of Japanese managers.

The impatience of younger managers

Why younger managers? Perceptions of time and accumulated 'reward points' are key. Traditional reward systems in Japan tend to be incremental, long-term and not least predictable and relatively transparent, particularly in comparison with many western organizations. Length of service is uniform and so non-negotiable: you either have the years behind you or you do not. Negotiable is the perceived quality or adjudged strategic value of an employee's service to the organization. HR and line-managers by means of the reward systems they set up and operate are in a position to open or foreclose these negotiations. If (in a performance appraisal discussion) manager 'x' claims to be doing 'more useful work' than manager 'y' (who's on a higher salary), the appraiser in question will decide whether this line of discussion (or accusation) is appropriate or relevant.

Under normal circumstances it would not be. Traditionally, Japanese employees are judged by how well they co-operate with their peers. Notions such as 'performance' and 'achievement' take on meaning by sharing information with one's colleagues; together they create the context for rewards (cf. Chapter 1). Ostensibly, a 'good' performance is measured against an organizational or industrial standard, and not against other members of staff. This convention releases individual line-managers from (formally, at least) having to respond to individualized challenges about what constitutes 'good' or 'useful' work. However, and as we saw in Chapter 6, comparisons between employees *are* in fact made and comparative scores *are* given (Box 6.3). Faced by the opaqueness of these procedures, individual employees are left with the choice of trusting in current procedures and being patient in anticipation of due rewards, or seeking out their own career path and rewards.

Global/local sources of tension

The tension therefore appears to be focused on interpretations of *achievement* and *ascription*, as presented in the Trompenaars and Hampden-Turner (1998) or 'TH-T model' discussed in Chapter 3. This tension directly challenges the 'seniority promotion' tradition in Japanese-style HRM (one of the so-called 'three treasures'). This represents an *ascriptive* value in that it is based on given status. In strategic HRM terms it promises stability and transparency and (so, together) predictability, given that the criteria refer to absolute measures such as age, length of service and (not least) gender. Any inefficiencies in terms of individual productivity/reward ratios could be tolerated and resourced where there was (1) continued long-term business growth, and (2) high and sustained levels of individual commitment and motivation from core staff and (3) high and sustained levels of individual commitment and motivation from individuals excluded from the benefits of seniority promotion, such as women and perhaps graduates of lower-ranking universities.

As illustrated through the course of our discussion so far, these three conditions no longer generally apply; or, at least, the growing perception is that Japanese HR and line-managers can no longer rely on them with confidence. Simultaneously, ambitious managers and employees appear less confident that HRM outcomes relating to processes such as 'seniority promotion' will benefit them in the short or even long term – an observation which led us (in Chapter 6) to re-assess our definition of 'trust' (cf. Cruise O'Brien, 2001). How each side *responds* to this problem or dilemma is indicative of their culture-specific experience and expectations (cf. Chapter 1). Insofar as one or both sides begin to respond in unfamiliar ways, we can talk about a shift in culture: or collectively, a change in the face of Japanese management.

In short, between the managers and the managed a local and unfamiliar tension has arisen, of which internationalized trends such as individualization, increasing loss of patience, and the emerging 'trust dilemma' (cf. Chapters 4, 5 and 6) may be regarded (i.e. for practical HRM purposes and in a time of fluctuating emotions and expectations) as both symptom and cause. We return to this theme in Chapter 8.

SECTION 2: MANAGING DIVERSITY

> Money and talent go and remain where they are treated well, and governments and businesses in the 21st century should realize this.
>
> (Foong, 1999)

Watanabe (1998) suggests four areas of challenge to established HRM systems in Japan:

- diversification in human resources being employed;
- diversification in recruitment;
- diversification in working styles, time and places;
- diversification in career courses.

> (Watanabe, in Hasegawa and Hook, 1998: 104)

The emerging scenario challenging existing HRM and (ultimately) reward structures in progressive Japanese organizations comprises 'a wide range of people of different age groups, gender, experience and nationality' (Watanabe, 1998: 104) needed to fill the talent deficit that increasing numbers of Japanese organizations are currently experiencing. This talent may be recruited through agencies on a short-term contract basis: these people will therefore skip the organization's culture-specific induction procedures. Increasingly, these and other core staff may be working part-time or at a distance (e.g. home-based working), thus further eroding established time–space parameters for cultural cohesion within the organization and/or the remit of individual line-managers. Where these 'interlopers' have and express strategically value-adding skills that the line-manager and his/her 'regular' core staff do not have, tensions arise that might serve to undermine the credibility of established ways of doing things. We recall the potential impact of *kikokushijo* on the value-laden authority of the Japanese education system (Box 3.5).

Hayafuji-san

Hayafuji-san represents what Watanabe (1998) identified as increased 'diversity' in terms of 'career courses' or the extent to which 'employees are encouraged to select for themselves a career course in line with their individual preference' (1998: 104). In Hayafuji-san's case, he had the confidence and opportunity to express this preference within the boundaries of an industry rather than within one organization.

Hayafuji-san had left his job at a major Japanese investment bank to join a French bank newly established in Tokyo. He was headhunted and is representative of a trend, if not in choice of action then at least in terms of aspiration among ambitious and 'free-thinking' Japanese managers. As Bird (2002: 399) states: 'The presence [in Japan] of Western firms, which no longer suffer a stigma as unstable employers, has served to amplify the different options open to new recruits: fast versus slow promotion, performance versus tenure.'

Hayafuji-san is in his early thirties and recently married. His wife's work takes her on frequent overseas trips so the long hours he routinely works (e.g. dining with major clients in addition to the twenty-four hour tracking of global markets) can be accommodated (he tells us) within his current personal circumstances.

Why did he quit the Japanese bank? 'I had a good job and an ok boss but the prospects of real promotion seemed too distant'. And now in the French bank?

Well, my promotion prospects are actually worse! All the senior jobs are taken by French [nationals]. I also didn't realize how 'snobbish' they are about which university you went to – just like in Japan. But in the French bank we're paid based on performance. I work hard; I get paid well. At the moment this arrangement suits our [he and his wife's] lifestyle. We'll save enough money to buy a flat and then think about starting a family. Maybe then I'll switch to a job with better promotion prospects.

How does he feel about his career prospects?

Good. The way we work [in the French bank] means I'll get better experience and qualifications more quickly than if I'd stayed in a Japanese bank. We specialize more: we work in teams on projects and I have my own portfolio of clients. I can see how I'm becoming more specialized. I know when I'm doing a good job as I can read the results – I don't need someone to tell me. The reporting lines [in the French bank] are clear, and not much different from my experience in the other [Japanese] bank. We work in English. But I know I'm not going to get to the top of this bank [where French is spoken]. This means I can just focus on doing what I know I do best and getting better at doing it.

Returning to O'Brien's definition of 'trust' – namely, that 'trust' is defined by an individual's 'confidence in the outcome of a situation' – we can conclude from Hayafuji-san's comments that he is confident about both the short- and long-term benefits of his current situation. Rather than concerning himself too much about promotion and a career in the context of one organization, he senses a degree of individual control over immediate outcomes (e.g. pay and bonuses) and longer-term outcomes such as skills which will enhance his future employability. This attitude, following Torrington and Hall (1998: 451), is the essence of the 'new' psychological contract (cf. Chapters 5 and 6). Hayafuji-san expects his situation to change. Simultaneously, he expects his attitude to his situation to change. But he and his wife see opportunities in change and so remain optimistic.

New problem areas in Japanese HRM

Hayafuji-san's attitude would very likely present a disruptive challenge to HR practitioners in 'traditional' Japanese organizations, unless these practitioners themselves took a more relaxed and internationalized view on such individual talents (cf. Suenaga-san, cited below). But, in times of tension and change, how traditional is 'traditional'?

Kono and Clegg (2001) have identified a series of 'new problem areas' in Japanese-style management. These include 'casualization' (e.g. the recruitment of short-term contract employees offering specific skills) and 'outsourcing' (e.g. transferring some customer service functions to call centres). These trends are already well established in western employment contexts (cf. Andersson, 1993; Sparrow and Marchington, 1998; Sparrow and Hiltrop, 1994).

Kono and Clegg also highlight a 'problem area' that challenges a fundamental value in traditional Japanese-style HRM: namely, the increasingly flexible interpretation of 'lifetime employment' (cf. Box 5.1). Increasing numbers of Japanese managers are being encouraged to take early retirement. They are either being 'bought off' with 'an increased retirement allowance of more than one month's pay per year of tenure' (2001: 270) or being offered special training (in the form of a 'career development holiday scheme') in order to facilitate their transfer to another organization. 'At the age of 60 all employees are encouraged to retire [or] find work with an affiliated or unaffiliated company' (2001: 272).

Hasegawa (1998) also sees parallels between the challenges that HR managers are facing in Japanese organizations and those faced by managers in European organizations. As Hasegawa explains, this challenge to local traditions and expectations arises as a logical consequence of globalization processes that either impinge uninvited (e.g. in the form of advances in information communications technology) or are actively sought out by Japanese companies who respond to global pressures by making a strategic choice to become more multi-national. Returning to our discussion of the 'TH-T model' in Chapter 3, we can recognize that the impact of globalization on 'local' attitudes to time and the environment may be regarded as increasingly standardized: examples include the impact of pollution and the real-time sharing of global market information. Much more 'local' are the *responses* to the 'problems' generated by these global pressures (cf. Chapter 1); both collectively (e.g. at the level of the nation, of industries and of organizations) and individually (e.g. in the perception and experience of individual managers).

Implications: a case study from the Japanese pharmaceuticals industry

These trends threaten to undermine traditional structures and values, particularly with regard to rewards and promotion (cf. Ariga *et al*., 2000; Sato, 2000). Part of the impact is illustrated by comments made to us by one senior HR manager who had spent his career working in the Japanese pharmaceuticals industry.

Suenaga-san

Suenaga-san is an HR manager in his early fifties. He has worked all his life in one of the higher-ranking Japanese pharmaceuticals companies. To begin with we asked him to describe the context for HRM given by the pharmaceuticals industry in Japan:

The Japanese pharmaceuticals industry

The Japanese pharmaceuticals industry was set up primarily to serve the domestic market – after the USA, the second largest in the world. Japanese producers have traditionally been shielded against non-Japanese competition by government-led price and quality controls together with the strength of relations between these companies and the Japanese doctors and health officials. Japanese producers were allowed (by domestic law) to copy drugs developed overseas. According to Roehl (in Bird 2002: 360) they did this 'merely by altering the process in making the pharmaceuticals'. The industry typically requires massive R&D investment: 10 to 20 per cent of sales revenue is the average and a ten-year development period for bringing new products to market is normal.

HRM policies were geared to steady and predictable growth. However, the strategic context for HRM in the Japanese pharmaceuticals industry is changing rapidly. Under pressure to reduce healthcare costs and speed up drug development (e.g. in response to a rapidly ageing population), the Japanese government has begun to reduce entry barriers to (lower-cost) foreign competition. Meanwhile, the industry has become distinguished by a series of large-scale mergers and acquisitions: GlaxoSmithKline (GSK) is one example. It is also becoming increasingly globalized, with

US American companies controlling over 40 per cent of the global market. The drive to survive is now (more than ever) focused on securing R&D and other strategic resources in order to bring the next 'blockbuster' product to market. Some Japanese pharmaceutical companies have tried mergers, but often unsuccessfully on account of clashes between company cultures and leaders: 'we are just not used to such strategic moves.'

Japanese pharmaceutical companies tend to be much smaller than their major international competitors. Furthermore, they tend to be undercapitalized and consequently vulnerable to foreign predators. Giant western MNCs such as (US) Pfizer and (Swiss) Novartis are already acquiring strategic shares in Japanese companies, hoping to acquire Japanese R&D and market share.

Suenaga-san's view

We asked Suenaga-san how recent global developments in the industry were impacting on his HRM activity, particularly in respect of promotion and reward. He explained how

> the style of management in our company has tended to be extremely conservative: very Japanese. Our top managers know the industry very well but do not feel confident about dealing with aggressive foreign competitors. But we know we will have to deal with them more. For example, we have brought in extra English language training: one hour of 'TOEIC' [examination preparation] classes each week. We know that some managers and employees will leave us, but we hope the talented ones will stay. We cannot yet offer better promotion prospects. But we can offer more interesting work, together with overseas experience. For example, we have set up a partnership with a distribution company in the United States. Our best 'monitors' [staff who liaise on drug sales and development with hospitals and doctors] have the chance to spend six months working in the USA. Some will leave us eventually, but others will see senior openings becoming available as more senior managers take early retirement.

And what about his own prospects? 'I'm confident. I think our company is strong enough to do well in the global market but in a "Japanese way". We may not have – or not have *yet* – the entrepreneurial drive of our US American and European competitors, but we have some good quality products coming up and I think we have time to adapt to the new markets. I'm sorry we are losing some good people. But we have enough good people to keep the company strong.' And autonomous? 'We'll see. I'm optimistic.'

We asked Suenaga-san whether the loss of these 'good people' could be arrested by reforming pay and promotion structures in his organization: for example, by extending the system of merit-based pay bonuses in addition to existing salary scales. Suenaga-san recognized that merit-based pay structures would at some time become the norm, as in other globalized industries (cf. Matsushita and Toshiba, cited below). However, he considers his organization to be still 'too conservative' for a radical restructuring at this time, calculating that the 'shock' of switching wholesale to merit-based pay and promotion structures would have a negative impact on motivation and productivity among current core staff. 'Perhaps if we're taken over by a foreign firm, we will have no choice but to accept a new system'.

SECTION 3: CONSTRAINTS TO MANAGING DIVERSITY

In Chapter 2 we spoke about 'face' as a means for describing and explaining – and perhaps even predicting – the constraints to individual decision-making in the context of Japanese management culture. We saw that face works at different levels: i.e. national, industrial, organizational; as well as individual. In this chapter – where one of our themes is the internationalization of Japanese management culture – we can identify and illustrate similar levels of constraint to the decision-making abilities of Japanese managers as they struggle both to adapt to global pressures and to manage diversity at local levels. In this and the following sections in this chapter we illustrate the nature of some of these constraints and conclude that there are sufficient grounds for confidence.

Constraints at the national level

> At the moment, Japan Inc is run by a group of old men who play golf together. The crunch for them – and so for Japan – will come when the cross-shareholding of Japanese blue chip companies comes increasingly under international ownership.
>
> (senior business analyst, Tokyo, 2002)

This comment represents a 'down-to-earth' view on analyses developed previously by Schaede (1995) and others. In November 2002 Prime Minister Koizumi's government published its report 'No Reform, No Growth: Part Two'. The title may suggest a Hollywood blockbuster sequel, but the behind-the-scenes wheeling and dealing associated with it (on golf courses and elsewhere) is very Japanese (cf. Box 2.5).

An editorial in *The Japan Times* (8 November 2002) puts the latest government reform attempts in context and reiterates in a generally supportive tone what 'must be done' as a matter of urgency to lift Japan from its economic lethargy:

- address the bad-loan issue: major Japanese banks have to clean up their act in order to become internationally credible (cf. Box 7.1);
- move people, goods and money smoothly from low-productive to high-productive sectors;
- improve corporate governance, focusing on efficiency;
- promote research and development.

The fact that the current Japanese government is being exhorted to undertake action is a legacy of its predecessors' heavy complicity in shaping and nurturing the current industrial landscape in Japan (cf. Johnson, 1985). The *Japan Times* editorial concludes as follows: 'That the Japanese-style managerial system must change also goes without saying. Here again, the real question is specifically what should be done to upgrade the outdated system.'

Box 7.1 The Japanese banking system

When the Yamaichi Securities bank – one of Japan's biggest and oldest – finally collapsed in 1997 (the government had previously bailed it out in 1964), its senior managers publicly wept their apologies on Japanese and international television. They had let down their customers and their employees. They had let down Japan.

The Japanese banking system emerged from the *ie* of merchant families during the pre-Meiji period (cf. Chapter 3). Their exchange houses became the banks at the core of the *zaibatsu* family business groups that, until the end of World War Two, controlled economic life in modern Japan (cf. Aoki and Patrick, 1994; Scher, 1996). The *keiretsu* networks (discussed in this chapter) that succeeded *zaibatsu*, maintained the structure of being organized around core banks.

The central Bank of Japan (BOJ), modelled on the nineteenth-century German *Reichsbank*, was re-chartered in 1952 under US American occupation on the condition that most of its power was transferred to a Ministry of Finance (MOF). MOF civil servants have thus overseen Japan's miraculous economic development since the 1950s and continue to wield enormous influence in the allocation of government funds (cf. Box. 2.3).

The boom years of Japanese exports were concentrated in capital-intensive industries, e.g. automobiles and electronics (cf. Kawahara, 1998). The MOF and banks together pursued a policy of supporting companies even when they were (by international standards) failing: a so-called 'convoy system' which would slow or adjust to allow the weakest to catch up. The system promoted social cohesion by avoiding mass redundancies, but also reinforced the view that, given time, even failing companies come good.

In any global comparison, the Japanese banking sector is massive. Bank holdings of cash and deposits (above all family savings accounts) in Japan run at double the levels of those in the UK and the USA *combined*. The Post Office savings bank in Japan represents the world's biggest singly managed fund (cf. Scher and Yoshino, 2002). Japanese people traditionally save in order to cover the costs of their children's education, weddings, and their own retirement. As many prices continue to fall and the bank rates hover around zero (December 2002), there is little incentive to withdraw savings and spend. As share prices continue to fall, many savers are switching to gold. As one respondent proclaimed: 'Japan is still the world's biggest creditor nation. The USA is the world's biggest debtor nation. The difference? Credibility, based on national self-confidence.'

The Japanese banking sector has traditionally offered graduates the prospect of lifetime employment with high salaries, bonuses and social status. Recently the Japanese sector has come into some disrepute, so some international banks in Japan are taking on this status. For a comprehensive discussion of Japan's banking system see Tsutsui (1999).

Global standards

> In the age of globalism the world is reduced to only one marketplace, which means there is just one set of rules. No longer can Asia afford to indulge in an 'Asian way' when it comes to business.
>
> (Backman, 1999)

From an individual perspective, 'the nation' exists as a perception. Its boundaries are encountered and experienced in the shape of institutions (e.g. schools and universities, city halls and other bureaucracies) and through the media (e.g. as a shape on a weather map or a set of economic statistics such as GDP). Equally, the perception and experience of globalization is transmitted in large part by news and other information media.

Currently, Japanese government and business management circles appear obsessed by abstract reference to 'global standards'. This reference is part of an agenda, particularly on the part of political and economic 'reformists'. Reference to 'global standards appears to have two main functions: first, to indicate what has 'gone wrong' with 'Japan Inc.' (cf. Backman – cited above); second, to express nostalgia and a determination to recapture something of the heady days when Japanese-style 'alliance capitalism' appeared triumphant (cf. Gerlach, 1993; Sakakibara, 1993).

Referring to 'global standards' has become a rallying cry for those whose intention is to reform traditional practices in 'big' Japanese business: e.g. corporate governance, financial accounting and measurement of corporate performance. Applying 'global' (i.e. as opposed to 'local') standards should make these more transparent and thereby internationally credible and attractive to investors. In practical terms it means recognizing that the main task for managers is to reconcile the interests of 'primary participants' in determining the strategic direction and performance of their organization (Monks and Minow, 1989; OECD, 1997a).

'No company is too big to fail'

This statement has been attributed to Heizo Takenaka, Prime Minister Koizumi's new state minister in charge of financial affairs in an interview with an American *Newsweek* magazine reporter in October 2002. Tanaka is an academic rather than a hardline LDP *apparatchik* (cf. Box 2.5). As a 'club outsider' he can say some of the things that an insider might not dare to. He has since described the nation's financial system as being 'in the middle of a grave illness' (IHT/*Asahi Shimbun* online, accessed 9 January 2003). The thrust of the statement about 'no company being too big to fail' is a warning that whatever its size or past glories no Japanese organization or institution (including the BOJ) is immune from the need to reform and adapt to the new global economic and strategic business environments. The days when Japan's *keiretsu* structures and attitudes were a source of global competitive advantage are gone (cf. Helou, 1991). Indeed, the current view among international (i.e. Japanese and non-Japanese) experts is that the residue of these attitudes and structures is stifling new strategic business growth (cf. Porter *et al.*, 2000).

Schadenfreude?

In discussing 'global standards' with Japanese managers, we kept returning to mention of Japan's relationship to the USA. In Chapter 3 we saw how the Japanese defeat at the end of World War Two was compounded – from the perspective of national loss of face – by a period of occupation which dictated the restructuring of basic industries (cf. Box 7.1) together with a restructuring of Japanese society: namely, the drawing up of a new (de-militarized) constitution; the promotion of a kind of belated post-feudal land reform; and (of perhaps more lasting impact) the imposition of a US American-style national education system. Any pre-war European-style models were largely eradicated. Against this background, it is easy to understand the sense of national pride fostered by watching regenerated Japanese companies penetrating US markets in the 1970s and 1980s. Similarly, we can imagine why the managers who started their professional careers during this period (approximately half of our sample) naturally refer to Japan's relationship to the USA in expressing their sense of 'being Japanese' (cf. Chapter 3).

By the same token, we should be able to understand something of the sense of disappointment or 'betrayal' (to quote one particularly irate respondent) generated by the current state (2002–03) of US-driven 'global standards' in, for example, the context of corporate accounting and governance. As one respondent told us: 'They [US politicians and business analysts] said our accounting standards weren't good enough. They repeatedly talked down our credit ratings. They said our global business successes were based on easy credit and bad debt. Then we read about Enron and WorldCom and the rest and we ask ourselves: "OK, so we were cheating. But now we find out that they've been cheating too." Whose "standards" are we supposed to believe now?'

Japan-bashing?

There is a strong sense of 'Japan-bashing' in the western media. We were referred to several headlines appearing in the London-based *Economist* magazine regularly over the past few years: e.g. 'Sad Japan' or 'The land that time forgot'. We pointed out that *The Economist* and others had taken to calling Germany the 'sick man of Europe' since economic growth there stagnated. German managers we have spoken to recognize in other UK-based media a form of *Schadenfreude* combined (at its basest) with some old and ingrained xenophobia. In other words, this form of media criticism (whether justifiable or not) is not limited to Japan.

Genuine frustration emerges when Japan is compared unfavourably to its East Asian neighbours. The rapid expansion of US American interest in China's economic and business development, in addition to improved international relations between the Chinese and US administrations, has led to a sense that Japan is becoming little more than a bridge for growing US interest in mainland China (Shimizuishi, 2002). We hear similar anxieties expressed by managers from Taiwan.

A special feature in *The Economist* (6 July 2002) caused particular upset. Under the title 'The lost (half) decade' the progress of reform in Japan is compared unfavourably with progress in South Korea. According to the article, after the national humiliation of IMF intervention in the late 1990s, South Korean politicians, business leaders and trade union representatives agreed to endure the pain of mass redundancies (there were homeless on the streets and underpasses of Seoul and other cities), push through a reform of the banking sector, and restructure the nation's *chaebol* (roughly similar networks to Japanese *zaibatsu* – cf. Box 7.1) to generate today's still fragile yet dynamic business environment where credit is competitive and reliable and there is increasing room for individual enterprise and innovation. Even allowing for massive differences in economic size and tradition, the message appears to be 'Why can't Japan be more like South Korea?'

This spiky form of comparison also features in the Japanese media: at least, in the *gaijin* Japanese media. An article by William Pesek Jr published in *The Japan Times* (18 November 2002) compares the Japanese 'Mizuho' and the Korean 'Kookmin' banks. After stating that 'Japan's embattled bankers deserve a place in the *Guinness Book of World Records* for inaction', the article (under the provocative sub-heading: 'Act more Korean') explains how South Korea's Kookmin Bank reformed its corporate governance by increasing foreign ownership, reassessing the (global) value of its assets, and saying 'no' to the advances of one of its traditional and powerful customers – a failing South Korean *chaebol*. This action (according to Pesek Jr) brought 'some of the respect that's long eluded Asia's fourth-largest economy'. Again, the implication is that this is the type of reformist action and international respect still eluding what is still Asia's largest economy: Japan.

We asked a western journalist in Japan why western media tended to be more pointedly critical of Japan than Japanese media. He suggested that one reason might be that western journalists are frequently excluded from government and other sources of information by the 'clubs' of Japanese journalists.

Constraints at the national industrial level

As seen in the example of the pharmaceuticals industry, the barriers to industrial and economic reform in Japan are part structural and part cultural. The traditional shape and nature of these barriers in Japan can be explained in terms of *keiretsu* – according to Backman (1999: 149), 'a fancy name for a stale concept'.

The term *keiretsu* signifies an industrial/financial network of separate but closely related or operationally integrated companies. *Keiretsu* roughly translates as 'succession' – the idea being of a chain of linked operations which, bound together, are strong and enduring. *Keiretsu* companies tend to be vertically integrated: for example, Mitsubishi Aluminium together with Mitsubishi Plastics and Mitsubishi Electric will supply Mitsubishi Motors whose products will be distributed and exported by Mitsubishi partner companies (notably the core trading company, *Mitsubishi Shoji*) together with Mitsubishi Warehouse and Transportation. These affiliations are not secret and can be checked in Japanese government publications and on websites.

The Mitsubishi companies hold shares in each other: a network of strategic ownership called 'cross-shareholding' (OECD, 1997). There is little incentive, therefore, for managers to perform in anything other than 'the Mitsubishi way'. To further stabilize and anchor the net, *keiretsu* tend also to be integrated horizontally around affiliated core banks (e.g. The Tokyo–Mitsubishi Bank). Thus organized, *keiretsu* have long acted as entry barriers to new (and particularly to non-Japanese) market entrants (cf. Janocha, 1995).

A state of mind

The heads of *keiretsu* companies meet and confer regularly, thus perpetuating a 'club' or 'reference group' that transcends industries and regions (cf. Kerbo and McKinstry, 1995; Flath, in Bird 2002: 190). The 'Presidents' Clubs' of *keiretsu* chiefs attract the 'golfers' euphemistically referred to at the beginning of this section. Sharing insider information is both a source of competitive advantage and of affirming group identity, notably when *keiretsu* companies launch into overseas markets. Kay (1993) likens the advantages of this type of corporate 'information architecture' to a football team playing a quick passing game to frustrate their opponents: 'The maintenance of a co-operative ethic relies on the underlying structure of relational contracts – the unwritten rules, the tacit understandings, the common purpose which is sustained by the expectations of all parties that these will be part of continuing relationships' (1993: 72). Kay's 'co-operative ethic' thus relates to Japanese traditions of *ie* and face. In strategic terms, this degree of interrelationship serves to reduce risk in response to environmental pressures and thus parallels the effect of the reference group outlined in Chapter 2.

Keiretsu form the industrial context for the emergence and sustenance of Japanese-style management traditions and expectations: e.g. the aforementioned 'three treasures' of Japanese-style HRM. *Keiretsu* companies routinely share staff. For example, a key stage in a manager's promotion – or near-retirement – will be to get sent to a regional or overseas subsidiary of the parent company. Staff from the *keiretsu* core banks may provide training in, for example, finance and accounting to staff in affiliated companies. Accordingly, and for as long as the group is doing well, individual managers could expect security of employment while HR managers could take a long-term view on use of strategic resources such as staff, information and experience or 'organizational learning' (as discussed in Chapter 5).

In less prosperous times, space could be made for the retention of core staff by releasing untenured staff at one or more of the less prestigious subsidiary companies. Put another way, for as long as senior members in the *keiretsu* 'club' *thought* they were doing well, they could assert (with the reliable accounting support of core banks) that they *were* 'doing well'. It is therefore helpful to understanding the *keiretsu* tradition (like reference groups) as a set of shared expectations or values; or a 'state of mind' (Gerlach, 1992;1993; Miyashita and Russel, 1994). This state of mind, like a set of culture-specific values, will (like an iceberg) move and change only slowly (cf. Laurent, 1983).

Case study: research and development

We saw how, in the case of the global and national pharmaceuticals industry, the growth of global markets means that individual organizations more than ever need to innovate in order to prosper and survive. We have seen (cf. in Box 5.3) how Japanese industrial culture has grown by virtue of its systematic pursuit of perfection rather than its leaps into the unknown.

The durability of a dominant paradigm or 'state of mind' comes under strain when challenged by exceptional circumstances: or, by exceptional individuals. Consider the case of Fujio Masuoka, as reported in *Forbes Magazine* (22 July 2002). According to the author of the article – Benjamin Fulford of Forbes' Tokyo office (cited here with permission) – Masuoka is the inventor of 'flash memory' – a system of memory chips that prevents data being lost when the power shuts off. An innovative and determined spirit, Masuoka worked 'nights and weekends' to produce the first versions of flash memory: 'I was senior enough that I could go to the factory without permission and order them to make me one.' According to Fulford's article: 'His seniority came as a result of innovations in his day job' at a giant electronics corporation that '[was] a good company in the sense that they give middle managers enough autonomy to do such things'. His 'flash memory' was a global hit, copied and developed by major US American chip and processor makers.

As the inventor of what is 'now a US$ 76 billion-a-year-industry', Masuoka was rewarded with some promotion but in terms of pay only 'a few hundred dollars'. He received job offers from US companies but 'in those days [the 1980s] in Japan, leaving your company was just not considered to be an option'. His reputation appeared to become a burden for the company's senior managers. He was told (in his own words) 'you are not a team player, you do not obey orders, you go off and do things on your own.' He quit the company in 1994 to become a university professor and lead his own research group.

The story of Masuoka is a startling illustration of how major Japanese companies are in danger of losing what Ohmae and other senior McKinsey executives now refer to as the new global 'war for talents'. That the talent is there in Japan was given high-profile confirmation by two Japanese scientists winning Nobel Prizes in 2002: like London buses, people wait ages for one and then several come along at once! But despite the national pride and public excitement, it is likely that these Nobel Prize winners will be offered greater rewards and resources outside Japan rather than inside.

We asked one long-time Japan observer about how Japanese companies – and Japanese society generally – usually respond to the challenge to change? 'They muddle through. That's always been the way. They keep their "dirty washing" indoors and together and over time, they get the problem sorted out. Or, they delay so long until the problem disappears or is no longer so important. Sometimes they get lucky and a solution drops into their lap.'

This informed but rather cynical view underpins the attitude of many managers we spoke to, ranging from: 'We know we have to change. Change will come from somewhere' and 'What do we need to change? I have a job, my family, the company will pull through' and 'What is this crisis they [politicians] are talking about? In our organization [public sector] we have more than enough work and demand.'

SECTION 4: CROSSING THE LIGHTS AT RED

> We lost the military war in 1945. And now it seems that
> we've lost the war of capitalism too!
>
> (retired senior manager, 2002)

One Japanese market analyst said this: 'It takes one person to cross the lights at red. You watch them, waiting at the pedestrian crossing, the light's at red but there's no traffic coming. One person steps out to cross, and immediately the rest follow.' In Chapter 3 we outlined how (among Japanese organizations) the Sony Corporation was one of the first 'to cross the lights at red' and effectively 'go global' at a time when the wind was in Japan's favour. The wind has since changed direction, a transformation which has been brewing for some time (cf. Kono, 1988). At the level of corporate leadership and innovation, it appears that foreign and/or hitherto unfamiliar winds are sweeping across Japan's industrial landscape.

From the perspective of individual managers, this development may be perceived as a threat or as an opportunity. As one retired senior manager (cited above) further said: 'It takes a foreigner to get Japan moving – to get Japan to realize the need for change.' He was thinking back to US American occupation after World War Two. Perhaps he was even thinking back to Commodore Perry's Black Ships. Representing a different generation, a female entrepreneur in her early thirties told us: 'Carlos Ghosn [at Nissan] is the new "global standard" for Japanese management.'

Foreign winds of change: *Nissan*

Nissan Motor Corporation used to be Japan's highest-ranking producer of automobiles until overtaken by Toyota in 1962. Despite a few global hits, notably its Datsun label, long-running industrial disputes and poor marketing saw it slip behind Honda in the Japanese car-manufacturers' rankings (cf. Box 8.2). In the late 1990s the French automobile manufacturer Renault took a majority shareholding in Nissan, taking advantage of the collapse of the one of the *keiretsu* network's core banks, Yamaichi Securities (cf. Box 7.1). In 1999 Renault installed Brazilian born Carlos Ghosn as Nissan president.

In an article entitled 'Carlos Ghosn: standing at the global crossing' (JCIC, 2002), Ghosn admits that his prior knowledge of Japan and Japanese business culture was 'very vague'. Despite (or because of?) this he felt unhindered and immediately set about closing down or selling off excess or loss-making capacity in Nissan's domestic and overseas operations. His initial target was to make Nissan – after ten years of incurring a loss – into a company capable of making a profit. Since 2001 Nissan Motors has been in profit.

In all respects Ghosn seemed to be foregrounding his credentials as a non-*keiretsu*-style manager. At first he was perceived as a 'slasher of jobs': according to Kono and Clegg (2001), Ghosn's policies and values were 'anathema' to established Japanese management practices. His Nissan Revival Plan was presented to the company and to the public – in English and Japanese – affirming again his *gaijin* status. However, he appeared to know how to tune into Japanese cultural (notably *bushido*) terms of reference: e.g. effort and perseverance against the odds. In English Ghosn talks about 'never making compromises' and 'enduring sacrifices'. In Japanese: 'To make the Nissan Revival Plan into a success, a tremendous amount of effort, pain and sacrifices may be necessary, and I recognize this. But please believe me, there is no alternative. Failure is not an option' (cf. *The Economist*, 21 October 1999; *Nikkei Business online*, accessed 19 November 2001).

The values he espoused appear unflinchingly Japanese: effort, sincerity, striving (even suffering) to achieve the desired goal (cf. Matsumoto, 2002; Nitobe, 1969). Japanese managers we spoke to (one of whom is a Nissan employee) did not consider his rhetoric a gimmick. 'He's been with us long enough, now. We know he means and acts on what he says.' In the many interviews he gives Ghosn come across as 'courteous and polite'. As Ghosn-san he has become something of a celebrity in Japan, a kind of leader/philosopher whose thoughts are sought out by the business media in Japan and overseas and who now also appears in a *manga* series dedicated to recounting his work and achievements.

In the context of HRM polices and procedures Ghosn has instituted changes designed to reform Nissan's organizational culture. For example, employees used to have the date of entry to the company permanently attached to their name in company documents: in 1999 Ghosn removed this practice and did much to open up established recruitment, training and promotion procedures. Unsurprisingly, the company began to recruit and promote people who are attracted by the Ghosn philosophy; English became the language of senior management, but 'Ghosn-san' is still happy to talk through an interpreter to sales and other employees, gleaning their views and suggestions on how the business is going: 'how many other western – or even Japanese – business leaders do that?'

Informal reports suggest that many more tradition-minded managers at Nissan feel squeezed, even threatened. Given that Ghosn was up-front about the crisis that Nissan had found itself in when he arrived, he was able to promote the setting up of 'cross-functional teams', similar in design and effect to those recently instituted at Matsushita (outlined in Chapter 5). New flexibilities and skills of horizontal communication and initiative taking thus become explicitly top–down promoted and rewarded. Doubtless, managers who perceive a threat to their own promotion prospects – earned over twenty or more years of cumulative commitment to the Nissan they committed their career to – feel threatened and suspect (or hope?) that Ghosn's reforms are no more than a 'quick-fix' attempt.

There are reports that some workers laid off at Nissan subsidiaries (cf. *Nikkei Business News*, 19 November 2001) resent the longer commute or relocation to plants still operating. In addition, many lower-level workers see their salaries and bonuses depressed while those of senior managers (including Ghosn) are rising as profits return. Middle-managers at Nissan see their reward and promotion expectations suddenly recast. Some senior managers see themselves as being 'frozen out' after refusing to become 'yes men' to Ghosn and his reform policies. 'Is this just a different type of bureaucracy?'

In terms of HRM values and priorities, the answer is almost certainly 'yes'. Speaking at the Seventh International Conference for Women in

Business (July 2002), Ghosn announced that Nissan was 'shifting from men versus women, seniority versus the young, and Japanese versus non-Japanese to the contribution and performance of a person.' However, where and when 'we maintain differences, we learn from it' (Kambayashi and Rutledge, 2002). In this sense he is tuning in to the Japanese 'learning organization' tradition while simultaneously knocking down many of the 'paper screen walls' that traditionally divided it. As an illustration of the company's new drive to reward individual talent and performance, the number of women in senior management positions at Nissan rose from ten in 1999 to twenty-eight in 2002.

Japanese winds of change: *Mitsubishi Corporation*

When a trading company and traditional *keiretsu* network with the size and status of Mitsubishi Corporation (in Japanese, *Mitsubishi Shoji*) undertakes a radical restructuring and shift of management focus everyone engaged in international management sits up and takes notice. One of the original pre-war *zaibatsu* (Box 7.1), the Mitsubishi name (which literally translated means 'three diamonds') was suppressed by US Occupation forces but then allowed to reform during the Korean War. Mitsubishi companies were major suppliers of products and materials used for military purposes such as aircraft, ships, metals, chemicals, heavy machinery, land vehicles, and energy.

Mitsubishi Shoji has always been one of Japan's most powerful *keiretsu* and, during the 1980s and early 1990s, 'was regularly listed by Fortune as the largest company in the world, in terms of trading transactions' (Rudlin, in Bird 2002: 316). Despite the recent economic slowdown, total company revenues during 2001 were around 14 trillion yen. The company continues to benefit from its close relations with successive Japanese governments and has acted (through its many subsidiary operations) as a major contributor to national economic growth, not least in its securing of precious energy sources (e.g. oil and gas) worldwide. The company has a tradition of sustaining an international outlook, as a recent strategic alliance with Germany's Daimler confirms. Furthermore, the company has a tradition of sustaining a strong organizational structure and a 'gentlemanly' and cautious culture (Rudlin, 2000; Rudlin in Bird, 2002). This might – or might not – explain why one of our female respondents referred to the company (pre-reform, it must be said) as 'one of the most sexist I've ever had dealings with'.

Managers in this mammoth *keiretsu* have recently undertaken some nimble and radical reforms. In an explicit response to changes in the company's global strategic environment, in addition to changes within the national economic structures, *Mitsubishi Shoji* has restructured its internal operations to a basis of more flexibly focused and specialized 'business units'; it now assesses corporate performance using a transparent in-house value-added measure modelled on the global EVA™ standard; and it has introduced a 'pay-for-performance' bonus system for its staff. The cost of restructuring has been high: a lot of cash was needed to fund a sweeping early retirement programme and an incentive bonus system. The company was big enough to absorb these costs.

The overall objective at *Mitsubishi Shoji* has been to integrate corporate performance measures with those of individual performance and reward and so recast the corporation's culture to one that is driven more by economic value creation than by attention to domestic market position or tradition. For example, they have taken a 30 per cent stake in the convenience store chain Lawson (cf. Box 8.3) to make money (unsurprisingly!) but also 'to promote transformation of our business models'. Organizational learning against global standards is the key; and, as the company website further proclaims: 'The key to success in today's fiercely competitive global markets is continuous reinvention, flexibility and new ideas' (Mitsubishi Corporation website, accessed 17 February 2003). This statement suggests a paradigm shift away from the traditional focus of Japanese corporations on competing and learning primarily against rivals within domestic markets.

Based on what younger Japanese managers spontaneously tell us (i.e. the generation identified by Kakabadse *et al.* as being most impatient for structures of pay and reward based on merit) *Mitsubishi Shoji* is now one of the most sought-after destinations of Japanese graduates, suggesting that forward-looking and internally oriented Japanese trading companies may again be coming into vogue among aspiring managers in Japan (cf. Box 2.4).

In terms of reforming HRM functions such as rewards management in line with international best practice, other high-profile corporations are following suit and creating new 'local' (i.e. Japanese national) trends. An article in the *Asahi Shimbun* newspaper (online edition, accessed 8 January 2003) reports how even Matsushita (cf. Chapter 5) has decided to outdo rival Toshiba by delegating not only the setting of (note) *merit-*based salary scales and benefits to divisional managers in the group; they are empowering them to set 'entirely different working conditions'. Taking these together with the Nissan and Mitsubishi examples discussed in this chapter, we can trace sources of regained confidence, pride and motivation among Japanese managers, irrespective of values ascribed to age, rank or gender.

SECTION 5: MAKE THE SYSTEM WORK FOR YOU

Japanese companies were, along with their US American rivals, among the first to become MNCs or multi-national corporations or enterprises. In similar fashion to their US American counterparts, the approach of Japanese MNCs has tended to be 'ethnocentric' – an approach that suggests either inordinate confidence or lack of confidence in one's own cultures and style of management, depending on the context, and on one's own point of view and experience (cf. Box 3.1). In generic terms, an 'ethnocentric' approach is taken by managers and their organizations where the objective is to pursue a 'global strategy' (typical for US American MNCs) or when driven by a need to export or re-import, typical for Japanese MNCs (cf. Daniels and Radebaugh, 1998; Yip, 1995). As a consequence, the strategic imperatives of the MNC will tend to be reflected significantly in the HRM values and norms operating in the overseas subsidiary.

Although marketing and recruitment might be delegated to local staff and agencies, most strategic (i.e. senior and middle-management) positions in overseas subsidiaries would be taken by Japanese expatriate managers and leave little room for promotion among non-Japanese managers. According to Kono and Clegg, 'the slow promotion of managers and ambiguous job descriptions are hard to transplant' (2001: 175). Japanese managers have also struggled to convince non-Japanese managers and staff of the intrinsic strategic value of *nemawashi* (Box 6.1), though they have won international friends for their focus on detail and quality, trust and respect, and (in the UK, at least) their offer of job security and/or relatively high salaries (cf. Dore, 1973; Oliver and Wilkinson, 1992; Kono and Clegg, 2001; Bird, 2002).

Japanese MNCs have long been established as a major factor in regional economic development in Asia (Hatch and Yamamura, 1996). Indeed, the volume of Japan's trade with its ASEAN partners currently exceeds its trade with Europe and the USA together (cf. Bird, 2002: 282). In Southeast Asia the ethnocentric approach to promotion and reward in

Japanese subsidiaries spawned the term 'bamboo ceiling' (Andrews *et al.*, 2002; cf. March, 1996). Some Japanese MNCs operating in Thailand have experienced calamitous communication failures. One year a major Japanese electronics multi-national refused to pay local staff the expected end-of-year bonuses on account of poorer than expected performance. In response the local staff rioted and burnt down the factory. It appears that senior managers in Japan had 'overestimated the cultural similarities' (e.g. Asian Buddhist) between Japanese and local staff (Andrews, 2001, private communication). The ethnocentric approach had failed.

Sukehara-san

Against this background we spoke to Sukehara-san. In his late forties, he had been working for three years on an expatriate management assignment in the UK for a Japanese white-goods manufacturer having worked in Hong Kong for two years previously. Married with two school-age children, he was now preparing to move with his family to an assignment for the same company and again in Hong Kong.

We asked Sukehara-san whether he wouldn't prefer to go back to Japan. What would taking the Hong Kong assignment do for his promotion prospects in Japan? He replied. 'First of all, it's difficult to say "no" to a foreign assignment. Second, I think my promotion prospects in Japan have suffered anyway because of the time I have spent abroad. But maybe when I go back to Japan the company will be more international and so my promotion prospects will be better as they look for people with my kind of international experience.'

What about your family? 'They're used to it. They accept it. My children went to an English school here and a Japanese school at weekends. We will have the same opportunity in Hong Kong. My wife looks forward to having a bigger flat in Hong Kong. Our quality of life there is better than it was in Japan. My salary is higher. We get special benefits for housing and schools.'

With all these positives, why don't more of your Japanese colleagues want to take overseas assignments? 'Because it's not normal. It's a risk. You are very much exposed in this position.' 'Exposed?' 'There are negatives. For example, the communication with headquarters is very difficult. You have to explain everything [about the overseas operation] in detail. On the ground you compromise and adapt to local conditions, but my bosses don't automatically accept that. They expect me to report to them nearly every day in the Japanese way. They keep strict financial control, which I think is right. But when they come to visit it's a nightmare for me – and my wife! Then I have to be the dutiful subordinate: arranging everything from visits to the plant and to suppliers and distributors to golf, shopping and sightseeing trips. I also have to be the strict boss with local staff when my bosses are here. My (English) friends and my wife notice a big difference in my mood when my Japanese bosses are here!'

We arranged for Sukehara-san to talk to a group of young Japanese who were preparing to graduate from business schools in the UK. We asked him to give them some career advice. He spoke particularly to those who expressed a wish to work for 'international companies' of Japanese organizations with widespread international operations. Sukehara-san's advice was (in summary): 'Go back to Japan; get a job in a good company with an international profile; gain experience for 3 or 5 years; learn how to work – learn about quality work and teamwork; then make it be known that you would be willing to go on an expatriate assignment; remind them of your overseas qualifications and experience.' Looking ahead, Sukehara-san also reminded them: 'After five years maybe you have changed your mind – or the company you're working for has changed – and you no longer feel you want to work outside Japan. Whatever you do, be optimistic, be ambitious, make a positive contribution, and at the same time make the system work for you.'

Summary

In this chapter we have illustrated how certain traditional forces and structures of political, economic and business management in Japan – what we could term a '*keiretsu* mentality' – have worked to constrain organizational responses to the emerging global strategic environment. However, we have also illustrated successful adaptation by major and highly influential Japanese companies.

We have seen how Japanese-style reward systems and structures are adapting (albeit slowly) to diverse demands. We have illustrated how increasing numbers of Japanese managers and their organizations are adopting reward management solutions from a range of sources, both non-Japanese and non-traditional. Overall in this chapter we have attempted to give enough examples of positive and optimistic developments based on traditional values and strengths of Japanese-style

HRM to suggest that there is sufficient cause for confidence in the career prospects of Japanese managers and the global business prospects of Japanese organizations.

Consider the following questions:

- What is it about the structures of promotion and rewards in your current organization that encourages you to stay or, alternatively, motivates you to look for another job?

- To what extent are your thoughts in considering question one reflected in the experiences of Japanese managers outlined in this and previous chapters in this book?

8 Facing the future

Introduction

> The ever greater demands being made on Japanese
> management are evident . . . Japanese companies are [. . .]
> standing at a crossroads where the future is not clear and at
> the same time [are] having to undergo substantial structural
> changes, described [in a 1994 government report] as the
> biggest discontinuity since the end of World War II.
> (Kakabadse, Okazaki-Ward and Myers, 1996)

In Chapter 4 we illustrated how Japanese managers commonly
experienced the processes of entry and induction to their first job, the
first step on a career path. In Chapters 5 and 6 we identified a growing
tendency among ambitious managers to lose patience with the pace
of career development determined by established ('classical') structures
and traditions of Japanese HRM, and in some cases begin to lose trust
in established HRM and career structures. In Chapter 7 we looked at the
emerging international context for Japanese HRM. Within these contexts
we can recognize that Japanese-style management does indeed 'stand
at a crossroads'.

In this final chapter we illustrate how Japanese managers are coping with
quitting, being transferred or retiring from their company – processes

generically termed *organizational exit*. We explore how different managers respond to this experience or prospect and the extent to which they feel prepared for this eventuality. From their examples we deduce the extent to which Japanese managers today feel prepared – or even inspired – to negotiate the challenges and opportunities of an increasingly uncertain professional future.

Our objectives for this final chapter are:

- to give voice to Japanese managers with experience of organizational exit;

- to trace features describing what appears to be the emerging face of Japanese management.

SECTION 1: THE EXPERIENCE OF ORGANIZATIONAL EXIT

Organizational exit is a super-ordinate term covering HRM processes such as the transfer, dismissal, redundancy or resignation of staff. There can be many reasons for organizational exit. These include:

- the employee's job disappears or becomes less important through a restructuring of the organization or a re-focusing of strategic objectives;
- the employee is no longer considered capable, appropriate [or, in Japanese terms, 'proper'] for carrying out his or her work effectively;
- the employee reaches a contractual retirement age and the organization feels obliged (or motivated) to let him or her go.

(adapted from Hannagan, 1998: 327)

These are essentially strategic HRM decisions and their basis is given by reference to time, as in the case of staff who either want or who are expected to retire at a certain age or date. However, the effectiveness of these decisions also relies on the quality of information available to senior managers and HR practitioners: they need to take care in deciding who, in the strategic interests of the organization, should be encouraged to stay or leave.

Most Japanese managers expect to retire – or be retired – by their late fifties. However, it is possible for organizations to keep people on after the normal retirement age, and indeed many companies offer a range of undemanding jobs from trainers of new recruits to uniformed lobby porters to loyal managers who officially have retired. Others will be seconded out to subsidiaries (see discussion of *amakudari* below) or moved sideways or 'upstairs' to some honorary (if hollow) title and function.

As we saw in Chapter 7, one enduring problem with the traditional '*keiretsu* mentality' is the apparent unwillingness of many core or higher decision-making groupings to bring in fresh blood and ideas: wariness of 'outsiders' and fear of loss of face are still strong drivers of organizational strategy. However, current demographic and technological trends in Japan are putting this tradition under strain: in Japan today there are more people of retirement age than there are in school. By some accounts Japan is becoming a 'childless society' (cf. Jolivet, 1997). Backman (1999) sees in this demographic trend a source of social inertia.

We have seen (in Chapters 3 and 7) how ambition and an enhanced sense of self-esteem among (usually, but not exclusively) younger Japanese managers is generating tension in the management of payment and reward systems based on ascriptive values (e.g. seniority promotion and salary increments linked to rank). One outcome of this tension is that the customarily smooth Japanese-style management of organizational exit is coming increasingly under strain, resulting in some untraditional and (at first glance) bizarre behaviour. For example, Melville (1999: 90) reports how 'some Japanese firms, in an effort to avoid the painful task of making a worker redundant, slip the names of their excess staff to head hunters in the hope that they will be pulled, rather than have to be pushed out of the company'.

Managing organizational exit

A problem with even routine HRM decisions on organizational exit is that these, from an individual perspective and depending on individual circumstances, may appear subjective and less than 'fair'. This perception mirrors those discussed in Chapter 6 in the context of *performance appraisal* and perceptions of trust; of course, with the added tension given by the finality that organizational exit implies. The need for HR and line-managers to manage organizational exit may arise not only in the natural course of time or as a result of a 'top–down' strategic intervention, but also out of a point of conflict or a perceived 'violation' of the social and psychological 'contracts' (cf. Robinson, 1996; Kasai, 1999).

These conflicts or violations can arise out of situations where:

- an employee loses trust in the organization's ability or commitment to develop his or her career: i.e. training and development becomes perceived as adding little in terms of professional 'market value' – this being determined by the career environment outside the organization (cf. Chapter 5);
- an employee gets a 'better' job or career offer (i.e. a more motivating appeal to their individual sense of self-esteem) from another organization or source: e.g. a headhunting agency or a rival company where different (and perceptibly more attractive) sets of HRM values operate (cf. Chapters 6 and 7);
- an employee is no longer willing to accept the conditions of work that the organization offers: e.g. in terms of promotion prospects, pay or other rewards (cf. Chapter 7).

As we saw in our discussion of face and control (Chapter 2), one common source of violation or conflict is where one side (i.e. the employee or senior managers of the organization) suddenly and without discernible cause appears to behave unpredictably or, depending on individual perception, irrationally or even 'chaotically' (cf. Box 8.4). An unexpected and apparently ungrounded decision by one side either to quit or to make an employee redundant is experienced as a shock that upsets the equilibrium of established and long-term-oriented norms and values. This impacts on fellow employees and may prompt a critical response across the organization, or even across the industry as in the case with recent mass redundancies in the electronic sectors in Japan-based plants. Once the 'dam' of established values and (above all) fundamental assumptions begins to crack, others fractures soon follow and a sense of compressed hysteria or even sullen fatalism can ensue. Alternatively, managers whose ambitions had been stifled may experience a sense of liberation through the prospect or experience of organizational exit. As in distinguishing between loss of face and embarrassment (cf. Chapter 2), time and future opportunity are key variables – the individual asks: 'Is there another or similar job to go to?' Space or location is also a key variable: 'Can I move to where the new jobs are?' The internationality of employment opportunities suited Sukehara-san and his family (introduced in Chapter 7). It did not (immediately) suit Mikimura-san and her family (introduced in Chapter 6). Whatever the individual response, the mood surrounding organizational exit is usually tense and the capabilities of HR managers and the structures in which they operate become stretched.

Threatening silence

For example, one senior HR manager (aged fifty-four) told us how much he was looking forward to his own retirement. His company had been laying off large numbers of staff: *risutura* (organizational restructuring). He had had the unenviable 'hatchet' role. Suddenly, he and his family began receiving frequent, and silent, anonymous phone calls at home. He interpreted these as desperate, even threatening: the communicative power of silence! He suspected the calls came from recently laid-off members of staff – they had his home number because he had often been called upon to counsel staff from home at weekends. These calls may or may not be as threatening as he suspected; however, the important point is that he and his family perceived them so. We asked if he could go to the police? 'What could they do?' Speak to his senior managers? 'It would appear to them that I hadn't done my job properly. And what could they do anyway?' He told us that his daughter was about to graduate from university: 'at last I can afford to retire!' She wants to make a career in HR. He warns her against. She persists.

Heaven or window?

As we saw in Chapters 4 and 5, one of the key functions of organizational induction and subsequent training and development is to socialize new or junior staff in the structures of expectations and rewards that define the culture of an organization. While accepting that circumstances change – and in reference to *kai-zen* philosophy (Box 5.3) we have seen how incremental change is accepted as normal and positive – managers who are moving towards the end of their career will have been carrying with them a bundle of fundamental expectations that may (like a good wine) have matured over thirty years. There is always the risk that opening the bottle offers a bitter surprise. Consider the case of Uchiyama-san.

Uchiyama-san

When we spoke to him Uchiyama-san was fifty-three years old and had been working all his post-university life in a major Japanese bank. He expected to retire (albeit reluctantly) at age fifty-five on a pension amounting to 50 per cent of his final salary. However, Uchiyama-san told us he felt under pressure to take earlier retirement. How did he know this?

First, because he had just been seconded to supervise the accounting procedures in a company that the bank held shares in.

Sometimes the move is associated with a decreased salary, thus reducing the parent organization's obligations for paying an 'exit bonus' and future pension contributions. The expectation is that, assuming the manager being transferred is a genuinely loyal member of staff, he or she will accept the cost-cutting as necessary and in the interests of the company. As another manager (fifty-five years old) told us: 'I realize that my [electrical supply] company need to reduce costs. At my age I'm expensive for them. But I want to keep working. This company is my life and I still have two children at university.' For many managers at this age, for whom work and the company has been central to their sense of identity, any respectable job is perceived as being better than no job at all. According to OECD statistics, apart from having a rapidly ageing population, Japan also has the greatest number of over sixty-fives officially in employment.

Amakudari

When we met him, Uchiyama-san was embarking on a process of *amakudari*. The term means 'descent from heaven' and refers to a process whereby managers of near-retirement age are transferred (traditionally from ministries or public to private sector organizations) to other organizations affiliated either by cross-shareholding or a history of business relations. *Amakudari* is a tradition going back to Confucian forms of centralized bureaucracy and attempts to standardize and maintain law and order 'in the provinces' while opening up vacancies for new blood in the central administration. The implication is that staff in the subsidiary company should feel honoured to receive these senior managers; however, the reality (based on stories told to us) is that they usually resent this top–down incursion into their way of doing things. Faced by the inevitable, they may however try to work *amakudari* to their advantage: 'welcome him, flatter him: he might just be in for a quiet life before retiring'. Others feel threatened, suspecting that this arrival from bureaucratic 'heaven' may, in reports he feeds back to headquarters about any 'delinquent' behaviour, scupper the chances of ambitious managers hoping to head the other way.

Did Uchiyama-san feel honoured to 'descend from heaven' at the subsidiary company? He smiled, thinly, but said little. It was 'a new challenge'. In fact, he didn't feel honoured at all, as his wife later explained to us with a level of detail and passion he apparently felt too ashamed or too angry to show. That something was amiss became clear when he had no *meishi* to exchange with us: after two weeks his bank had not yet provided him with one for his new job. 'He feels hurt and is determined to make them pay', explained his wife: 'after all he has sacrificed in the interests of the bank over the years!' The most effective way to 'make them pay' was to hang on for as long as possible before retiring. Overall this was a dispiriting interview, uncovering little of the 'respect' that Kono and Clegg (2001) so readily ascribe to Japanese-style HRM. Consequently, we can assume that Uchiyama-san's experience is exceptional.

Madogi-wa

When we told Uchiyama-san's story to other Japanese managers we encountered little sympathy. 'It could be worse: they could have "sent him to the window".' 'Sending someone to the window' (*madogi-wa*) refers to a notorious form of exclusion from the mainstream work group whereby an employee who is no longer deemed to 'fit' has his or her desk moved to a position near a window, has the telephone and PC removed, and thereby all communicative responsibility removed also. The idea is that this employee can turn up each morning and spend the day looking out of the window until the loss of face becomes so unbearable that he or she quits. However, for older workers, to quit is to lose one's social identity. As one retired manager told us: 'not to work is to disappear from view'.

The fact that Uchiyama-san had worked in a bank also appeared to act against him: 'These guys get such high salaries anyway, twice as much on average as [similar aged] managers in other industries. What he loses in terms of salary is still more than most other people of his age earn.' So, not much respect here either! Overall in our discussions we felt an antipathy towards banks; younger and more enterprising managers tended to blame banks for many of Japan's current economic problems (cf. Box 7.1); aspiring entrepreneurs complained about the difficulties of getting start-up capital or credit. However, such views – stoked by the Japanese and international media, as we saw in Chapter 7 – probably reflect a mood of tension and apprehension among Japanese managers generally (cf. Box 8.1).

Box 8.1 *Salaryman*

When asked, most Japanese people consider themselves 'middle-class' (Box 4.3). The *salaryman* image has emerged as the archetypal middle-class, salaried, usually male employee whose lifetime job and social status overlap (cf. Sugimoto, 1997). Uchiyama-san (discussed in this chapter) is one of the *salaryman* elite. Born in the late 1940s or early 1950s, *salaryman* has grown to expect continued economic growth, social stability, secure employment, and high-quality education for his children. Although the majority of Japanese managers never attained these rewards to the full, *salaryman* has stood as 'an ideological reference group' for at least two generations (Usui, in Bird 2002: 390).

Most of the managers we interviewed for this book can be categorized as *salaryman* – though this is no longer a label they would choose for themselves: it would be like calling an ambitious manager in the UK a 'yuppie'. For female *salaryman* the term 'career woman' (*kyaria woman*) has been coined, which (being relatively new and dynamic) carries less of the negative irony of the timeworn *salaryman* tag.

JTB (1997) offers a semi-serious insight into the world of *salaryman*. Now in his mid-thirties to mid-forties, his main daily worries include: his children (How are they really doing at school? Are they being bullied?); his wife (Is she being unfaithful? Will she find out about his affairs? Is she looking after his elderly parents?); and paying off the family home, particularly when the company passes him over for the promotion he feels he deserves or reduces his twice-yearly bonus.

The Hakuhodo Institute conducts regular surveys of the mood of Japanese society, exposing trends in 'middle-class' norms and values. One survey (Hakuhodo, 2000: 82) confirms that most Japanese claim to have little idea where Japan is heading. Obsessive saving is one result, with negative consequences for the Japanese retail industry (Box 8.3). According to Hakuhodo, 'core beliefs and values are crumbling' (2000: 86), and 'the institutions of family and work that anchor [individual] lives are eroding' (2000: 88). Particular reference is made to middle-aged Japanese men 'whose lives centred on work [and who] feel that they are losing their place in the company, in the family and in their circle of friends' (2000: 90). On the upside, the survey identifies greater general use of advanced information technologies as people strive to become 'better informed'. More than 50 per cent of Japanese households are connected to the internet. The challenge now, according to some experts, is for Japanese managers and their organizations to learn how to use it competitively (cf. Porter *et al.*, 2000).

SECTION 2: SOURCES OF INSPIRATION

The experience of organizational exit generates a personal and professional crisis: the essential question becomes 'What do I do next?' Consistent with the theme of this book, we asked ourselves a different though related question: 'From where do individual Japanese managers take inspiration for deciding what to do next?'

Self-help guides

Given the respect accorded to expertise and the written word, it is unsurprising that 'self-help' books should be selling well. One (Covey, 1989; reissued 1999) was instantly recognized by several managers we spoke to. Entitled *The 7 Habits of Highly Effective People* it reminded us of the Confucius quote that opened our own Chapter 1. Covey's book guides people into developing the 'habits' required for moving from a state of dependence, then independence ('self-mastery'), then on to an advanced and 'more mature' state of 'interdependence'. Here, an individual is 'self-reliant and capable' and able to identify and affirm his or her inner 'sense of worth'. The way is then clear for proceeding towards the 'public victories' of 'teamwork, cooperation and communication' (Covey, 1989: 51).

The attraction of this lesson among the Japanese managers we spoke to was the affirmation of individual worth within a clear social or group-oriented context – values assumed to be embedded in Japanese culture. One respondent drew a parallel at national level: Japan should strive towards a 'mature' state of political and economic 'interdependence' with western countries such as the USA and Japan's East Asian neighbours rather than the current and 'miserable' state of dependence (i.e. on the USA) or the chimera of independence (i.e. towards China and other of Japan's Asian markets). Another (younger) manager lamented: 'I wish the dead hand of many [existing] business and social structures in Japan would allow us to become "highly effective people" more easily'.

Perennial bestsellers among Japanese managers and business people are the biographies of inspirational leaders such as Sony's Akio Morita, Soichiro Honda (see below) and (more recently) Nissan's Carlos Ghosn, in standard biography and in *manga* form (cf. Box 3.6). Those with a more international view and aspiration (along with countless of their non-Japanese counterparts) also read about figures such as the USA's Jack Welch and Lee Iaccoca.

Leadership

> Never has strong leadership been more earnestly sought
> from corporate top management than it is now.
>
> (Kakabadse *et al.*, 1996)

According to Hannagan: 'Leadership is the process of motivating other people to act in particular ways in order to achieve specific goals [. . .] Leadership involves other people, who by the degree of their willingness to accept direction help to define the leader's status' (1998: 38). By invoking notions of status and the context given by 'other people', Hannagan thus affirms 'leadership' as a socio-cultural construct. Accordingly, inspirational or 'charismatic' business leadership in one culture-specific context might not function as effectively in another.

Contexts of leadership

In Chapter 3 we spoke about culture being interpreted as 'the myths and stories' that a group of individuals tell to themselves about themselves, usually over generations. These myths and stories help inspire individuals and so shape the cultures of nations: William Tell in Switzerland; Robert Bruce in Scotland; Napoleon Bonaparte in France; George Washington in the USA.

In Chapter 7 we saw examples of innovators who become leaders in respect of the inspiration their work and attitudes transmit. They and their products become myths and legends that can shape the management and business cultures of nations (e.g. the Anglo-French Concorde project; Nokia in Finland) or of industries (e.g. Sony's 'Walkman'). Business myths can be parochial and anecdotal and help shape the cultures of departments or sections: 'Remember the time when Smith made that massive sale and then immediately told the boss to *****?!' Inspiration is about learning, and in discussing the inspirational influence of business leaders on individual managers in a Japanese context we should recognize the norms and values informing *sensei/gakusei* or *senpai/kohai* relationships (cf. Chapter 3) and, by extension, expectations of the relationship between subordinates and line-managers (cf. Chapter 4).

Honda: daring to be different

When asked to name a Japanese business leader (living or dead) who could stand as a role model for inspiring today's Japanese managers, the most popular response – from young and not so young, male and female – was: Honda.

Soichiro Honda (1906–1991) was an inventor and co-founder of the Honda Motor Company (Box 8.2). He grew up the son of a small-town blacksmith. He decided he wanted to build cars when he was in elementary school. He studied metal casting in his spare time and, after two years of failure and rejections, sold a new-design piston ring – and in 1940 a whole production plant – to Toyota. On the proceeds 'he made whiskey and spent a year partying with his friends' (Craig, in Bird, 2002: 181). He drove racing cars, until a crash ended his career. Honda the man was notorious for 'having a good time' and seeking out his own path to 'quality of life'.

Box 8. 2 *Honda*

Soichiro Honda (1906–1991), the co-founder (with Takeo Fujisawa in 1949) of the Honda Motor Company, gained fame as an engineer who was expert at getting high performance from small and inexpensive engines. Honda first went into mass vehicle production in 1946 by converting ex-military radio generator engines into bicycle engines. He later inspired the adaptation of lawnmower engines towards producing highly efficient and reliable motorbike engines. 'You meet the nicest people on a Honda' was the advertising slogan that swept the US American market in 1962. Honda inspired other Japanese motorcycle manufacturers such as Yamaha, Suzuki, and Kawasaki, and their combined market onslaught caused the disappearance of several competing brands (e.g. BSA and Triumph in the UK) and the US government to bail out Harley Davidson, as Japanese managers are keen to remind westerners who complain about so-called 'anti-trust' business practices in Japanese industry.

Honda brought innovation into the design of cars; an example is the decision to place sideways the engine in the Honda Civic (a global hit product) in order to create more space for passengers.

Honda was one of the first large-scale Japanese vehicle manufacturers to relocate production overseas: e.g. to the USA in the 1960s. Given that Honda cars were seen as practical and fuel efficient, the company was ideally positioned to exploit global (and, above all, US American) markets during the 1970s oil price crises (cf. Mair, 1999). Honda is now the world's largest motorcycle manufacturer, and the US market currently accounts for twice as many Honda vehicle sales as the domestic Japanese market (*The Financial Times*, 27–28 April 2002).

Today, Honda the company is generally recognized as one of the most open, innovative and internationally oriented of all Japanese companies. By the 1990s the company was producing more cars overseas than in Japan. In 1999, Honda's share of sales in the global automobile market overtook those of Nissan, precipitating the decision by Renault to appoint Carlos Ghosn to lead Nissan's Japanese operations (cf. Chapter 7). Managers we spoke to (none of whom worked for Honda) cited the company's reputation for flexible recruitment and reward policies 'based on talent and individual merit'. Honda 'is consistently rated among the top ten companies preferred to work for in Japan [and] is renowned for its commitment to excellence in engineering through individual initiative and experimentation' (Bird, 2002: 180).

Honda the business leader appears to have a contemporary and dynamic appeal. Striking remains the extent to which his and his company's approach to business and management – and indeed to life generally – so contradict many of the stereotypical images of Japanese management styles (cf. Sakaiya, 1982; 1997). As an innovator and 'maverick' entrepreneur (cf. Bird, 2002: 319), Honda's legendary status resembles that of Akio Morita, founder of the Sony Corporation, whose achievements were outlined in Chapter 3.

Honda's example acts as a source of inspiration above all to forward thinking Japanese managers, business leaders and entrepreneurs or those who feel constrained in their ambition. As Porter and colleagues state categorically: 'Honda's penchant for being different was backed up by an almost fanatical devotion to independence and a maverick disregard for conventional wisdom' (Porter et al., 2000: 93), citing phrases such as: 'Don't be afraid to make mistakes' and 'Don't imitate others' (2000: 94). In short, Honda the maverick is an integral part of the *existing* face of Japanese management and his example proves how striving to 'be different' can bring business success. Paraphrasing from Kakabadse et al. (1996), Honda's example inspires 'a new breed' of manager who is 'tough, resilient uncompromising and results-driven' and who does not shy from '[disrupting] the expectation of lifetime employment'.

Trendsetting: the 'Uniqlo effect'

> Our clothes are not branded on the outside, because we
> want to promote your sense of style, not our brand name.
> (Uniqlo advertising slogan, 2002)

Uniqlo is a brand name of the Fast Retailing Corporation Limited, a Nikkei listed Japanese fashion retailer. The name is itself an example of internationalized Japanese inventiveness, combining the English words 'unique' and 'clothing'. Uniqlo's emergence on the Japanese (and now European) clothes retail markets has been spectacular and sudden. Sales quadrupled in fiscal 2001 – a remarkable performance given the state of the Japanese retail trade (cf. Box 8.3). Uniqlo's segmentation encompasses lower to mid-price sensitive middle class, which can mean just about everyone in Japan except the extremely rich or the extremely poor (cf. Box. 8.1). The slogan cited above illustrates this inclusive customer focus. 'The company has made basic staple fashion items acceptable to a highly brand-conscious consumer group and has been credited with, among other things, "turning fleece into fashion"' (Mindbranch, 2003).

Box 8.3 The Japanese retail industry

The history of modern through-store retailing in Japan really begins with the Mitsukoshi department store, founded in 1904 (Wong, in Bird, 2002: 385). Rapid post-war urbanization created a demand for fast and commuter friendly shopping that was met by large shopping malls in railway stations and self-service supermarkets. Brands such as Kinokuniya and Daiei rose to challenge Mitsukoshi and other 'general merchandise stores' (cf. Larke, 1994).

The first significant international influence in shaping the Japanese retail industry came from the now ubiquitous 'convenience stores' (*konbini*) such as Lawson or Seven-Eleven Japan. Their names reveal their US American inspiration. Competition in this sector is fierce. For example, several Seven-Elevens will stand in competition on one city street within metres of each other. Differentiation may come in terms of use of space on the premises (e.g. offering a hot food counter or cafe area); opening hours (e.g. variations on the 24/24, 7/7 and 365/365 themes); and technology (e.g. offering photocopying or film developing services, fax and internet access, or ATM cash machines). Sophisticated point-of-sale inventory and distribution (logistics) management systems have been standard in Japan since the 1980s. The 1970s oil-price shocks benefited specialist retailers (i.e. those focusing on one main line of merchandise and/or on one strand of customer service). Ito-Yokado Company became the most strategically focused and profitable among these. Their example set a trend for establishing smaller-scale outlets in large shopping centres. Fast Retailing's Uniqlo label falls into this tradition.

Distinctive features of Japanese retailing include:

• focus on high quality, notably in terms of design and other aesthetic features, and a 'no-haggle' policy if customers return damaged or even unwanted goods (cf. Melville, 1999);

continued

- obsessive attention to wrapping and packaging, particularly during the several 'gift-giving' seasons (cf. Herbig, 1998);
- imported goods being more expensive than domestically produced goods, but simultaneously offering attributes and benefits that Japanese-made goods cannot (cf. Kotler 1997; Melville, 1999);
- discounting (e.g. 'sales') without reliable or trustworthy endorsements in 'normal' economic times suggests goods are faulty or otherwise of low quality (cf. Rice, 1991).

In a significant development discounting is now 'in' as salaries and consumer spending continue to fall (December 2002).

The Uniqlo effect: what aspiring Japanese managers think

When Uniqlo opened its first retail store in the UK in September 2001, we asked a group of Japanese business students (average age twenty-five) to analyse what made Uniqlo 'unusual' in the context of the Japanese wholesale/retail industry. These were their results:

- *Strategy*: systematically deriving their marketing effort (i.e. as opposed, for example, to product development) from foreign rivals; notably GAP and to a lesser extent Benetton.
- *Segmentation/USP*: addressing and setting trends simultaneously for the *freeter* generation (cf. Box 4.1) and for consumers of all ages currently motivated by the 'quality of life' trend in Japan. For example, Uniqlo's 'Precision Basics' are designed to appeal to a wide range of consumer age groups in Japan by being well made, affordable, fashionable, and international and assume growing opportunities for leisure time and demand for 'smart casual' wear (cf. Oumi, 2000).
- *Price*: consciously differentiating their products with a lower retail price against foreign rivals' (e.g. GAP) benchmark price while simultaneously recognizing that there is virtually no tradition of wearing 'cheap' or throwaway casual clothes in Japanese public life.
- *Product*: focusing on a limited product range (e.g. in terms of colour) to achieve economies of scale. Uniqlo clothes are made under licence in mainland China and South East Asia under strict design and quality controls. In doing this they confront a common consumer prejudice that clothes 'Made in China' must be cheap and therefore of low quality. This prejudice does not apply to all foreign made goods (cf. Melville, 1999; Box 3.3)

- *Packaging*: conforms to (high) Japanese standards, is understated and effective and carries English language translations of important product specifications and marketing concepts: appears confident and future-oriented.
- *Distribution*: individual store managers appear to have considerable opportunities for responding to local customer demand: The point-of-sale inventory system is directly linked to production, storage and transport operations in mainland China. Delivery usually takes less than a month. Shop displays are changed on average every two months (cf. Okamoto, 2000).
- *Customer service*: customers are 'allowed' to shop freely: i.e. without the immediate and individual attention of shop assistants, as is normally expected in the Japanese retail sector. Online shopping is also available, thus further freeing up time and space for individual customer choice.
- *Brand/overall image*: Uniqlo appears young and dynamic without appearing brash or aggressive. It presents itself as international but also as Japanese. The colour mix ('Japanese' red and white together with 'universally fashionable' black) and the understated 'post-logo phenomenon' message (cited above) reinforce this image.

Uniqlo's effect on the Japanese retailing industry

Industry experts have since confirmed these conclusions. For example, Uniqlo's (2001) pricing policy flies in the face of strategies adopted by major Japanese rivals such as Ito-Yokado Co. who are (June 2002) raising prices on their 'Made-in Japan' line, following Japanese retail tradition by 'touting higher quality as a trade-off for higher prices' (*Nikkei Net Interactive*, 17 June 2002, accessed 21 June 2002). Another expert industry view is that 'Uniqlo has virtually subverted the traditional Japanese retail business model by retaining manufacturing, distributing, selling and marketing under one roof' (Mindbranch, 2003).

In contrast, Nagura (2002) explains how rival fashion chain Shimamura – a 'once dowdy chain store' – has brightened up its prospects by imitating and then adapting some Uniqlo techniques: for example, combining China-based production and distribution with an assessment of (future Japanese) consumer demand based on (current European) fashions. In the context of falling retail prices together with a slowdown in consumer spending (the risk of so-called 'deflation' looms large in Japan)

Shimamura President Fujiwara is quoted as saying: 'When prices go this low, fashionability leads sales' (Nagura, 2002). Shimamura shares (14 November 2002) are outperforming those of similarly buoyant Uniqlo in Japanese share trading.

Uniqlo's effect on Japanese retail management

Despite the brand's overtly modest image (see slogan cited above), Uniqlo's top managers have achieved a high profile. In response to Uniqlo's entry to the UK market, Thorne (2002) introduces Tadashi Yanai, 'Fast Retailing's dynamic CEO' who is fifty-two years old and 'unusual among Japanese executives in sourcing ideas from abroad. In addition to US college co-ops, he reportedly took note of cheap Chinese-produced merchandise in Hong Kong during his extensive world travels as a young man, and later applied the same approach to Uniqlo. His innovative, nonconformist business practices have made him something of an outsider in Japan's somewhat conservative retailing world' (cf. Box 8.2). Thorne's article further reports how Yanai has 'ruffled feathers with Uniqlo's low prices and unusual management system, which focuses attention on individual store performance'.

Uniqlo's effect on aspiring Japanese managers

Our Japanese business students claimed to recognize in Uniqlo one of 'a newer generation of young, entrepreneurial companies' (Porter *et al.*, 2000: 186): however, as one which did not belong to the much-hyped – and now much-dissipated – e-business sectors; but rather as one which had 'brought fresh air' into an otherwise 'fossilized industry' (cf. Box 8.3). The Uniqlo effect becomes clearer when we compare retailing to another conservative and related industry in Japan: hotels. *The Economist* magazine's online 'Cities Guide: Tokyo' (accessed 16 October 2002) explains how foreign companies are behind a significant proportion of new hotel construction in central Tokyo. According to *The Economist* Guide: 'Most of Tokyo's hotels date back to the 1960s – and look it. Typically owned and run by Japanese, many of them suffer from inflexible management and outdated practices (almost all permanent staff have to be Japanese and promotion tends to be by age). The upcoming competition may mean existing hotels will have to stretch themselves in new ways.'

In summary, Uniqlo's national and industrial impact is about 'stretch' and shaping future attitudes. It is a company which through its strategic decision-making and product marketing enters not only the consciousness of aspiring Japanese managers through media coverage; the Uniqlo vision locates itself in the sphere of their social life and lifestyle choices. As one of our Japanese business students concluded after working on the Uniqlo case: 'I have seen the future of successful Japanese business.' When we asked members of the group: 'Is Uniqlo the type of company you would like to work for after graduation?' the majority answered 'yes'.

Further retail trends: individualization

Foreign retailers are making inroads while convenience stores and high-volume outlets are setting the trends in retailing and wholesale distribution (cf. www.nihondatabank.com, accessed 24 January, 2003). Another common phenomenon during economic recession is for middle-range producers and retailers to suffer most: top-range (luxury) and bottom-range (bargain) operations tend to thrive. Japan is no exception. However, there are notable developments to be observed. One example is the '100-yen' (*hyaku-en*) shops that sell a wide range of goods – often 'Made in China' and other Asian countries with low labour costs – on a single-price policy: a throwback to the old 'Woolworth' tradition in the USA and Europe.

At the top range are fashion goods and cosmetics carrying Japanese brand names such as Issey Miyake, Hanae Mori and Samantha Tabatha. These are unusual in that the full name of the producer/designer is branded: in Japanese business culture usually only family names are referred to: an *ie/zaibatsu* tradition. Indeed, Japanese fashion designer Keizo uses only a first name. The influence in this sector is likely to be derived from foreign brands/designers such as Giorgio Armani and Louis Vuitton. The new Louis Vuitton store in Tokyo (on Omotesando boulevard, Tokyo's 'Champs Elysee') is currently the world's largest.

The branding of full names on Japanese 'lifestyle' products is symptomatic of the *individualization* identified in Chapter 7. The explicit use of 'Made in China' (etc.) labels on fashion or utility goods is a pragmatic recognition of the 'new economy' in retail. Added to this scenario is the increasing 'price consciousness' among consumers meaning that 'the retail industry will have to focus on delivering goods and services that satisfy consumer needs at reasonable prices' (*Nikkei Net*

Interactive, accessed 17 June 2002). Uniqlo managers appear to have caught this trend precisely, and indeed are instrumental in setting and sustaining it. How long this status can last in such a fast-moving industry is open to question.

SECTION 3: THE 'WAR FOR TALENT'

> My young son is a good runner. I recently saw him at his school sports day, running and surely about to win. But he slowed down and allowed some of the others to catch up. I thought: 'This is what we teach kids in school here. This is how kids learn to suppress their individual talent for the sake of the group. There isn't enough stretching of talent.'
>
> (senior manager and parent, DOB 1955, media industry)

In 1998 and again in 2001, Ed Michael, the US director of McKinsey, a business consultancy, urged companies worldwide to prepare systematically for the 'war for talent' (cf. *The McKinsey Quarterly* magazine, Number 4, 2001 – online edition accessed 18 February 2003). McKinsey America is the former employer of Kenichi Ohmae, who in his recent writings has popularized the idea among Japanese managers and employers that this is the future of employment and professional achievement in an increasingly 'borderless world' (cf. Ohmae, 1995).

In response to Michael's appeal, a study by 'Fast Company' (2001) suggested how senior managers and organizations could win this war for talent. Recommended strategies include:

- 'a rigorous and candid' review/appraisal process based on individual performance;
- an approach to HRM which emphasizes trust and respect and 'delivers on your people's dreams' (one recalls Matsui and the Yomiuri Giants, discussed in Chapter 6);
- 'attractive compensation' as this not only 'buys the house' it 'equally represents recognition and fairness'. The authors go on: 'Talented people expect their contributions to be acknowledged and their compensation to reflect their impact';
- an aggressive searching out and recruiting of talent, at 'even senior levels';
- creating 'stretch jobs' combined with 'informal feedback, coaching, and mentoring';
- a systematic 'moving on' of under-performers.

Tension: achievement and ascription

Applying the notion of 'stretch' at the level of corporate strategy (cf. Hamel and Prahalad, 1996) is familiar to successful Japanese organizations and business leaders: we think of Honda, Morita and Matsushita among others who form an outstanding tradition. Also, we recognize how several of these recommendations tune in to what is established practice or tradition in Japanese-style HRM: in this sense, the rest of the world is catching up with Japan.

However, based on our discussion so far it should be clear which of these recommendations – should they be incorporated systematically into traditional Japanese-style HRM – would likely generate most tension between employees and senior or line-managers. For example, there is the obvious problem of contextualizing and satisfying 'dreams' (individualization) and rewards. Furthermore there is the buying in of talent at 'even' senior levels, thereby undermining the seniority promotion tradition. Together these represent an appeal to promote and reward *achievement* above *ascription* (cf. Trompenaars and Hampden-Turner, 1998 – discussed in the context of the 'TH-T model' in Chapter 3). This, we conclude from our research, is one of the major sources of tension challenging Japanese managers today and can be traced as a theme through all of the case studies we have presented in this book. Consider the following case.

Miura-san

In Chapter 4 we illustrated experiences and expectations of organizational induction. We reported on the experiences of Miura-san who, having enjoyed several years of career progression, left her original company to work abroad, returning to Tokyo some years later to work in a different company and in a different industry. We caught up with her in Tokyo to ask her about whether she had re-established contact with any of her former work colleagues. In fact, Miura-san told us about a reunion party she had recently attended. This is what she said:

> I really enjoyed meeting my company 'family' at the reunion party. I always enjoyed my time at the company and I kept in touch with some of my colleagues while I was away, particularly my former boss [now head of HR in the company]. He continued to give me good [personal] advice even after I left the company. I didn't contact him so often, but I always knew he would be there if ever I needed advice. He surprised

me once when he told me that I would always be remembered as a 'good and reliable colleague' –which is, in fact, just how I remember him and my other colleagues.

The party was a success and in many ways just like old times. But still I noticed a kind of tension in the behaviour of some of my former colleagues. One of them told me that sales and R&D activity at the company were stagnating and, seeing what was happening or being written about other companies [in the same industry] many managers and other [core] staff worry about a hostile takeover or an enforced merger with another Japanese – or even a non-Japanese – company. I know from my own analysis that, in global terms, Japanese companies in this particular industry are increasingly under threat from foreign predators.

Towards the end of the party my former boss told me he was particularly worried about the career prospects of two talented women in the company's sales department. If there were to be a takeover or redundancies, he thought that one or both of these might be among the first to go. Unexpectedly, he asked me whether I'd be willing to return to the company, perhaps in a part-time consultancy role, in order to advise these and other female staff on how to manage their careers in 'the new international employment environment'. I asked him 'why me?' and he said something like: 'I can give them career advice, but surely it's better if they get advice from someone [i.e. another woman] who's actually "gone out and done it"'.

We asked ourselves: What is going through this HR manager's mind? Professional concern and respect are there, certainly. There is also a recognition that his experience and perhaps his and his organization's competence and vision are overtaxed – or overstretched? Collectively they appear to have hit the buffers (cf. Box 8.4). Yet the problem is real. How should they deal with it?

Box 8.4 Thriving on chaos?

Research by Kakabadse, Okazaki-Ward and Myers (1996) identifies distinctively high levels of harmony among senior and general or line-managers in Japanese organizations. Harmony emerges where operational expectations of senior and middle-ranking managers in respect of motivation, trust, performance improvement and intra-organizational relationships converge (1996: 78–79). In comparison with their European counterparts, the views of both manager groups in Japanese organizations tend to converge in terms of strategic vision and direction, preferring a long-term orientation to HRM decision-making.

Relative chaos emerges when harmony is disrupted and where responses to change in the strategic environment appear sudden and radically divergent from established or perhaps predicted norms of behaviour. Following Gleick (1988) and others, we regard 'chaos' as a superficially random manifestation of deeper systematic trends. Globalization can be regarded as one of these covert but discernible trends as it challenges accepted management assumptions in Japan as elsewhere (cf. Watson, 1994).

It is significant that back in the early to mid-1990s Kakabadse *et al.* identified what can in hindsight be regarded as a significant key chink in the armour of Japanese managerial harmony: namely, 'the inability [of managers collectively] to address known sensitive issues that exist within the organization' (1996: 85). Kakabadse *et al.* contrast 'sensitive' with 'safe' issues: i.e. those that require less in terms of a critical response or innovation and which are backed up by established mainstream tradition (i.e. without emphasizing 'mavericks' such as Honda, discussed in this chapter).

In practical terms, we can imagine that HRM structures built on 'ascriptive' values (e.g. promotion according to age, length of service or gender) are 'safer' to manage than, for example, pay structures based more explicitly on more controversial measures of individual merit and/or performance.

Managers in large-scale organizations and *keiretsu* networks with a tradition of reliable business growth probably could afford (until recently, at least) to spend more time dealing with 'safe' issues for the purpose of generating organizational 'harmony' and strategic stability. In Japan as elsewhere, managers in less well-resourced organizations (e.g. SMEs and family businesses) or entrepreneurs are likely to have fewer opportunities to dwell on 'safe' issues, needing more frequently to respond to turbulence in the business environment by, for example, laying off staff and struggling to defend their prices and orders with major customers and suppliers: in other words, to 'thrive on chaos', recalling the title of Peters' (1991) bestseller. As suggested in this chapter, the experience and expectations of these managers appears to be becoming more the norm in the context of Japanese management culture.

Does the answer to this particular HR manager's dilemma lie 'out there', along tracks other than those laid down by the established structures and systems that appear to limit his and his organization's choice of HRM and career development options? Where should he take his inspiration from? From books and the vision and experiences of successful business leaders; from the example set by other (currently successful) companies; or (and in this particular case) from the experience of former employees – all possibilities presented in this chapter? To what extent can he rely on his senior managers to offer guidance which will motivate staff threatened with organizational exit while simultaneously motivating the remaining staff – and future recruits – to support the organization in its attempts to achieve specific goals?

SECTION 4: THE ENTREPRENEURIAL SPIRIT

We believe that the HR manager in Miura-san's story showed something of an 'entrepreneurial spirit' in recognizing that he and his organization needed help and a new path towards solving the forthcoming 'organizational exit' dilemma on behalf of the two female employees mentioned. Could this presage a new HRM policy? As in systematically adopting the 'war for talent' paradigm, any move in this direction would need to be promoted and supported by senior management (cf. Box 8.4). But it is likely that these senior managers – or, let's say, the least 'productive' of these – would perceive that they have most to lose by adopting such an approach. This HR manager is probably acting on his own initiative.

Although saying that he displays something of the 'entrepreneurial spirit' is not to claim he is a budding entrepreneur. Entrepreneurs are people who 'undertake the risks of establishing and running a new business [and] are characterized by their initiative and enterprise in seeking out new business opportunities; inventing and commercializing new goods and services and methods of production' (Pass, Lowes, Pendleton and Chadwick, 1995: 224). According to Webber (in Pitman/FT, 1997: 7), entrepreneurs 'tend to be loners, primarily interested in personal achievement and uncomfortable with exercising power over a large organization. Their personal career anchors tend towards "autonomy/independence" or "functional/technical" rather than aspiring personally to lead a large company. They are uneasy with the interdependence that management requires.' Described thus, their character resembles that of the Japanese R&D specialist whose story we presented in Chapter 7: despite inventing a global hit product, he was accused of not being 'a company man' and so was effectively expelled from the 'company family'. We recall he went off to found his own research group.

Nakamura-san

Or consider the much lower-profile case of Nakamura-san. He asked us to meet him at his favourite Shinto shrine in central Tokyo. He is thirty years old, trained as a graphic designer, and together with his young female partner he was praying for good fortune as they both prepared to set up their own graphic and art design business. Confidently they handed us business cards for a company that was not to see the light (officially) for another six months. Why did they choose this time to go freelance? The company they were still working for (a foreign-owned media conglomerate) was beginning to outsource more and more projects. It was only a question of time (they assumed) before one or both of them would be asked to leave. Together they had decided to 'get a head start' on the inevitable.

Why arrange to meet us in a shrine? We were told that worshipping at this shrine should bring prosperity and luck to new ventures, as evidenced by the many young parents and mothers-to-be who visit. Also, Nakamura-san's family has long-standing connections to this shrine. Much of it had been transported from Kyoto when the then Emperor moved his capital to what later became Tokyo. One of Nakamura-san's ancestors had been a teacher in the imperial household. Nakamura-san had always maintained his family's traditional links to the shrine and, more pragmatically, he was in negotiation with the shrine administrators about work his nascent company could do for them. Through the shrine authorities he had also taken up negotiations with the local (Tokyo prefecture) government.

Nakamura-san spoke English well but he had never been outside Japan: his holidays had been spent tending to traditional family matters in Japan. His great-grandfather had been to England, and Nakamura-san would also like to go there one day 'just to see what he might have seen'. These budding entrepreneurs clearly had confidence and a number of very useful social and business connections. But what was the main difficulty? 'Money. The banks won't help us, or they want to know more about us and our project than we are willing to say at the moment. Fortunately, office property in this area – though expensive – is far less expensive to rent than it was even a few years ago. We're optimistic we can make a success of our business.'

The problem of securing venture capital was one we heard frequently in our discussions with entrepreneurs in Japan. As we discussed in Chapter 7, the banking system in Japan is currently in a state of some disarray. Furthermore, several aspiring entrepreneurs we spoke to are reluctant to resort to the type of 'easy credit' offered by companies that, apart from charging extremely high rates of interest, are suspected of operating too closely to the activities commonly attributed to *yakuza* or organized crime networks. Are they being too cautious? More likely the situation is that, for as long as established sources of venture capital or debt- and credit-management are overstretched, agencies from the 'parallel economy' will continue to move in to satisfy a growing demand.

Beware over-generalizations

Nakamura-san's case should remind us that not all enterprising Japanese managers can or will become self-starting entrepreneurs. So how does this insight help Miura-san's former HR manager and his problem of managing organizational exit? At a superficial glance, the apparent lack of encouragement to 'be a loner' and 'take risks in establishing a new business' may be embedded in the structures and traditions of Japanese management culture. However, perhaps this reluctance will last only as long as the norms and values of traditional Japanese management 'culture' are dominated by the interests of giant corporations: the '*keiretsu* mentality' referred to in Chapter 7. As increasing numbers of Japanese managers experience a formal and perhaps (until recently) unexpected 'exit' from organizations, new reference groups will emerge and (if prominently successful) should come to inform benchmarks for the norms and values which shape HRM and career decision-making among current and future generations of Japanese managers.

Convergence with other national models and experiences?

We have already seen how Japanese managers and their organizations have proved themselves adept at learning from management experience and ideas in other countries (cf. Chapter 5). At the risk of upsetting some of our Japanese colleagues (cf. Chapter 7), a possible way forward is illustrated by the strides taken in this direction by South Korean managers and their organizations (notably the massive *chaebol* networks) since their recent and (by several accounts) painful and humiliating experience of economic and industrial restructuring at the end of the 1990s (cf. Bae, 1998). Chen (1995) illustrates the apparent facility among South Korean managers to focus their loyalty on specific people (e.g. a senior or line-manager) rather than on the organization, as their Japanese counterparts tend to do: i.e. the organization as 'family', as discussed in Chapter 3. Accordingly, when *chaebol* industrial networks restructure, it is likely that South Korean managers are prepared to set up smaller entrepreneurial units that, by choice and opportunity, continue to add value to the former 'parent' organizations.

The globalization/localization debate

However, and as Bae and Rowley (2001) conclude in their multi-faceted study of the 'impact of globalization' on the structures and cultures of HRM in South Korea, pressures to change fundamentally established HRM practice at 'local' levels may well be formulated and instituted at the policy level, but not then accepted at the level of implementation (e.g. middle management) and of individual experience. In Japanese organizations this transfer could be expected to work relatively smoothly. However, this is to assume that senior and middle management – under new strategic conditions – continue to share common interests and values (cf. Box 8.4). This line of thinking informs practical HRM considerations in response to the 'localization/globalization debate' among management theorists. It further illustrates the challenge of managing diversity, as discussed in Chapter 7.

Certainly in the case of Japan, there is such perceived strength in 'tradition' (examples of which we have referred to throughout our discussion) that the collective response to global pressures will (in this crisis period) tend to be 'local': i.e. essentially 'Japanese'. Traditional structures and expectations are ingrained not just in respect of perceived time and familiarity. There are also sufficient embedded interests held by groups in Japanese business and society who are unwilling (or unable, perhaps, in terms of the limits of their competence and vision) to relinquish direct control over the interpretation of how people should be managed. As a result, 'even in an era of globalization, national systems of HRM remain robust in their individuality and usefulness' (Bae and Rowley, 2001: 423). 'Useful' is a relative term.

Entrepreneurs as role models?

As Webber reminds us: 'Entrepreneurs seldom provide models of general management in large corporations' (Pitman/FT, 1997: 7). In the context of Japanese management, the 'large corporation model' still dominates. Consequently, although we are keen to emphasize 'change' in this discussion we must be aware that currently it is the voices of 'continuity' in Japanese management culture that are still trying to claim the last word (cf. Maswood, Graham and Miyajima, 2003).

For example, not all budding entrepreneurs in Japan have the type of contacts that should help Nakamura-san and his partner get started in their new venture. Not all budding entrepreneurs in Japan can expect to be like Honda or Morita – their time and place are very different – though such legendary figures can offer profound inspiration. As important a variable is the confidence and optimism that Nakamura-san personifies. A minority of Japanese managers have the interest, courage, vision and other resources needed to become successful entrepreneurs. It is possible to make a comparative generalization and claim that in parts of China the attitude would be very different. For example, Mead (1998: 380) citing Wong (1986) explains how 'a Shanghainese at 40 who has not yet made himself the owner of a firm is a failure, a good-for-nothing'.

This generalization is one which preoccupies several Japanese managers we spoke to. As one said to us: 'Think of the size of China's population. Think how many smart and talented and entrepreneurial people they have compared to the numbers in Japan. Even if the proportion [of would-be entrepreneurs] is the same, the numbers are very different. If we don't wake up to this we will soon see an erosion of our [i.e. Japanese] markets and our way of doing business.' This (mid-thirties) manager perceived a growing threat to his own position and prospects as his company had begun buying in 'talent' from among Japanese-speaking Chinese graduates, of which there are increasing numbers in Japan.

Emerging reference groups

Time will tell; it usually does. At the moment there is probably more value in focusing on individuals who are nearer the mainstream of internationally aware managers and would-be entrepreneurs in Japan; managers such as Takeguchi-san, whose story we recounted in Chapter 3. He is the middle-aged manager who – after his organization went bankrupt – set up a professional headhunting agency, demanding of his successful candidates that they should be 'culturally adaptable' and 'confident, not only in [respect of] foreign cultures, but also in the management [culture] which is emerging in Japan now'.

Returning to the boy who wouldn't win the race (cited at the beginning of this section): why didn't he choose to finish first? One reason is probably his reluctance to set himself up as a lone 'reference group': he instinctively sought the support and affirmation of his peer group and wanted to avoid his own embarrassment and their loss of face. We asked Nakamura-san whether he was worried about 'going it alone'. 'I'm not alone. I have my partner, my contacts, and my family name and tradition.'

Slowly groups of practising and budding entrepreneurs are beginning to emerge; or, more precisely, their voice is beginning to be heard – and noticed, not least because the voice is often female (cf. Kambayashi and Rutledge, 2002).

We have consciously made a balanced presentation of Japanese women and male managers in this book. However, and beyond gender, when we compare the backgrounds of these several individual cases and, for example, the three of Takeguchi-san (Chapter 3) and (in this chapter) Miura-san and Nakamura-san, we see that no standard picture emerges: they are male and female, young and not so young, graduates from high-ranking or not so high-ranking universities, with extensive or not so extensive social connections, and with or without experience of working and living outside Japan. Apart from nationality, what these three individuals do appear to have in common is experience of working in large-scale (Japanese and non-Japanese) companies: the experience of the requirements of 'management' as defined by Webber (1997, cited above). They thus confirm the recommendations made by Sukehara-san to aspiring Japanese international managers, presented in Chapter 7. In this sense, the forces of continuity can be seen to be nurturing the seeds of change.

What further appears to unite the diverse individuals whose stories we have told in this book is the courage and sense of occasion to pursue an idea, a challenge, and thereby assert their sense of professional self-esteem. Together they form an emerging reference group in Japanese management culture.

SECTION 5: VOICES FROM THE FRINGE

> As the core of Japan's economy yawns its way into a
> second decade of stagnation, dynamism can be found on
> the fringes, where many of the entrepreneurs, innovators
> and risk takers just happen to be women.
> (Kambayashi and Rutledge, 2002)

In their article, Kambayashi and Rutledge (2002) cite the stories of several women who have either started their own business or are working to inject a new dynamism into standards of management practice and vision in Japanese organizations. We can read examples of women who have set up training and venture capital agencies designed to help other women set up their own business. Many have chosen to escape the binds of expectation of 'just' being a housewife or an 'also-ran' in the race for promotion in traditional Japanese organizations: 'the energy from their outrage helps trigger the launching of their business' is the view of one female entrepreneur.

One female university professor's view is that 'men's viewpoints don't always meet the market demand precisely'. In other words, Japanese women tend to be more flexible and pragmatic, less loyal to companies and more aware of what's happening in the employment market generally – unsurprisingly, given that for generations they have been systematically excluded from most traditional career structures in Japan (cf. Chapter 4). The professor goes on: 'Since the fields of service and welfare are expected to expand more hereafter, I think women's points of view could be put into practical use more often.' In this statement we see an overlap with the growing scope for career and entrepreneurial opportunities in the not-for-profit sectors in Japan, as suggested above.

Another chance

These opportunities are open to men and women managers of all ages and backgrounds. In an article entitled 'Senior workers reboot their careers', the *Nikkei Net Interactive* (14 October 2002) explains how increasing numbers of Japanese retirees are re-entering the world of work and, simultaneously, redefining their own and other people's experience of a career. The example is given of one '62-year-old' former engineer, who now teaches computer skills to other retirees (average age 57) at a local 'non-profit' organization: for his contribution this former engineer earns the equivalent of US$20,000. 'We regard individual members as entrepreneurs, and help them establish businesses', explains a spokesperson for the organization.

Among this generation of 'entrepreneurs', the businesses being founded are concentrated in the non-profit sector and in industries such as education, social care and catering. However, the seed money (sometimes supported by government grants) that these organizations can provide has made it possible for retirees to set up profit-making companies in, for example, the cosmetics, marketing and entertainment industries – anywhere where there is a niche and where the retirees can re-apply their skills. One fifty-five-year old is quoted as saying: 'My income is half, but I'm happy that my skills are still needed.' While the head of another agency specializing in the re-integration of retired managers into enterprise is quoted as follows: 'New approaches to work are needed for those older employees to result in the happy medium of working and being self-employed.'

A shift in values

The reference to a 'happy medium' is topical. Increasingly, surveys and newspaper articles indicate a change of attitude in Japanese society. We have already referred to the *freeter* phenomenon as indicative of a shift in public attitudes to work (Box 4.1). Perhaps theirs is in part a reaction to the shocking rise in the suicide rate in Japan, particularly among middle-aged employees and managers fearing or having experienced redundancy (cf. *The Financial Times* online 25 September 2001). Seldom spoken about openly, but a shadow hanging over families across Japan nevertheless, this most desperate of answers to the question: 'what to do next?' may be one outcome of the strain of trying (often desperately) to adhere to traditional work-related values. Masui (2002) suggests that Japan might be going through 'a transitional period' where people are 'preparing for a new shape for the country'. He identifies a significant shift towards 'taking life easy' and concludes: 'One thing is certain. The economy and money are no longer foremost in people's minds.'

Sone (2002) cites sixty-three-year-old Tsutomo Okuda, brother of Toyota Motor Corporation's chairman Hiroshi Okuda, and president of Daimaru Inc, a major player in the Japanese retail and wholesale (department stores) and real-estate sectors. Okuda says: 'The Japanese have pursued expansion and growth so aggressively in the past, and we now deserve more ways to enjoy our leisure time.' In Okuda's case this means spending more time listening to his favourite music (Bach) and watching movies. His company, meanwhile, is bucking the retail trend among department stores in Japan by dramatically improving earnings.

A shift in perspectives

The non-profit sector or field of activity for non-governmental organizations (NGOs) is currently the fastest growing sector for employment in the world. We spoke to several Japanese NGO managers during our research.

As the management for development literature suggests (cf. Taylor, 1996), managers who succeed in non-profit sectors tend to have a more heightened sensitivity than many of their private-sector counterparts towards the political dimensions of management decision-making and (correspondingly) 'sufficing' rather than seeking to 'control' outcomes to complex 'people-focused' decision-making processes. In respect of the 'politics' of management decision-making, one (male) NGO manager explained that, in seeking to manage change, the first step is to identify what it *is* that needs changing, and then communicate this insight to other 'change-makers': 'To manage change effectively, we have to have the necessary words to be able to label what we see.' We are talking here about the 'management of meaning'. Also, we are not suggesting that all Japanese managers who are seeking a new direction in their career development are going to move into the NGO or not-for-profit sector. Rather, we are talking about what managers in the private and public sectors (i.e. comprising the vast majority of managers and jobs in Japan) can learn from these sectors.

Claiming the language of change

This NGO manager's views about 'identifying what needs changing' was shared by a (female) manager who used to work in a private-sector company but who now works as a freelance consultant advising women who are trying to set up their own business. This is how (in her own words) her 'eyes were opened' to the sexism which persists in many Japanese social and work environments:

> I used to hear some of the comments made by my male colleagues. They would ask me – jokingly – what colour underwear I was wearing that day. This went on for years and it wasn't until I actually heard the [Japanese] word '*sekuhara*' from a close [female] colleague working for another company that I understood what 'sexual harassment' actually was. My antennae are now primed. I'm able now to hear and recognize *sekuhara* wherever and whenever it happens – at work, in the media, in everyday conversation. And believe me, I make sure I let other people know that I recognize it when it does happen!

Facing facts

The identification and labelling of this particular 'problem' was for this manager a crucial step towards a more critical awareness of how 'people are often unconsciously biased in how they deal and work with each other. Their mutual lack of real comprehension means that problems – and I mean the essential problems that shape our lives and our relationships to others – go unrecognized and so, inevitably, unsolved. We need to face up to these problems, give them a name, and then work together to solve them.' As one manager of a Japanese NGO explained to us: 'In order to manage the future we need to know where we're starting from – we need to understand our present. We need to face facts, pleasant or unpleasant as some of these may be.'

Facing the future

It is possible to regard the voices from the 'dynamic fringe' of Japanese management as representing the tip of a very large iceberg, moving slowly but with modest confidence towards an uncertain future. These opinions and voices from the fringe echo many of those we have presented throughout this book. They still represent a minority in Japan. But equally, they almost certainly indicate a shift in values that will continue to have a significant resonance among those people whose combined efforts and aspirations and whose individual and collective response to current problems and dilemmas we generalize on and label 'Japanese management culture'. And, as this 'dynamic minority' struggles to break free from the structural and culture-specific constraints that work to hold them back, they simultaneously represent the changing face of Japanese management.

Summary

In this final chapter we have looked at how Japanese managers commonly – and exceptionally – deal with the experience and prospect of organizational exit. We have explored the extent to which existing HRM and employment structures facilitate their negotiation of this experience. We have looked at past and present sources of inspiration that, in addition to helping them formulate and achieve their individual career or business objectives, allow them to respond to current challenges with confidence and simultaneously develop and express a growing sense of achievement. The picture of the 'face of Japanese management' that emerges from these individual and collective experiences is one that can be future-oriented and international, entrepreneurial and vital. However, it is also one shaped by conflict with some of the ingrained structural problems in Japanese business and society.

In this and previous chapters we have also seen the positive legacy of Japanese-style HRM traditions: how to manage and nurture individual talent; how to sustain a working environment based on respect and concern for the individual. We have illustrated areas where exceptional Japanese managers and entrepreneurs have been able to build on some of these traditional strengths in order to negotiate the professional and business challenges of both their present and of their likely futures, and in doing so gain a stronger sense of self-esteem.

Finally, consider these questions:

- What would / did finally motivate you to change job or career path? What aspects of your professional or personal experience and working environment would make/made this decision easier or more difficult?

- Imagine a close friend or colleague is preparing for an expatriate assignment to manage a project in a partner organization in Japan. What practical advice would you give, and why?

 # Glossary

[Numbers in brackets] denote chapters where the term is discussed in detail.

amae traditional socio-economic patterns of expected dependency (e.g. between child and mother, wife and husband) [4] (cf. Doi, 1971/2002)

amakudari 'descent from heaven', traditionally describing a situation where senior civil servants transfer to private-sector companies or company subsidiaries [8]

aotagai a process whereby Japanese organizations 'jump the gun' on the graduate recruitment windows informally agreed among industry insiders and government ministers [4] (cf. *naitei shiki*)

bento carefully pre-packaged meals usually containing specially prepared rice (*sushi*) and raw fish or cooked meat and sold in convenience stores, supermarkets, department stores and at railway stations and on trains [2 and 8]

bucho middle-ranking manager or line-manager, usually with accountability for the financial performance of a department or division [5 and 6] (cf. *kacho*)

bushido chivalric code of honour and ritual among Japanese *samurai* warriors [2] (cf. *ronin*)

chusan socio-economic term describing Japan's 'middle class' [4] (cf. Ishida, 1993)

doki a group of people who begin a stage of their career path together (e.g. school or university; or during organizational induction, where they're also known as *shinsotsu*) [2, 3, 4, 6 and 7]

freeter a recently coined term applied to Japanese people who appear to emphasize 'quality of life' over dedication to work or commitment to a company [4 and 8]

gai-jin foreigner (i.e. non-Japanese person): *gai* = 'outside', *jin* = 'person' [3 and 7]

ganbaru to persevere, try hard. The common phrase *ganbatte kudasai* means 'please do your best', usually emphasizing sheer effort over achievement [3, 4, 5, 6 and 8]

giri a sense of obligation and duty towards people perceived as having higher social status [3] (cf. *on*)

han a study group at school and (in culture-specific terms) a precursor of the work or project group in Japanese companies [3 and 4]

haragei 'belly language', suggesting that Japanese people are so culturally and socially attuned to each other that they can communicate without words [1]

hensachi (or 'T-score') a normalized test score used nationally by Japanese high schools and universities as the basis for student selection [3 and 4]

honne what a person actually feels and thinks in specific contexts as opposed to what is expected in terms of individual and collective behaviour [1, 2, 6 and 7] (cf. *tatemae*)

ie originally describing a feudal merchant house, the term also connotes 'family' and 'the company as family' [3, 4, 7 and 8] (cf. *kaisha*)

ippan shoku clerical or general administration career track, traditionally the preserve of women recruits to Japanese organizations [4] (cf. *sogo shoku*)

Japan Inc. an ironic term that evokes the image of Japan as one large nationally motivated and co-ordinated company family [4, 7 and 8] (cf. *ie, kaisha*)

juku/yobiko commercially run cramming schools to train students how to survive Japan's school 'examination hell': *yobiko* cramming schools specialize in getting students into higher-ranking Japanese universities [3 and 4] (cf. *ronin*)

kacho middle-ranking manager or line-manager with accountability for monitoring individual employee performance in a section or department [2, 3, 4, 5 and 6] (cf. *bucho*)

kaisha generic term for a Japanese company or organization (cf. Abegglen and Stalk, 1985; Yoshimura and Anderson, 1997)

kai-zen a philosophy of continuously striving towards incremental and detailed improvement [2, 3, 4, 5, 6 and 8]

kanban an innovation in inventory management and an integral component of the revolutionary Toyota Production System (TPS) [5 and 6]

kanji written form of Japanese language which originates from Chinese [1 and 3]

karoshi death from over-working [5]

keiretsu post-World War Two industrial networks of vertically and horizontally integrated companies, banks and trading or distribution companies [2, 3, 7 and 8]

kikokushijo 'returnee children' who have spent part of their upbringing and education outside Japan and face the task of reintegrating themselves into Japanese society [3 and 7]

kohai younger 'apprentice' member in a dyadic learning relationship where the younger and less experienced member is given guidance by the older *senpai* member [1, 3, 5 and 6]

kyakusama wa osama 'the customer is king' [2]

kyariawoman (or 'career woman'), a recently coined label applied to Japanese women who choose to pursue a professional career rather than subsume their interests and ambitions to family and husband [4 and 8] (cf. *amae, ryosai kenbo, salaryman*)

madogi-wa a euphemism to describe an often undignified process of forcing an employee out of an organization [8]

manga enormously popular Japanese-style comic book and artwork form covering topics as wide-ranging as pornography, politics and management education [3, 7 and 8]

meishi generic term for business card, usually referred to as o-meishi (the 'o'-prefix denoting respect) [1 and 7]

naitei shiki formal and extended recruitment and selection process instituted by HR staff in Japanese organizations [4] (cf. *aotagai*)

nemawashi a process of consensual strategic decision-making commonly used in Japanese organizations and in their subsidiaries overseas [6 and 7] (cf. *ringi-sho*)

nihon (also pronounced *nip-pon*) 'Japan' and means literally 'sun-origin' or (in subsequent westernized usage) the 'land of the rising sun' [1]

nihonjinron academic term denoting the study of Japanese people and the alleged 'uniqueness' of Japanese culture [3]

on an expectation of paternalistic benevolence from superiors towards their subordinates [3] (cf. *giri*)

pachinko a form of entertainment whereby players flick small balls around in a Las Vegas-style slot machine; gaudily-lit *pachinko* parlours are ubiquitous in Japan, very often near shopping centres and railway and bus stations [5 and 8]

ringi-sho (also *ringi seido*) a process of decision-making which requires all involved parties openly to express their consent to a proposed change [6] (cf. *nemawashi*)

risutora an imported term for (organizational) 'restructuring' [7 and 8]

ronin formerly a term to describe a Japanese *samurai* warrior who had lost his master; it is now used to describe students who are still cramming to get into the university of their choice [4] (cf. *bushido, juku/yobiko*)

ryosai kenbo 'good wife, wise mother', assumed to be the traditional career aspiration of Japanese women [4] (cf. Renshaw, 1999)

salaryman (also *sarariman*), the cliché image of a salaried (for life!) male Japanese office worker or manager [4 and 8]

-san attached to people's names as a sign of respect, particularly when talking about direct or indirect acquaintances; for example, 'Sato-san' could in English be translated as 'Mr' or 'Mrs' or 'Ms' Sato, as appropriate; out of modesty, Sato-san would never refer to him/herself using the '-san' form

sekuhara an imported term for 'sexual harassment' [8]

senpai older and more experienced member in a dyadic learning relationship; *senpai* informally 'teach the ropes' to younger and less experienced *kohai* [1, 3, 4 and 5] (cf. *sensei*)

sensei formally 'teacher', but evoking the image (derived from Confucian tradition) of an older (male) person as wiser, socially senior, and so acting as a role model for younger people (*gakusei* = student or pupil) [1, 2, 3, 4, 5 and 8] (cf. *senpai/kohai* relationship)

shimbun newspaper; for example, the *Nihon Keizei (Nikkei) Shimbun* was founded in 1876 and is the Japanese equivalent of the UK's/Europe's *Financial Times* and the USA's *Wall Street Journal* (cf. Bird, 2002)

shinkansen revolutionary high-speed 'bullet train' and railway network linking all Japan's major cities [2 and 3]

sogo shoku managerial career track, particularly used in reference to women employees [4] (cf. *ippan shoku*)

sogo shosha generic term for traditional large-scale Japanese trading companies [2 and 7] (cf. *keiretsu*)

tatemae the sense of what is publicly expected in terms of individual and collective behaviour [1,2, 6 and 7] (cf. *honne*)

wa absence of open conflict, often translated as 'harmony' [2, 5 and 8]

wagamama acts of individual selfishness or self-indulgence [5 and 6]

yakuza underground criminal and business networks, often compared to western *mafia* [8]

zaibatsu family-based industrial and commercial networks, dismantled during the US Occupation after World War Two and subsequently reformed as *keiretsu* industrial networks [3 and 7]

 # Bibiliography

Abegglen, J. C. (1958) *The Japanese Factory: Aspects of its Social Organization*, Glencoe (IL): Free Press

Abegglen, J. C. and G. Stalk Jr (1985) *Kaisha: The Japanese Corporation*, New York: Basic Books

Adler, N. J., N. C. Campbell and A. Laurent (1989) 'In search of an appropriate methodology: from outside the People's Republic of China looking in', *Journal of International Business Studies* spring, pp. 61–74

Ambler, T. and M. Witzel (2000) *Doing Business in China*, London: Routledge

Andersson, T. (ed.) (1993) *Japan: A European Perspective*, London: Macmillan

Andrews, T., B. J. Baldwin and N. Chompusri (2002) *The Changing Face of Multinationals in South East Asia*, London: Routledge

Aoki, M. and H. Patrick (eds) (1994) *The Japanese Main Bank System*, Oxford: Oxford University Press

Argyris, C. and D. A. Schon (1978) *Organisational Learning*, Reading (MA): Addison-Wesley

Ariga, K. (1999) *Japanese Human Resource Management at the Crossroads*, The Monthly Journal of the Japan Institute of Labour 474, pp. 50–61

Ariga, K., G. Brunello and Y. Ohkusa (2000) *Internal Labour Markets in Japan*, Cambridge: Cambridge University Press

Avruch, K. (2002) *Culture and Negotiation Pedagogy* in www.pon.harvard.edu (pdf file accessed 29 July 2002)

Ayto, J. (1990) *Bloomsbury Dictionary of Word Origins*, London: Bloomsbury

Backman, M. (1999) *Asian Eclipse: Exposing the Dark Side of Business in Asia*, Singapore: John Wiley & Sons

Bae, J.-S. (1998) 'Beyond seniority-based systems: a paradigm shift in Korean HRM', *Asia Pacific Business Review* 3 (4), pp. 82–110

Bae, J.-S. and C. Rowley (2001) 'The impact of globalization on HRM: the case of South Korea', *Journal of World Business* 36 (4), pp. 402–408

Barnard, C. (2003) *Language, Ideology and Japanese History Textbooks*, London: Routledge

Bayyurt, Y. (1996) 'The analysis of the concept of face in TV talk shows in Turkey', *Lancaster Papers in Linguistics*, 85: University of Lancaster (UK)

Beasley, W. G. (1999) *The Japanese Experience: A Short History of Japan*, Berkeley: University of California Press

Beechler, S. and A. Bird (eds) (1999) *Japanese Multinationals Abroad: Individual and Organizational Learning*, Oxford: Oxford University Press

Benedict, R. (1946) *The Chrysanthemum and the Sword: Patterns of Japanese Culture*, Boston (MA): Houghton Mifflin

Bennis, W. G. (ed.) (1968) *Leadership and Motivation: Essays of Douglas McGregor*, Boston: MIT Press

Bird, A. (ed.) (2002) *Encyclopaedia of Japanese Business and Management*, London: Routledge

Blackman, C. (1997) *Negotiating China: Case Studies and Strategies*, St Leonards (Australia): Allen and Unwin

Briscoe, D. (1995) *International Human Resource Management*, New Jersey: Prentice-Hall

Brislin, R. W. and T. Yoshida (1994) *Intercultural Communication Training: An Introduction*, Thousand Oaks (CA): Sage

Brown, C., Y. Nakata and I. Ulman (1997) *Work and Pay in the United States and Japan*, New York: Oxford University Press

Butcher, D. (2002) 'It takes two to review', *Management Today* November, pp. 54–59.

Chen, M. (1995) *Asian Management Systems*, London: Routledge

Clammer, J. (1997) *Contemporary Urban Japan*, Oxford: Blackwell

Cohen, T. (1987) *Remaking Japan: The American Occupation as a New Deal*, New York: The Free Press

Cole, R. E. (1991) *Strategies for Learning: Small Group Activities in American, Japanese and Swedish Industry*, Berkeley: University of California Press

Covey, S. (1989) *The 7 Habits of Highly Effective People: Powerful Lessons in Personal Change*, London: Simon & Schuster

Cruise O'Brien, R. (2001) *Trust: Releasing the Energy to Succeed*, Chichester: John Wiley and Sons

Cummings, W. K. (1980) *Education and Equality in Japan*, Princeton: Princeton University Press

Dahl, S. (2002) *Communications and Culture Transformation: Cultural Diversity, Globalization and Cultural Convergence* in www.stephweb.com/capstone (html/pdf file accessed 5 June 2002)

Daniels, J. and L. H. Radebaugh (1998) *International Business: Environments and Operations*, Reading (MA): Addison-Wesley

Deming, W. E. (1982) *Out of the Crisis*, Cambridge (MA): CAES

De Mooij, M. (1994) *Advertising Worldwide: Concept, Theories and Practice of International and Global Advertising*, London: Prentice-Hall

Devanna, M. A., C. J. Fombrun and N. M. Tichy (eds) (1984) *Strategic Human Resource Management*, New York: John Wiley

Doi, T. (1971/2002) *The Anatomy of Dependence*, Tokyo: Kodansha International

Dore, R. (1973) *British Factory Japanese Factory: The Origins of National Diversity in Industrial Relations*, London: Allen and Unwin

Dore, R. (1987) *Taking Japan Seriously: A Confucian Perspective on Leading Economic Issues*, London: The Athlone Press

Dore, R. and M. Sako (1998) *How the Japanese Learn to Work*, London: Routledge

Dower, J. (1999) *Embracing Defeat: Japan in the Wake of World War II*, New York: W. W. Norton

Drucker, P. (1999) *The Frontiers of Management*, New York: Penguin

Etzioni, A. (1975) *A Comparative Analysis of Complex Organisations*, New York: Free Press

Etzioni, A. (1988) *The Moral Dimension*, New York: Free Press

Ezrati, M. (1999) *Kawari: How Japan's Economic and Cultural Transformation Will Alter the Balance of Power among Nations*, London: Aurum Press

Fast Company (2001) *War for Talent II: Seven Ways to Win* in www.fastcompany.com (accessed 17 February 2003)

Fisher, R. and W. Ury (1997) *Getting to Yes*, London: Arrow Books

Foong, W. F. (1999) *The New Asian Way: Rebuilding Asia through Self-reliance*, Selangor Darul Ehsan (Malaysia): Pelanduk

Fujimoto, T. (1999) *The Evolution of a Manufacturing System at Toyota*, Oxford: Oxford University Press

Fukuyama, F. (1995) *Trust: The Social Virtues and the Creation of Prosperity*, New York: Free Press

Fukuyama, F. (2000) *The Great Disruption: Human Nature and the Reconstitution of Social Order*, London: Simon & Schuster

Gao, B. (1997) *Economic Ideology and Japanese Industrial Policy*, Cambridge: Cambridge University Press

Geertz, C. (1973) *The Interpretation of Cultures*, New York: Basic Books

Gerlach, M. (1992) 'The Japanese corporate network: a blockmodel analysis', in Ghauri and Prasad (1995)

Gerlach, M. (1993) *Alliance Capitalism: The Social Organization of Japanese Business*, Berkley (CA): University of California Press

Ghauri, P. N. and S. B. Prasad (eds) (1995) *International Management: A Reader*, London: Dryden Press

Giddens, A. (1989) *Sociology*, Oxford: Polity Press

Giffard, S. (1994) *Japan Among the Powers 1890–1990*, London: Yale University Press

Gleick, J. (1988) *Chaos: Making a New Science*, Harmondsworth: Penguin

Goffee, R. and J. Hunt (1997) 'The end of management? Classroom versus the boardroom', in Pitman/FT (1997)

Goffman, E. (1959) *The Presentation of Self in Everyday Life*, London: Allen Lane/Penguin Press

Golding, D. and D. Currie (eds) (2000) *Thinking about Management: A Reflective Practice Approach*, London: Routledge

Goodman, R. (1990) *Japan's 'International Youth': The Emergence of a New Class of School Children*, Oxford: Oxford University Press

Goodman, R., C. Peach and A. Takenaka (2002) *Global Japan*, London: Routledge

Goto, A. and H. Odagiri (eds) (1997) *Innovation in Japan*, Oxford: Oxford University Press

Graham, J. L., S. Ichikawa and Y. Apasu (1995) *Managing Your Sales Force in Japan and the U.S.*, in Meloan and Graham (1995)

Guest, D. (1989) 'Personnel and HRM: can you tell the difference?', *Personnel Management* (January) London: IPD

Hakuhodo (2000) *The Annual Data Book on the Japanese People*, Tokyo: Hakuhodo Institute of Life and Living

Hall, E. T. (1976) *Beyond Culture*, New York: Anchor Press / Doubleday

Hall, E. T. (1983) *The Dance of Life*, New York: Anchor Press / Doubleday

Hall, E. T. and M. R. Hall (1987/1990) *Hidden Differences: Doing Business with the Japanese*, New York: Anchor Press / Doubleday

Hall Chamberlain, B. (1905) *Things Japanese*, London: Murray

Halmos, P. (ed.) (1966) *The Sociological Review Monograph 10: Japanese Sociological Studies*, Keele: The University of Keele Press

Hamel, G. and C. K. Prahalad (1996) *Competing for the Future*, Boston: Harvard Business School Press

Handy, C. (1991) *Gods of Management: The Changing Work of Organisations*, London: Arrow Books

Hannagan, T. (1998) *Management Concepts and Practices*, London: Financial Times/Pitman Publishing

Hasegawa, H. (1998) 'Japanese global strategies in Europe and the formation of regional markets', in Hasegawa and Hook (1998)

Hasegawa, H. (1998a) 'The rise of flexible and individual ability-oriented management', in Hasegawa and Hook (1998)

Hasegawa, H. and G. Hook (eds) (1998) *Japanese Business Management: Restructuring for Low Growth and Globalization*, London: Routledge

Hatch, W. and K. Yamamura (1996) *Asia in Japan's Embrace: Building a Regional Production Alliance*, Cambridge: Cambridge University Press

Hawthorn, G. (1998) *The Future of Asia and the Pacific*, London: Phoenix

Hayashi, S. (1988) *Culture and Management in Japan*, Tokyo: University of Tokyo Press

Helou, A. (1991) 'The nature and competitiveness of Japan's Keiretsu', in Ghauri and Prasad (1995)

Henderson, B. D. (1989) 'The origins of strategy', *Harvard Business Review* November–December

Hendry, J. (1995) *Understanding Japanese Society*, Oxford/London: Nissan Institute/Routledge

Herbig, P. A. (1995) *Innovation Japanese Style*, Westport (CN): Quorum

Herbig, P. A. (1995a) *Marketing Japanese Style*, Westport (CN): Quorum

Herbig, P. A. (1998) *Handbook of Cross-Cultural Marketing*, New York: IBP/Haworth

Hickson, D. (ed.) (1997) *Exploring Management Across the World*, Harmondsworth: Penguin

Hijino, K. (2001) *SURVEY – JAPAN: Taste of freedom starts to turn sour as choice narrows: YOUNG PEOPLE* in *The Financial Times* (online edition, accessed 25 September 2001)

Hiromura, S. (1990) A presentation given at a conference of the World Association of Opinion and Marketing Research Professionals (Esomar®), Monte Carlo, cited in De Mooji (1994: 96–97)

Hofstede, G. (1980) *Culture's Consequences: International Differences in Work-Related Values*, Beverly Hills: Sage

Hofstede, G. (1984) *Culture's Consequences: International Differences in Work-Related Values*, Beverly Hills: Sage (abridged edition)

Hofstede, G (1991/94) *Cultures and Organisations: Intercultural Cooperation and Its Importance for Survival*, London: HarperCollins

Hofstede, G. (2001) *Culture's Consequences: Comparing Values, Behaviors, Institutions, and Organizations Across Nations*, New York: Sage

Hook, G. and H. Hasegawa (2001) *The Political Economy and Japanese Globalisation*, Sheffield/London: The Sheffield Centre for Japanese Studies/ Routledge

Hori, I. (ed.) (1989) *Japanese Religion*, Tokyo: Kodansha International

Hsu, R. (1994) *The MIT Encyclopedia of the Japanese Economy*, Boston: MIT Press

Iida, Y. (2002) *Rethinking Identity in Modern Japan*, London: Routledge

Imai, M. (1975) *Never Take Yes for an Answer*, Tokyo: Simul Press

Inohara, H. (2000) *Human Resource Development in Japanese Companies*, Tokyo: Asian Productivity Organization

Ishida, H. (1993) *Social Mobility in Contemporary Japan: Educational Credentials, Class and the Labour Market in a Cross-National Perspective*, London: Macmillan

Ishida, H. (1998) 'Educational credentials and labour-market entry outcomes in Japan', in Shavit and Mueller (1998)

Ito, T. (1992) *The Japanese Economy*, Cambridge (MA): MIT Press

Iwata, R. (2000) *Japanese Style Management*, Tokyo: Asian Productivity Organization

Izeki, T. (1995) *ONE to ONE Maaketingu: Kokyaku Rireishon Senryaku*, Tokyo: Daiyamondosha

Jackson, K. (2003) *International Management*, (Learning Module 7: 'Managing risk and uncertainty') in P. Franklin: *An on-line course in English for German students of management* in www.fhk-mba

Janocha, P. (1995) *Japan: Wegweiser zur Erschließung des japanischen Markets für mittelständische Unternehment*, Munich: Oldenbourg Verlag

JETRO (2002) 'Foreign firms employ 1 million in Japan', in JETRO (*Japanese External Trade Organisation*) press release, online edition (22 October 2002)

Johansson, J. K. and M. Hirano (1995) 'Japanese marketing in the post-bubble era' in Meloan and Graham (1995)

Johnson, C. (1985) *MITI and the Japanese Miracle: The Growth of Industrial Policy 1925–1975*, Stanford (CA): Stanford University Press

Johnson, C. (1992) *Japan: Who Governs?: The Rise of the Developmental State*, New York: Norton

Jolivet, M. (1997) *Japan: The Childless Society*, London: Routledge

JTB (1997) *Illustrated 'Salaryman' in Japan*, Tokyo: Japan Travel Bureau Inc.

Kakabadse, A., L. Okazaki-Ward and A. Myers (1996) *Japanese Business Leaders*, London: International Thomson Business Press

Kambayashi, T. and B. Rutledge (2002) 'Outstanding individuals', in *J@pan Inc. magazine*, October

Kaplinsky, K. and A. Posthuma (1994) *Easternization: The Spread of Japanese Management Techniques to Developing Countries*, London: Frank Cass

Kariya, T. (1995) *Taishu kyouiku shakai no yukue* (*The Future of Mass Education*), Tokyo: Chuo Koron Sha

Kariya, T. (1998) 'From high school and college to work in Japan: meritocracy through institutional and semi-institutional linkages', in Shavit and Mueller (1998)

Kasai, N. (1999) 'Why do Japanese employees work for foreign multi-national companies as opposed to Japanese companies?' Unpublished masters research project: Lancaster University Management School

Kawahara, A. (1998) *The Origins of Competitive Strength: 50 Years of the Auto Industry in Japan and the U.S*, Berlin: Springer Verlag

Kay, J. (1993) *Foundations of Corporate Success*, Oxford: Oxford University Press

Keeley, T. D. (2001) *International Human Resources Management in Japanese Firms*, London: Palgrave Macmillan

Kerbo, H. R. and J. A. McKinstry (1995) *Who Rules Japan: The Inner Circles of Economic and Political Power*, London: Praeger

Kidd, J. B. (1998) 'Knowledge creation in Japanese manufacturing companies in Italy', *Management Learning* 29(2), pp. 131–146

Kluckhohn, F. R. and F. L. Strodtbeck (1961) *Variations in Value Orientations*, New York: Peterson

Kodansha (1997) *The Inscrutable Japanese*, Tokyo: Kodansha International Ltd

Koike, K. (1988) *Understanding Industrial Relations in Japan*, New York: St Martin's Press

Koike, K. and T. Inoki (1991) *Skill Formation in Japan and Southeast Asia*, Tokyo: Tokyo University Press

Kono, T. (1988) *Corporate Culture Under Evolution*, Tokyo: Kodansha

Kono, T. (1990) *Strategy and Structure of Japanese Enterprise*, London: Macmillan

Kono, T. and S. Clegg (2001) *Trends in Japanese Management: Continuing Strengths, Current Problems, and Changing Priorities*, New York: St Martin's Press

Kossek, E. E. and S. A. Lobel (1996) *Managing Diversity: Human Resource Management for Transforming the Workplace*, Oxford: Blackwell

Kotler, P. (1997) *Marketing Management: Analysis, Planning, Implementation, and Control*, New Delhi: Prentice-Hall

Kotter, J. P. (1997) *Matsushita Leadership: Lessons from the 20th Century's Most Remarkable Entrepreneur*, New York: The Free Press

Kovach, K. A. (1987) 'What motivates employees? Workers and supervisors give different answers', *Business Horizons* September–October, pp. 58–65

Kudo, A. (1998) *Japanese–German Business Relations*, London: Routledge

Lam, A. (1992) *Women and Japanese Management: Discrimination and Reform*, London: Routledge

Lane, H. W., J. J. DiStefano and M. L. Maznewski (eds) (2000) *International Management Behavior*, Oxford: Blackwell

Larke, R. (1994) *Japanese Retailing*, London: Routledge

Laurent, A. (1983) 'The cultural diversity of Western conceptions of management', *International Studies of Management and Organisations* 13(1), pp. 75–76

Laurent, A. (1986) 'The cross-cultural puzzle of international human resource management', in Ghauri and Prasad (1995)

Lincoln, J. R., H. Kerbo and E. Wittenhagen (1995) 'Japanese companies in Germany: a study in cross-cultural management', *Journal of Industrial Relations* 25, pp. 123–139

Lo, J. (1990) *Office Ladies/Factory Women: Life and Work at a Japanese Company*, New York: M. E. Sharpe

Lu, D. L. (1987) *Inside Corporate Japan: The Art of Fumble-free Management*, Cambridge: Productivity Press

Mabey, C. and P. Iles (eds) (1994) *Managing Learning*, London: Routledge

Mabey, C., G. Salaman and J. Storey (eds) (1998) *Human Resource Management: A Strategic Introduction*, Oxford: Blackwell

Mabey, C., G. Salaman and J. Storey (eds) (1998a) *Strategic Human Resource Management*, Milton Keynes: Open University Press / Sage Publications

Mackie, V. (2001) *Gender in Japan*, London: Routledge/Asian Studies Association of Australia

Mair, A. (1999) 'Learning from Honda', *Journal of Management Studies* 36 (1), pp. 25–44

Makin, P., C. Cooper and C. Charles (1996) *Organizations and the Psychological Contract*, London: BPS Books

March, R. (1996) *Reading the Japanese Mind: The Realities behind their Thoughts and Actions*, Tokyo: Kodansha International

March, R. (1996a) *Working for a Japanese Company: Insights into the Multicultural Workplace*, Tokyo Kodansha International

Martin, D., P. Herbig, C. Howard and P. Borstoff (1999) 'At the table: observations on Japanese negotiation style', *American Business Review* 17 (1), pp. 65–71

Maslow, A. H. (1970) *Motivation and Personality*, New York: Harper and Row

Mason, M. (1997) *Europe and the Japanese Challenge: The Regulation of Multinationals in a Comparative Perspective*, Oxford: Oxford University Press

Masui, S. (2002) 'Poll shows shift in attitude toward "taking life easy"', *The Daily Yomiuri* (22 November)

Maswood, J. J., J. Graham and H. Miyajima (2003) *Japan: Change and Continuity*, London: Routledge

Matsumoto, D. (2002) *The New Japan: Debunking Seven Cultural Stereotypes*, London: Nicholas Brealy

Matsunaga, L. (2000) *The Changing Face of Japanese Retail: Working in a Chain Store*, London: Nissan Institute/Routledge

Matsushita, K. (1988) *Quest for Prosperity: The Life of a Japanese Industrialist*, Kyoto: PHP Institute

Matsushita, M. (1993) *International Trade and Competition Law in Japan*, Oxford: Oxford University Press

Mead, R. (1998) *International Management*, Oxford: Blackwell

Mead, R. (2000) *Cases and Projects in International Management*, London: Routledge

Meloan, T. W. and J. L. Graham (eds) (1995) *International and Global Marketing: Concepts and Cases*, New York: Irwin/McGraw-Hill

Melville, I. (1999) *Marketing in Japan*, Oxford: Butterworth-Heinemann

Mercer, D. (1996) *Marketing*, Oxford: Blackwell

Mindbranch (2003) *Uniqlo: Company profile* on www.mindbranch.com (accessed 25 February, 2003)

Mintzberg, H. (1979) *The Structuring of Organisations*, Englewood Cliffs (NJ): Prentice-Hall

Mintzberg, H. (1983) *Structure in Fives: Designing Effective Organisations*, Englewood Cliffs (NJ): Prentice-Hall

Miyashita, K. and D. Russel (1994) *Keiretsu: Inside The Hidden Japanese Conglomerates*, New York: McGraw-Hill

Mizuno, S. and Y. Shiom (2002) 'A review of "Doing Business with Japan" by Kazuo Nishiyama', *Intercultural Management Quarterly* (online edition, accessed 16 April 2002)

MOL (1994) *White Paper on Labor: Tasks for Enriching Working Life Based on Stable Employment*, Tokyo: Japanese Ministry of Labour

Monks, R. A. G. and N. Minow (1989) *Corporate Governance*, Oxford: Blackwell

Morgan, G. (1989) *Creative Organisation Theory*, London: Sage

Morgan, G. (1997) *Images of Organisation*, London: Sage

Morita, A. (1986) *Made in Japan: Akio Morita and Sony*, New York: E. P. Dutton

Morris-Suzuki, T. (1994) *The Technological Transformation of Japan*, Cambridge: Cambridge University Press

Morrison, E. W. and S. L. Robinson (1997) 'When employees feel betrayed: a model of how psychological contract violation develops', *Academy of Management Review* 22 (1), pp. 226–256

Morrison, T., W. A. Conway, G. A. Borden and H. Koehler (1995) *Kiss, Bow, or Shake Hands: How to Do Business in 60 Countries*, Holbrook (MA):Adams Media

Mueller, F. (1998) 'Human resources as strategic assets: an evolutionary-based theory', in Mabey, Salaman and Storey (1998a)

Murdoch, J. (1996) *A History of Japan*, London:Routledge

Nagura, K. (2002) *Shimamura copies Uniqlo?* in the *Nikkei Net Interactive* (online edition, accessed 5 August 2002)

Nakata, H. (2002) 'Corporate whistle-blowers still left out in the cold', *The Japan Times* (13 November 2002)

Nathan, J. (1999) *Sony: The Private Life*, Boston/New York: Houghton Mifflin

Nishiyama, K. (2000) *Doing Business with Japan*, Honolulu: University of Hawaii Press

Nitobe, I. (1905/1969) *Bushido: The Soul of Japan*, Tokyo: Tuttle

Noh, T. and J. C. Kimura (eds) (1989) *Japan: A Regional Geography of an Island Nation*, Tokyo: Teikoku Shoin

Nonaka, I. (1994) 'A Dynamic Theory of Organizational Knowledge Creation', *Organizational Science* 5 (1), pp. 14–37

Nonaka, I. and Y. Kobayashi (1998) 'The essence of knowledge management for continuous innovations among future organizations', *Harvard Business Review* 1, pp. 84–90

Nonaka, I. and H. Takeuchi (1995) *The Knowledge-Creating Company: How Japanese Companies Create the Dynamics of Innovation*, Oxford: Oxford University Press

Nonaka, I. and H. Takeuchi (1995/1998) 'The knowledge-creating company: how Japanese companies create the dynamics of innovation', in Mabey, Salaman and Storey (1998)

Nonaka, I., Y. Yamashita, A. Kokubo, and Y. Sakuma (1997) *Innovation Company: Conditions for Constant Innovation*, Tokyo: Diamond

Odagiri, H. (1994) *Growth through Competition, Competition through Growth: Strategic Management and the Economy in Japan*, Oxford: Oxford University Press

Odaka, K. (1966) 'The middle classes in Japan', in Halmos (1966)

OECD (1997) *OECD Economic Survey*, Japan, Paris: OECD Publications

OECD (1997a) *OECD Economic Survey*, United States, Paris: OECD Publications

Ogasawa, Y. (1998) *Office Ladies and Salaried Men: Power, Gender, and Work in Japanese Companies*, Berkeley (CA): University of California Press

Oh, T. K. (1991) 'Understanding managerial values and behavior among the gang of four: South Korea, Taiwan, Singapore and Hong Kong', *The Journal of Management Development* 10 (2)

Ohmae, K. (1982) *The Mind of the Strategist*, New York: McGraw-Hill

Ohmae, K. (1995) *The Borderless World*, New York: HarperCollins

Ohmae, K. (ed.) (1995a) *The Evolving Global Economy: Making Sense of the New World Order*, Boston: HBS Publishing

Ohmae, K. (2001) *The Invisible Continent: Four Strategic Imperatives for the New Economy*, London: Nicholas Brealy

Ohta, H. (1998) *nihonteki koyo no henbo* ('Changes in the Japanese employment system') in Yoshiro and Harada (eds)

Ohtsu, M. and T. Imanari (2001) *Inside Japanese Business*, New York: M. E. Sharpe

Oishi, I. (2002) 'Politicians blur facts to save face during internal disputes', in the *Nikkei Net Interactive* (*Nikkei Shimbun* online edition, accessed 5 August 2002).

Okamoto, H. (2000) *The UNIQLO System*, Tokyo: PAL

Okuchi, K., B. Karsh and S. Levine (1988) *The Japanese Employment Relations System*, London: Routledge

Ono, A. (1989) *nihonteki koyokanko to rodo shijyo* (*Japanese-style Employment and Labour Markets*), Tokyo: Toyo Keizai Shinpo Press

Ono, A. (1999) 'Changes in Japanese employment practice', Tokyo: *The Monthly Journal of the Japan Institute of Labour* 446, pp. 1–9

Oliver, N. and B. Wilkinson (1992) *The Japanization of British Industry: New Developments in the 1990s*, Oxford: Blackwell

Otsuki, S., F. Tanaka and Y. Sakurai (1996) *Good Mileage: The High-Performance Philosophy of Soichiro Honda*, New York: Weatherhill

Ouchi, W. G. (1981) *Theory Z: How American Business Can Meet the Japanese Challenge*, Reading (MA): Addison Wesley

Oumi, N. (2000) *The Secret of UNIQLO's Rapid Growth*, Tokyo: Apple

Parsons, T. (1951) *The Social System*, New York: Free Press

Pascha, W. (ed.) (2003) *Systematic Change in the Japanese and German Economies*, London: RoutledgeCurzon

Pass, C., B. Lowes, A. Pendleton and L. Chadwick (1995) *Collins Dictionary of Business*, Glasgow: HarperCollins

Paton, R., G. Clark, G. Jones, J. Lewis and P. Quintas (1996) *The New Management Reader*, London: Routledge / Open University Press

Peters, T. J. (1991) *Thriving on Chaos: Handbook for a Management Revolution* London: HarperCollins

Pitman/FT (1997) *Mastering Management*, London: Financial Times/Pitman Publishing

Porter, M. E. (1990) *The Competitive Advantage of Nations*, New York: Free Press

Porter, M. E., H. Takeuchi and M. Sakakibara (2000) *Can Japan Compete?*, Cambridge (MA): Perseus

Prasad, S. B. and P. N. Ghauri (1993) 'A network approach to probing Asia's invisible business structures', in Ghauri and Prasad (1995: 285–292)

Ptak, C. L., J. Cooper and R. Brislin (1995) 'Cross-cultural training programmes: advice and insights from experienced trainers', *International Journal of Intercultural Relations* 19 (3), pp. 425–453.

Pugh, D. S., D. J. Hickson and C. R. Hinings (1983) *Writers on Organizations*, Harmondsworth: Penguin

Renshaw, J. (1999) *Kimono in the Boardroom: The Invisible Evolution of Japanese Women Managers*, Oxford: Oxford University Press

Rice, J. (1991) *Doing Business in Japan*, London: BBC Publications

Robinson, S. L. (1996) 'Trust and breach of the psychological contract', *Administrative Science Quarterly* December, pp. 574–599.

Rohlen, T. and C. Björk (eds) (1998) *Education and Training in Japan*, London: Routledge

Rudlin, P. (2000) *The History of Mitsubishi Corporation in London: 1915 to Present Day*, London: Routledge

Sakaiya, T. (1982) *Honda Motor: The Men, the Management, the Machines*, Tokyo: Kodansha International

Sakaiya, T. (1997) *Twelve People Who Made Japan*, Tokyo: PHP

Sakakibara, E. (1993) *Beyond Capitalism: The Japanese Model of Market Economics*, London (MD): University Press of America

Sako, M. and H. Sato (eds) (1997) *Japanese Labour and Management in Transition*, London: Routledge

Saso, M. (1990) *Women in the Japanese Workplace*, London: Hilary Shipman

Sato, A. (2000) *nihon no rodosha no rodoishiki* ('Japanese labour and the experience of employment') *kikan rodoho* (*Journal of Labour Law*) 194, pp. 55–59

Sato, K. (ed.) (1980) *Industry and Business in Japan*, New York: M. E. Sharpe

Schaede, U. (1995) 'The "old boy" network and government-business relations in Japan', *Journal of Japanese Studies* 21 (2), pp. 293–317

Schein, E. (1985) *Organizational Culture and Leadership*, San Franciso: Jossey-Bass

Scher, M. J. (1996) *Japanese Interfirm Networks and their Main Banks*, London: Macmillan Press

Scher, M. J. and N. Yoshino (2002) *Postal Savings Systems in Asia*, Tokyo: United Nations University Press

Schneider, S. C. and J.-L. Barsoux (1997) *Managing Across Cultures*, Harlow: Financial Times / Prentice-Hall Europe

Schwartz, F. J. (1998) *Advice and Consent: The Politics of Consultation in Japan*, Cambridge: Cambridge University Press

Segal-Horn, S. (ed.) (1998) *The Strategy Reader*, Oxford: Blackwell

Selmer, J. (2003) 'Winds of change? Japanese human resource practices and industrial relations', *BRC Paper in Industrial Relations*, Hong Kong Baptist University, http://net2.hkbu.edu.hk/~brc/CCMP200102. (pdf file accessed 17 February 2003).

Senge, P. (1990) *The Fifth Discipline: The Art and Practice of the Learning Organisation*, London: Random House

Shavit, Y. and W. Mueller (eds) (1998) *From School to Work: A Comparative Study of Educational Qualifications and Educational Destinations*, Oxford: Clarendon Press

Shimizuishi, T. (2002) 'Have American interests shifted from Japan to China?', masters paper presented at the University of Texas at Austin, 14 November 2002

Shuki, H. (1988) *Culture and Management in Japan*, Tokyo: University of Tokyo

Smith, P. B. and J. Misumi (1994) 'Japanese management: a sun rising in the west?', in Hickson (1997). Originally Chapter 4 (pp. 117–57) in C. L. Cooper and I. T. Robertson (eds) *Key Reviews in Managerial Psychology: Concepts and Research for Practice*, Chichester: John Wiley & Sons

Sone, H. (2002) 'Younger Okuda ready to lead Kansai', Tokyo: *IHT/ Asahai Shimbun* (online edition, 25 December 2002)

Sorrels, K. (1998) 'Gifts of wisdom: an interview with Dr. Edward T. Hall', *The Edge, The E-Journal of Intercultural Relations* Vol 1(3) on www.interculturalrelations.com (accessed 14 September 2002)

Sparrow, P. (1996) 'Transitions in the psychological contract in UK banking', *Human Resource Management Journal* 6 (4), pp. 75–92

Sparrow, P. and J.-M. Hiltrop (1994) *European Human Resource Management in Transition*, Hemel Hempstead: Prentice-Hall

Sparrow, P. and M. Marchington (1998) *Human Resource Management: The New Agenda*, London: Financial Times/Pitman

Steinhoff, P. G. and K. Tanaka (1993) 'Women managers in Japan', *International Studies of Management and Organization* 23 (2), pp. 25–48

Stewart, P. (ed.) (1997/2001) *Beyond Japanese Management: The End of Modern Times?*, London: Frank Cass

Storey, J. (ed.) (1989) *New Perspectives on Human Resource Management*, London: Routledge

Storey, J. (1992) *Developments in the Management of Human Resources*, Oxford: Blackwell

Sugimoto, Y. (1997) *An Introduction to Japanese Society*, Cambridge: Cambridge University Press

Sullivan, J. J. (1992) *Invasion of the Salarymen: The Japanese Business Presence in America*, London: Praeger

Sumiya, M. (2001) *A History of Japanese Trade and Industry Policy*, Oxford: Oxford University Press

Tachibanaki, T. (1996) *Wage Determination and Distribution in Japan*, Oxford: Oxford University Press

Taka, I. (1997) 'Business ethics in Japan', *Journal of Business Ethics* 16, pp. 1499–1508

Tames, R. (1993) *A Traveller's History of Japan*, Moreton-in-the-Marsh: Windrush Press

Tanner Pascale, R. and A. G. Athos (1981) *The Art of Japanese Management*, Harmondsworth: Penguin

Tanouchi, K. (1983) 'Japanese-style marketing based on sensitivity', *Dentsu Japan Marketing/Advertising* 23 (July) pp. 77–81

Taylor, H. (1996) 'The applicability of HRM concepts to less developed country contexts', *Human Resources in Development Group Working Paper 2* Manchester: IDPM

Thorne, S. (2002) 'After conquering Japan, UNIQLO takes on the UK', for the International Confederation of Shopping Centres (ICSC), website accessed 6 January 2003.

Tonnies (1922/1987) *Gemeinschaft and Gesellschaft*, Berlin: Curtins

Torrington, D. and L. Hall (1998) *Human Resource Management*, London: Financial Times/Prentice-Hall

Townley, B. (1991) 'The politics of appraisal: lessons from the introduction of appraisal into UK universities', *Human Resource Management Journal* 1 (2), pp. 27–34

Toyota Motor Corporation (1996) *The Toyota Production System*, Nagoya

Triandis, H. C. (1972) *The Analysis of Subjective Culture*, New York: Wiley-Interscience

Trompenaars, F. (1993) *Riding the Waves of Culture*, London: Nicholas Brealy

Trompenaars, F. and C. Hampden-Turner (1998) *Riding the Waves of Culture: Understanding Diversity in Global Business*, New York: McGraw-Hill

Tsutsui, W. M. (1998) *Manufacturing Ideology: Scientific Management in Twentieth-century Japan*, Princeton (NJ): Princeton University Press

Tsutsui, W. M. (ed.) (1999) *Banking in Japan*, London: Routledge

Uchida, Y. (1995) *Shosha*, Tokyo: Kyouikusha

Usunier, J.-C. (1996) *Marketing Across Cultures*, London: Prentice-Hall

Wakabayashi, M. (1980) *Management Career Progress in a Japanese Organization* (monograph) Tokyo: ProQuest UMI Research Program: ASIN

Watanabe, T. (1998) 'The rise of flexible and individual ability-oriented management', in Hasegawa and Hook (1998)

Watson, T. (1994) *In Search of Management: Culture, Chaos and Control in Managerial Work*, London: Routledge

Webber, R. A. (1997) 'Modern imperatives', in Pitman/FT (1997)

Whitehill, A. M. (1991) *Japanese Management: Tradition and Transition*, London: Routledge

Williams, R. (1985) *Keywords: A Vocabulary of Culture and Society* Oxford: Oxford University Press

Wong, S.-L. (1986) 'Modernization and Chinese culture in Hong Kong', *China Quarterly* 101, pp. 306–325.

Woodall, B. (1996) *Japan under Construction: Corruption, Politics, and Public Works*, Berkeley: University of California Press

Woronoff, J. (1981) *Japan:The coming economic crisis*, Tokyo: Lotus Press

Yamamura, K. (ed.) (1997) *The Economic Emergence of Japan*, Cambridge: Cambridge University Press

Yip, G. S. (1995) 'Global strategy as a factor in Japanese success', in Meloan and Graham (1995)

Yonekawa, S. (ed.) (1990) *General Trading Companies: A Comparative and Historical Study*, Tokyo: United Nations University Press

Yoshihara, K. (1982) *Sogo Shosha: The Vanguard of the Japanese Economy*, Tokyo: Oxford University Press

Yoshimura, N. and P. Anderson (1997) *Inside the Kaisha: Demystifying Japanese Business Behaviour*, Cambridge (MA): Harvard Business School Press

Yoshino, A. (2002) 'This may make you choke on your sushi', *The Times Higher Education Supplement*, 31 May

Yoshiro, N. and Y. Harada (eds) (1998) *nihonteki koyo no kokumin seikatsu* (*The Japanese employment system and people's life*), Tokyo: Toyokeizai Press

Young, N. (1998) *Basic Business Japanese*, Tokyo: Kodansha International

Index